The Shining Light

All rights reserved 2015.

Printed in the United States of America

First Printing, 2016

ISBN 978-0-692-61596-6

The Shining Light Press

R. Adams

Reverend Gyoko Saito (1927–2001)

I made two trips to Los Angeles where Reverend Saito was installed as Rinban (Head Minister) of Higashi Honqwanji Main Temple (Jodo Shinshu), having left the Buddhist Temple of Chicago to go there in 1981. My first trip was in 1984 and my second trip was in 1987. At that time he was Bishop of the North American District. In the first trip Rev. Nobuo Haneda was present on a visit and he took our picture.

The second trip took place wherein I stayed in the Temple itself for almost a month in the small tea room where he allowed me to stay. The intention here was to give up my place in Chicago, move to Los Angeles, find a job there, and rent an apartment, and so forth; whereas I could listen to more of his teachings. So with my portfolio in tow, I went around to the various studious seeking employment. But I failed to get a job, so I had no choice but to return home.

But I think he recognized this, the fact of my wanting to continue on receiving more of Buddhist teaching, so he sought a way of dealing with this situation. Coincidentally, Rev. Nobuo Haneda expressed the desire to have his own sangha in which he too, could continue with his study. He wanted to set up a study center called: "The Maida Center of Buddhism" in Berkeley where he lived with his wife. Therefore, this gave me the opportunity to once again pursue my interest by attending his sessions, which I did. The first one was held in their small apartment, by a small number of people. Rev. Saito also attended along with his wife, Toshiko, and a friend from Japan who belonged to Shuichi Maida's study group for which Rev. Haneda's place was named after. Rev. Haneda was mainly a student of Shuichi Maida; and, by the way, was also a student of Reverend Saito, having attended several A. B. A. discussion group meetings along with the rest of us. So he was also part of our study group early on here in Chicago.

A place solely dedicated to the teaching of Buddhism in this country that was specifically dedicated to Buddhist studies alone was sorely needed, as in my case for instance; so he encouraged and helped Rev. Haneda set up his study center which has grown to a large proportion of attendies, and is really quite a contribution.

Since my visit coincided with Shinran Shonin's birthday, an outdoor ceremony was held in which a good number of people attended at the main temple in Los Angeles. I clearly and distinctly heard the words of Shinran given by Reverend Saito; who in a booming voice shook up the audience with: "I will grind my bones into powder, and tear my flesh into pieces to hear the teachings". This is the journey I took to hear it.

Rev. Gyoko Saito was born on July 6, 1927 in Kumomoto, Japan.

1945 - After the 2nd World War, he was released from the military academy. He then entered University of Kumamoto majoring in electrical engineering.
1946 - He met his teacher Rev. Akegarasu. Began attending his lectures.
1950 - Received Bachelor of Science degree. He then entered Otani University where he studied directly under Rev. Akegarasu in Kyoto, Japan.
1954 - Gyoko married Toshiko Yoshida. Two years later they had a son Shin.
1956 - He earned a Bachelor's and Master's degree in Shin Buddhism. He came to the Buddhist Temple of Chicago to assist Rev. Gyomei Kubose.
1958 -.His wife Toshiko and son joined him in Chicago and later daughters Dawn and Maya were born.
1962 - He began translating Rev. Akegarasu's writings.
1966 - He became head minister of Buddhist temple of Chicago.
1977 - He published "Shout of Buddha", a large collection of Akegarasu's work. During the period from 1956 till 1981 he also translated many other Japanese writers, wrote many of his own articles, conducted study groups, took care of a fairly large congregation of parishioners - plus the needs of his own growing family - all within the span of 25 years of his administering to this temple.
1981 - He and Toshiko left Chicago and moved to Los Angeles main temple.
1981 - 1993 - He was Rinban (Head Minister) at Los Angeles Betsuin (temple).
1985 - 1991 - He was Bishop of the North America District.
1993 - He retired as Rinban but continued to serve as minister at the Los Angeles Betsuin.He was active as a speaker in the districts religious retreats.
2000 - He and Toshiko left Los Angeles to serve as Head Minister (Rinban) in Hawaii Betsuin. Soon he initiated a Buddhist educational program. Later that year, however, he was disabled by a congestive heart failure.
2001 - In February of that year, due to further medical complications, he was hospitalized. Several friends and family gathered and he was in good spirits. But then his conditioned deteriorated. He passed away March 10th in peace.

CONTENTS

10	The Gateless Gate
11	In Reverence
13	Dedication
14	Seeds of Life
17	Origins of the Nembutsu
18	What the Teacher Means to Me
20	The Shining Light
25	The Rhythm of Life
27	The Spiritual Journey
28	The Human Spirit
29	A memorial
30	Introduction: The Trip to Japan
47	Freedom of the Infinite
54	The Will and the Spirit
56	Shakyamuni
57	In Pursuit of the Truth
63	Life of the Temple
64	Dialogue and Nembutsu
66	The Face
69	Joan Sweany
71	Goodmorning!
72	Birth of the New Year
73	Where I found New Year's
75	Too Difficult to Live: I Am Grateful
77	San Gan Yennyu (The Three Gates)
92	Greed, Anger, and Ignorance
94	Notes on "Late Summer's Delight"
97	Eternal Life
101	Amaryllis
102	Song of the Flame
106	About Nature
109	From Death to Life
110	For Orchids
113	The Glowing Jewel of Hope
115	Shining Hope
115	Sunday Morning Awakening
118	Mind of Embracing All Things
120	The Garden of Life
122	Suffering of Break Through

124	Kingdom of the First
127	In Such Praise
129	Preparation for Birth and Birth
130	Upon the Third Birth
132	Young Grasses
135	"Onceness"
141	Thoughts about Destruction
142	The Eternal Life Sutra – The Larger Sutra
192	Mind of the Pure Clean Truth
193	Living the Life of Shakyamuni
203	Seeds of a Revolution
210	An Article on War
211	An Article on Love
218	Transcendental Wisdom
221	Our Deepest Wish
225	Studentship of the Ordinary Person
230	Biography of Reverend Haya Akegarasu
232	Letter to Mrs. Saito
233	Memorial for Toshiko Saito
234	The Sutra of the Quiet Person
244	Addenda Refresh
249	Dear Rev. Martin Harada
252	Farewell Message
256	Water That Flows Into the Sea

The Shining Light

Preface: Articles Reflecting on Pure Land Buddhism.

By Roger Adams

> If someone were to ask me why they should come to Buddhism, I would answer the same as Reverend Haya Akegarasu: "Do you know yourself?"
>
> "Seeking the truth is itself the truth", as my teacher, Reverend Gyoko Saito said.
>
> Coming to Buddhism therefore, means that we are willing to seek the truth about ourselves in light of the Buddha-Dharma in order to be emancipated into the world of freedom and spaciousness, and to experience the spiritual life of an awakened human being.
>
> The aspiration to seek one's true self is to seek one's true life, and to find our living voice that gives us the means to express it.

THE GATELESS GATE

Difficult it is to meet with the Buddha.

Difficult it is to meet with the Tathagatha.

Difficult it is to find the living essence of life within oneself.

Difficult it is to come up with one's very own shout of total freedom and independence.

Difficult it is to forsake or have removed one's attachment to self and seek the life within nothingness and the interrelatedness of all things.

Difficult it is to express the fresh life gushing from the core of one's being.

Difficult it is to transcend the world.

Difficult it is to follow the Way of the Buddha, the Way of the Spirit.

What solemn joy and fervent reverence to come across the Teachings that allow me to cross over to the other shore of happiness and enter the Pure Land of life itself.

The struggle in seeking the truth begins with my seeking, and within the seeking itself an unimaginable truth enters within this difficulty and impossibility; with the transcendence and entry into an unknown and unknowable life.

The one flash moment that empties the mind which opens and feels flexible, soft and yielding – as I feel the fresh breezes that come in the way that I live within the world focused on the Teaching. Delighted in meeting others with which I greet with an open heart. The world itself is the Pure Land the moment as I am at one with it. Here is where the truth is clearly understood within this moment while in the very world as it is.

IN REVERENCE   4/12/2004

When I awoke this morning with various kinds of thoughts and feelings all seeming to come and go, and yet all ended up as rather empty. Eventually I thought of what is it that I am seeking? It seems that out of a sense of emptiness one has the desire to seek one's real life, or at least a sense of direction that has real meaning; not just a bunch of attachments to this and that. In that sense it is a universal question shared by all. In this milieu of confusion one seeks to straighten up one's sense of direction and focus on what is the most essential point. This can happen on a daily basis, even. If we really look carefully, we can be easily confused by the secular world and our relative way of thinking. To transcend this, which represents a form of suffering, we are forced to seek into our real life. Otherwise, we will continue to suffer needlessly. We can return to external forms of pleasures to help relieve the problem, but these are only temporary solutions that don't really help in the end. Indeed, in our attempts to make such solutions permanent, we may actually cover up our true instinct as truth seekers and end up with an artificial life-style that totally denies entrance into the truth; i.e., we have then, to work even harder to get to the truth. So in that sense, it is important for us to be honest truth seekers and get rid of the clever or lazy mind that seeks easy external solutions. In my case, I can visualize the image of the teacher to gather what I need to stimulate a fresh, new direction. So the teacher is very important. Even his image, within my memory, is all need. In time, this leads to total dedication, and total respect. It is this human quality that sets up the new directions and refreshes my mind as to what is the true direction.

Without the spiritual life there is no life in the true sense, and the spiritual life I'm speaking of is contained and encompassed by the Nembutsu, that which is bowing to the indescribable essence of life which is verbalized as "Namu Amida Butsu". In that sense, I cannot help but focus on the teacher's nembutsu, that feeling that all along he imparted to me, but slowly. It is a function of time before one realizes its full essence; it doesn't come all at once because of our unawareness, but it has such a significance to have this feeling towards a person you deeply respect and towards all life as well.

This is what moves me as it sets up a direction. Past, present and future are at one as the eternal light, that of going forward with my total effort.

So the proper teacher is the most important one, for he is the living manifestation of the ever moving, ever changing life. Indeed, he is the living manifestation of the living sutra. He made it. As such, he fulfilled the wish of his own teacher, Reverend Haya Akegarasu, to bring and share the feeling of nembutsu and the teachings that manifest it to this country by living it. This is what really strikes me, and why I too, continue to learn from his efforts. He changed my life, and in that sense, I have no estimation.

January 6, 2015

    The brightness that shines through the window, the open door, and the fresh snow that has fallen last night, all speak of freshness. My mind is lit up in delight. The pure clean atmosphere of blowing snow, brilliant sun, and mind as well. The whole world comes to me without my thinking. A new world is born this morning. And with this whole new world comes to life, joyously.

    This pure clean mind touches the universe. And within all things are alive. I don't need to seek it actually. And I don't need to study it, either. Effortless life emerges here, and I am open to enjoying it. How can I think of anything other than an awakening to a new day, with a fresh new insight?

    Through all the efforts and difficulties in finding the essence of what I was seeking, and so putting it into a book that I wanted to put in. And the book is within the multitudes of things that enlightened me, taught me, and served as a way to see this moment of infinite life as represented by the clear sun, the window, and the open door. Where there are no flowers blooming, I am blooming. And where there is no darkness that overshadows my clear wish, life itself opens up. In this brightness that moves me the light within shines, and it is this light within that is brighter than the sun itself, as it is organic.

    This simple life, these simple things, all contributes to my happiness. In losing myself I keep finding myself. I dwell in a world where all things come together in *onceness*. And in knowing this to be true, I have found the essence of Buddhism and my life. The essence of the teaching for me alone, now becomes the essence of the teaching I want to share with others.

    Even facing difficulties, nothing can tarnish this moment-to-moment life that I feel at this very time which opens and unfolds before me.

    I will go to work giving life to others who come with honest minds to live their life to their fullest potential, reaching into the unknowable life.

    Smiling, as I discover and realize my own fullest potential. That is of Amida Buddha shining its essence throughout the world in all directions. Buddha contemplating Buddhas mutually is the nembutsu of bowing that transcends past, present, and future as the formless infinite life. The <u>Tathagata</u>: Sans. Agata: "coming", and gata: "going" – "thus comes"– as the continuous, discontinuous, continuity of life. Thus impermanence is the basis of Shakyamuni the Buddha's awakening. And deep and careful introspection is the way to get there. This is the light of wisdom in the ever-fulfilling potential.

Dedication

Every time I think of the Teacher my being bows. For he gave me the teaching that enabled me to fulfill my deepest aspiration for freedom and independence, for which otherwise I could never have found. He taught me how to be a human being, the most important but difficult of all. As I think of him the feeling is of such respect, for he was this person, this giving person who also had the power to remove one's ignorance.

Therefore, soon after he had passed away in 2001, I thought what a shame it would be if his life's work were not recorded and documented. How could I just let it slip by, as if he came to this country, America, for nothing? With tears I decided – no way. I will do my very best. You, who changed my life, shall have a book. With this determination I proceed, for even if it takes a long time, it will be done. You shall not be forgotten for all your efforts to help me and others to cross over to the other shore of emancipation; for this world as it is can become confused and one can travel within it aimlessly without any real direction, without any real spiritual life. And without this you have nothing, no real self- realization, and no real self-recognition – just nothing. What satisfaction I have then in contemplating the Buddhas and you in particular, who I feel close to. Through all those years, I have no regrets, but am fully involved and happy. So it is giving back in a sense, for that which I know he would like to have done. Anyway, if for no other reason, I want to do it for myself alone; for in a real sense the teaching is for me alone.

Furthermore, in the process of seeking, I want to examine and re-examine his life which includes his writings, for I am still learning from him and being reprimanded by him. Once, when attending a Buddhist retreat in Berkeley, Ca. and not having seen each other for some time, he asked, "Are you keeping up the direction?" "Yes I am." I answered.

Thus he was always concerned about my life and the direction I was taking as he was about so many others who showed interest in Buddhism, for he knew the importance that it had on our life in seeking into it, and in so doing discovering one's own life.

This book then, is both the aspiration and out-pouring I have for him before me now along with the will and deep desire to do it. Thinking of his spirit that has kept him alive in me and all the things that transpired, how could I not come up with a book? Little did I know at the time that it would be about his life with me bowing in reverence to the life that he unselfishly shared with all of us.

R.A. 2/24/08

SEEDS OF LIFE R. Adams   2/5/2009

   Reality is made to exist by Eternal Life. All the wondrous things happen within this eternal life, including the Tathagata of continuous change which gives me the freshness I need to inspire a new creation and to feel the freshness of the world as I begin the new day. I don't need anything other than this to enliven a spiritual life. Without this spirit there's no sparks but just a kind of existing. But when I first started out I didn't know anything about all of this. But I did have an instinct for what it was that I was seeking religiously or spiritually.
   Inadvertently I became a student of this spirit when I began to realize that I was not just a person with a body wandering around aimlessly, but wanted to discover who I really am. Yes, formal education gave me certain skills, especially in terms of language and other skills in order to obtain a job, but did all these skills including jobs answer my most essential question? So in other words, the secular world had no answer for my problem. Yet, I lived in this world on a day-to-day basis, got my sustenance from it, met with others who were going about their business just as I, so what is so wrong with that? But it still doesn't answer the main question that lay buried in my mind as to "Who am I?" Thus I left home to find out a spiritual discovery to this enigmatic question resting in the back of my mind.
   While it is true that I was seeking, it is also true that I was being pushed out by some unknown power of instinct. Now that I think about it, this power that both called me and at the same time pushed me out from my parents house was to discover a world within a new insight coming out of the Orient, mainly China or Japan that spoke of Zenism and "Enlightenment" and new ways to seek my life within the area of religion. So I had a deeper sense of what it was that inspired me.
   So I prepared, left home, following the famous "Route 66", where all such people like me joined with the "hippy crowd", and went the way of such brightness all the way to California where I hoped to set up shop as a muralist and seek out a "Zen Master", or someone who was knowledgeable in oriental spirituality and wisdom. Such a youngish dream I had back in the late fifties. Then I eventually landed among the hippies – what a crowd! I got tired of them – besides, it was getting too confused, noisy and even immoral. So I found a place near the ocean, a small cabin sitting near a beach called Muir Beach backed by the beautiful Muir Forest and further on, Mt. Tammilpious. A perfect spot for Zen meditation as I was in paradise!
   I could watch the brilliant sun going down into the ocean. I found a cute

stray puppy and then found a job as a painter. Yet, despite the fact that I was surrounded by all this beauty and naturalness, I became increasingly lonely. Something was missing. Family, friends, I began to miss them terribly. A sense of emptiness entered that I had no answer for. Besides, I'd seen the world that I wanted to experience. Thus I could not find the answer here. I must move on and come back to Chicago.

The adventure ended with my returning home with a junky car that was held together underneath with 2 x 4's and bailing wire tied to the underbelly to make sure that the car wouldn't break in half. Ha! – If I pushed the mat aside I could see the road underneath! Miracle – I returned home with .75 cents in my pocket! What a trip, the whole thing! (Those were the days before credit cards). Being back I met with my parents who were glad to see me still intact. Next thing I had to attend to was my girlfriend who I loved and who I knew wanted to get married with me and set up a family on a small acreage somewhere in Michigan and to raise horses, and all. But I knew that if I got married with her then I couldn't pursue my wish to discover the world, cure my irresolvable skin problem (psoriasis), and meet with the "Zen Master", and etc. Marriage had to wait – pushed aside – because of my strong feeling for what I now see as my essential wish, or, "Who am I?" was becoming something of a destiny.

Now however, after a period of seven months, I was ready to get married and settle down. But she was nowhere to be found. In that sense I was ready to return to normal life. Spirituality would have to come through living a normal life. Aside from normal life there is no spirituality. Normal life is the reality of the world as it is. As Rev. Akegarasu stated, "I do not understand why Gautama Buddha did not return to his family." Once you find the essence of your being through self-recognition, then how could family life disturb your meditation, but in fact deepen it? But anyway, coming back, I once again pursued my original instinct. That which was an enigma when I first began my journey was now becoming a deepest wish to find out.

In my mind at the time, the world was divided essentially into two parts; on one hand you had the secular world, and on the other hand you had the spiritual world. The secular world was the finite world where we as human beings were born, worked, lived our lives, and died. The other was that of the unknown or infinite. In the secular context we as finite beings played out our desires and various attachments all controlled by the self, thus all our selfish desires and attachments came from here. Self-love is at the basis of this. Then the individual develops a distinct identity which we know as the ego, which insists on its own self-based independence. This self-affirmed ego becomes hardened into a shell-of-self. As the self hardens, we become more isolated, and as such, our life becomes difficult.

The thing about the ego, driven as it is by self-power, is that it won't admit defeat, or guilt. Yet it is standing on the wobbly seat of evil thinking that it is worthy of recognition; or conversely, by comparing itself with others, depreciating on one's self. It thinks of itself as the center of the world, yet the center of this world is not moving – it is static, inflexible (except in the case of convenient motivation), and as such, no life. No joy, no brightness, stinginess, coldness; often becoming mundane scholars who judge others based upon their limited understanding of should and shouldn't. Thinking of themselves as good people who are morally pure and self-righteous and who are trying to force themselves to be so – but aren't. Sentimentally loving, attached humans are so cute. See on the stage of human affairs how human beings practice their "devil-ship" on one another under such lies, cover-ups, deceits, disguises, fake-outs, subterfuges, and corrupt contrivances that you wouldn't believe!

Yet despite all this, we all yearn to be at one. Here we are expressing the human being in our almost subconscious desire to be at one with each other. This is akin to our true aspiration, isn't it? We suffer as a result of not being at one with each other and the world at large. This is so because the infinite is represented by the One alone. The infinite is not devisable, yet ever moving, ever changing – like a great wind or soft breezes – like torrents of water or a still pond – the infinite in all its descriptions is boundless. And it hits us. It is this "compassion" of the infinite that teaches us real compassion by compelling us to make our own real confession as to our absolute ignorance before life itself. It is here where we taste the real absolute; and, compelled to bow before it, we draw tears, and these hot tears melt the cold ice of our minds. <u>Now</u> we are made into humans who can experience true spirituality at one with the infinite, the eternal life that we cannot understand with our small relative knowledge, but in our rebirth as true human beings. Here is where our noble being is at one with the ever- moving and flowing essence of life.

The whole point is being naked before Eternal Life, is the birth shout of Shakyamuni, as indicating his total independence from all external entities:

> Above the heavens,
> and below the heavens,
> alone, I am most noble.

The seed becomes a plant, and the plant sends forth a bud to greet the sun and to become a flower, opening to shine its essence. How noble is its life. We can be that flower that unfolds its petals to meet with the spacious skies.

Origins of the Nembutsu 11/12/2012   R.A.

    The origin of the nembutsu began for me when I met the teacher. For there was something about him that I could not describe, but attracted me to him and which led me to listen to what he had to say in regards to Buddhism. That was way back in 1963 when I was just beginning my study of Buddhism (I was 27 years old and was seeking a Buddhist teacher). At that time he was an assistant minister along with a head minister Rev. Kubose, and another minister Rev. Ashikaga, here at the old temple called Chicago Buddhist Temple (Jodo Shinshu).

    Prior to meeting him I was studying with Rev. Kubose for about six months in his Thursday evening discussion class studying from D. T. Suzuki's book, <u>Zen Buddhism</u>, a subject that was rather popular among Caucasians during that period. And while the class on Zen was interesting and all, it didn't really touch my life. Interesting though it was, there was no nembutsu here. But how did I know that? I didn't even know the word, let alone know its meaning! But there was something going on in my subconscious that for all the miles of travel that I was looking for wasn't being satisfied. However, when Rev. Kubose left the temple to get his doctorate in Japan, Reverend Gyoko Saito became head minister, and took his place as head of the discussion group as well.

    I began to notice a change in the atmosphere. After a while we switched from Zen into Shinshu Buddhism with the introduction of Reverend Haya Akegarasu. Rev. Saito knew Rev. Akegarasu and studied under him for some two years while becoming a minister at Otani University in Japan and his respect for his teacher was absolute, so when he came to this country his main wish was to translate his writings so that all the members of the temple could read them and learn from them. This included the now dwindled down size of the discussion group (all the "fashion minded" people began to fade away). This was his nembutsu, the depth of which I was going to observe as time went on, and which directly influenced my life. Here is a man who touched my life; again, it was so quietly intuitional you would never know. It had to be felt. Was that what we were really learning all that time? Yes, because this is the way he thought about his own teacher, Rev. Akegarasu.

    He was this person, a man of the nembutsu. Yet, he never stunk of religion, but being such a dedicated student, an ordinary person, loving us as ordinary persons; learners, seekers, just like him, never putting himself above others. Never parading around as a "learned one" – even telling us once that he was a paid minister. Oh, how I loved this man, and can't help it, that is the cause of my nembustu. Tears come now…. "How difficult it is to be human", he said. Yes, how difficult it is to express the very feeling that makes me come up with such hot tears. As these tears melt ice into water, the water turns into the shining essence of life itself. This is what the teacher gave me of himself.

    Then right after his memorial a confession came of my ignorance and stupidity. "How stupid I am, beyond stupidity! Why did you even waste your time with me?" How the hot tears just came gushing down uncontrollably as they were falling on the old table outside the temple.

What the Teacher Means to Me

I am at a point where I want to dwell on the importance of the nembutsu in relation to the teacher. This feeling for the teacher has to do with the respect and absolute trust I had in him. It is a solemn feeling that causes me to bow before his essence. Now that he has passed away, this feeling has increased, which has made the relationship I had with him even more significant. Among so many other things, the two that are most important are the Nembutsu and the Tathagata. Yet, he never actually taught them, they were something that was incorporated into his being in such a way that they were implied, which means that he manifested them without his actually having to teach them to us as such. This is importantly significant, a unique way in which he led us to the Teaching. To that extent he was the Dharma itself. He didn't need to teach it, he was it. He was the vehicle for it. Without his presence we wouldn't have had a vehicle. This is the significant importance of the teacher. Without this trust, this solemn feeling, none of us would have learned anything about Buddhism, which has to do with the life of continuous change and that of the nembutsu, which is our actual spiritual life.

Reverend Akegarasu once said: "I have nothing to teach, no students to teach to." What is it that cannot be taught? This is the very point that the teacher was most careful of; not to treat us as a separate body of students to "teach down to" in a dualistic manner as is the case within secular education. If the latter were the case, he would have been teaching to us in the way we *should* feel as a form of preaching, rather than evoke from us a feeling that naturally occurs from our own feeling itself.

Here too, he never allowed us to think that with our own limited intellectual ability we could gain some insight into the truth of the Buddha-Dharma which is based on impermanence or the tathagata, life of continuous change. Thus, he never gave us truth in the static sense which we could then store as so much head knowledge which he would then have to remove. This was in fact, our very problem – we tended to store everything as head knowledge, thus turning it into dead knowledge. In that sense we tried to promote ourselves by acquiring knowledge in order to gain for ourselves an elevated position. And, by this attempt, to let the other person(s) know that we have greater understanding in our grasp of the truth. But in fact, it's all in the head! This is intellectual, not spiritual.

Here we can live the life of pretense in our conceit; for in our blindness we can see only as far as our nose. The teacher could detect even subtle differences in our sincerity or smartness and cut it off if it were false, or wait for the proper time. We should know about the truth of ourselves which is that we are in error for thinking that with our self-power abilities alone can gain access to the living truth. The shout of truth itself is of other-power which is to say that it is beyond our limited and relative self-power. (At that time we knew nothing about power beyond the self.) As naïve as we were, this is what we had to struggle with – so difficult! We have difficulty with this understanding because we are so indoctrinated into thinking that we do things alone by self-power, leaving us oblivious to Other-Power.

What is it that is not teachable and yet communicated? Dogen, a well known Zen teacher and a contemporary of Shinran Shonin, stated that it is better not to study Buddhism without a teacher. When I read Dogen I could not help but feel his nembutsu upon meeting his teacher. There is something hidden from our surface consciousness that we are seeking from religion, some unknown and unknowable source; there is a void in our life without it. We don't exactly know what it is — could it be our inherent desire to be at one with the world and with others? Away from our agitated mind, do we not seek peace within the one? Beyond that, do we not seek a rhythm to life within our own bodies just is in nature? What is it that motivates us to become seekers of the truth? What is the essence of life that we are seeking? Something motivates us, inspires us in this direction, otherwise we are living in a kind of spiritual void. Without the spiritual essence of life, we are somewhat like half-dead people, just wandering around not really knowing what to make of our life, and not having a focus. The focus is on one's nembutsu, the depth of which turns everything around. This is the power behind the Tathagata of continuous change and truth of "thus comes". It is the power beyond self that we are seeking. It is that which converts everything into human feeling; otherwise it is not the true nembutsu. And this is what Dogan is talking about. The teacher can expose us to the truth of continuous change (Tathagata) and the power beyond self which is the nembutsu (being at one with Amida's embracing light). Otherwise, the teachings and sutras may not be understood properly without the guidance from the teacher, so that we may get confused or misdirected. The teacher is the embodiment of that which we are seeking. So in time, as we listen to the teacher our feeling deepens.

From an old letter I received from Joan Sweany, is an article which both she and Rev. Saito translated some years earlier from Reverend Haya Akegarasu's writings. A partial excerpt:

> ... But when I am sitting quietly by myself, I feel such a warm communion with others, such gaiety! — A longing, yet such a cheerful mood! Without reading and writing, hearing or speaking, I melt into that rhythm of nature which cannot be read or written or heard or spoken. Then I shed tears, and I smile. Out of the depths of tears, the miraculous spring comes forth.
>
> I know all beings in the lonely self and taste communion in this loneliness. It is not enough to say I am thankful or reverent — these words do not express my mind. As I walk I bow my head, and my eyes move with the rhythm of nature that flows under my feet. Tears form and fall; the blood dances in my veins. I go to the unimaginable One.

THE SHINING LIGHT

    What a beautiful day, huh? This is the first day the temperatures have been above freezing after some 14 days of below freezing temperatures. The sun is streaming through the windows and the plants are all lit up. Outside in the white glistening snow sparrows are chirping gaily. My mind is lit up also. The thought comes to my mind on the subject of identity and how one's identity changes from one's self-identity to universal identity which involves the infinite. Then I thought as a question, what is a name or word that I can give to this brilliantly lit up scene that I was witnessing and enjoying? Then a name or word popped up in my mind as "Amida" (as in Amida Buddha) that best describes this beauty of mind. In Shinshu Pure Land Buddhism we have words to describe this boundless life that is one of its main features. The eternal light that shines throughout the universe has been given a name. Spiritually, we can have a name that best describes it, or that opens up to a set of teachings that have value to our lives. Indeed, from here I can have a whole palette of words, expressions, and teachings that I can use to describe this essence. But keep in mind that life comes first and then come the words to describe it.

    Scholars are the ones who set out to describe things a-priori so as a result there is no life behind what they say. Life is not a concept. To catch words just as they come alive is the best way to express my life. Even the thoughts I have, if they are fresh insights to what it is that I'm studying, then I'm okay with it. I can love words, but they have to be living words that create sparks. Our thoughts and words may be just chit-chat without any real content. Words and thoughts just strung together like so many building blocks. So it is not easy to come up with one's life, just as it is not easy to be human. Yet my being itself is alive, why then is it so difficult to express it?

    Somehow, when we get into thinking for the sake of thinking we get misled and covered up with so many dead and useless thoughts. These dead thoughts that seem to pile up kill our instinct for life. My teacher was the one who insisted on the fact that we should express our very own life, and not merely use quotations from others'. At the very moment as life just pops up or unfolds is the very moment when the words I use are so living and create life in others as well. And by listening to the spirit of others' as they have expressed their life has so deepened my own understanding.

In Buddhism we have a name for that infinite identity and the name is Amida Buddha of Immeasurable Light and Immeasurable Life (from the Sanskrit: as in Amitabha and Amitayus). In the <u>Larger</u> <u>Sutra</u> these words are characteristics of a king who became an aspiring monk called Dharmakara (storehouse of knowledge) and who completed all the vows necessary for himself to become a Buddha known as Amida Buddha. In temples he is depicted as a wooden statue faced in gold leaf at the top center in the Hondo (altar) area in order to provide visual optimization and a focal point for the interior of the temple itself. In no way is he considered as a Buddhist God or linked to a form of idol worship, and etc. He is simply there to visually represent the Name that describes the two qualities that in the shortest number of words describe for us aspects of Pure Land Buddhism and specifically Jodo Shinshu Buddhism in particular. It was written from verbal transmissions about two centuries B.C. (?), which in a story form represents the Buddha's own life. Both popular and decisive, it is a spiritual way of life that has taught millions of people how to be true human beings.

The Larger Sutra is an abbreviated title which essentially means: "The Larger Vehicle" or "The Larger Basket" since it was created universally for the largest number of people, many who were illiterate at the time of its inception and who needed a spiritual direction that applied directly to their lives. With words they could easily chant that would engage their trust of Amida's transforming power that would lead them to the Pure Land of bliss and fulfillment (Nirvana). Buddhism itself contains many, many sutras and commentaries on sutras that go into the thousands, but this one focuses its whole emphasis on Shakyamuni's original intent for all people and not just for monastic's, monks, priests, and the educated. The power behind it is one's deepest wish to be free of suffering caused by the three poisons of greed, anger and ignorance.

Associated with the word Amida Buddha is another word consisting of six syllables: Na-mu-a-mi-da-butsu, which means bowing before the Immeasurable Light that comes in the form of a chant called the *Nembutsu*, i.e., from *nem*, meaning: *Buddha thinking of Buddha's mutually*; as the solemn worship and bowing praise before the truth of Immeasurable Life. Here we must be humble and passive, for otherwise we cannot be true listeners for the solemn life within us. It is the point in which our attachment to self-love ego simply vanishes as it is focused entirely in the Dharma of infinite light and life.

So in Buddhism we have in very simple words that which succinctly describes one's spiritual life; as is the main protagonist, Dharmakara, who has found Nirvana in the Pure Land of peace and bliss, after completing 48 Vows.

The Larger Sutra consists of four main characters: the Buddha, his cousin Ananda; and two others about in which the story is related: Lokesvararaja who is the Buddha, and the monk or bodhisattva Dharmakara. Through his aspiration to be just like his teacher, he eventually becomes Amida Buddha.

To begin with the nembutsu is universal, that is, with hands clasped and in reverence the humbled person confesses his or her own ignorance and stupidity before the very tathagatha of life itself. It simply comes, as it is free of any intention on my part. It is within a power beyond my control. As it is beyond my power, it is inconceivable. If someone thinks or imagines that they can control the use of the nembutsu towards their own personal gain, it is false. Perhaps we will be going through such surface nembutsu's until the day comes when we will meet with the true and solemn nembutsu within oneself which will gush out and crush our ignorance and artificial posture. Isn't that our human condition? Thinking that we can gain our way into spirituality by adopting various pious practices? Isn't it therefore universal to all people? Our true spirituality is based on our humility, not on our postures as we are conditioned to be as good people. It is a kind of subtle conceit, isn't it? If the nembutsu practice is a way to make ourselves look humble – then isn't it showing to others our false humility? The real nembutsu is our humble confession before the truth as being so terribly sorry.

It is here, at the teacher's memorial service shortly after his death, and after listening to all the speeches and thinking of him during the service and at the end as people gathered expressing their feeling, I began to tear up. I went outside to the rear of the temple and sat down on an old picnic table as it came out as a loud shout, "I am so stupid, beyond stupidity! Why did you even bother with me?" At that point tears began to gush out. My body bent over the table as I lost myself in these hot tears hitting the table. Then a quiet came over me as I sat for a while and went back into the temple.

Once when in Berkeley, he quoted a friend who said that we can live without worldly things, but we cannot live without the nembustu.

The nembutsu that can be written on the blackboard or explained is for explanation purposes and one might call it the blackboard nembutsu.
All such studies are preliminary and provisional. But if it is a confession of one's ignorance before the truth itself in communion with another person then the true nembutsu gushes out "in the flesh" within the solemn mind.

In the beginning there was life, and then came the word. The way we describe life is with words. But words are abstractions that are used as symbols or sounds that represent actual life. So often we cling to the words overlooking the life behind them. We cling to name and form in such a way that they become part of our self-identity; in this case we become bounded by them, and they control our mind and our way of thinking. It's all part of our limited and relative self. Here we act like scholars and philosophers. In the area of the existence of things, we look for abstractions, concepts, and theories. But do we look for life itself? This is the question we have to ask as we get into the meaning of the nembutsu physically, not just formally.

As a result of our pedagogic educational system if you will, and since words that are used are in the form of abstractions that are dichotomized and that lack an organic expression of life itself. We therefore, and without knowing it, develop a dualistic and habitual use of words that creates a conceptualized understanding of life. As a result of our academic and sophisticated education along with our relative self we become estranged and disconnected from life itself. Our spiritual life will not take place if we are disconnected from it. We have to have our eyes opened by discarding a relative self that creates it and that can stand in the way of our seeing. This process is called: an awakening, enlightenment, and/or emancipation. The more our eyes are opened the more we can see and understand. Thus our perspective on life increases, while our judgmental and hardened positions decrease. We soften and are able to flow with the stream, whereas going against the stream will cause agitation and unrest. The more we go in this direction the more we will be in touch with the living spirit within ourselves. This will encourage us to go forward. Above all, we will become students and listen to our predecessors and teachers who themselves studied from the Dharma. Our aspiration to be born will be awakened when we study with the teacher who himself has gone through the same process that we are. Don't look for a holy person or a know-it-all or someone who will "improve" you. Just look for a dedicated student as one who won't put himself above others. Buddhism is not a therapy; it is a spiritual process of awakening; not merely for improving the self, but the inconceivable transforming of one's total self.

So it is true that the teacher is as such because he is the best student who himself is awakened. By the way in which he studies with an open and sincere mind he demonstrates to us the proper attitude that we must have in order to progress in our understanding. For instance, the truly awakened person lives humbly in regards to him; not thinking of himself as something special, but rather free from any ego-based self-affirmation. Indeed, he places himself as the last of the unenlightened ones. He also feels that all others are expedient means towards his own enlightenment. This leaves him open to learn from others. He has gone to the other shore and returned as an ordinary person. He does not live as an isolated person, nor does he exist as a mystic guru, but lives right here on the earth as such. He has transcended the other-world of deities and Gods. He also has discarded the fantasy land of heavenly bliss. He has no claim to any virtue of his own making. As such he may charactorize himself as a serious but playful person, not conforming to the worldly conventions of logic. But he is very active and creative and lives a creative life. Simply he is himself, and goes his own way as a free person. He does not follow but creates his own way. This one is known as a Tathagata, one who exemplifies the life of continuous change.

The Rhythm of Life　　　　　　　　　　R. Adams, Dec. 5, 2015

"The oneness of all things" – this is Reverend Manshi Kiozawa's (1863 – 1903) statement in which he describes the interdependence and interrelatedness of all things and all people. We may have trouble understanding this because of the various problems occurring in the world today, but that's because we haven't investigated fully the cause and conditions of the very multitudinous karma's that play out and effect each other on the worldly stage we face today, where everything we see is ugliness and tragedy. The causes and conditions are due to self. Self-love, self-centeredness, selfishness, greed, and anger, lead to the paths that many follow out of pure ignorance, inhumanity, and utter coldness – what suffering they bring upon themselves and others. Their ego as one's own supreme being is the cause.

Yet even here there exists an interrelatedness that represents a light of redemption and transcendence of the human condition of devil ship upon other human beings, as all must learn of the oneness of all things. This too, must be the goal of religion which is to bring us together and to teach us how to be true human beings, for without that there is no feeling within ourselves to ever discover who we really are. We can go around and around endlessly with no real focal point and in a world of confusion and endless debate over what is the real truth.

Referring to self, Reverend Kiozowa made the following statement: "Self is nothing more than sitting back and observing the phenomena of life." How relaxed and natural I feel when hearing these two statements, and how different they are when compared to the political scene that involves the secular world. Here we have self-enhancement, self-promotion, and stupidity going on, in which people become so attached to themselves, insisting on their most important "I". They have no idea for seeking a spiritual life, but just being bounded and entrapped by a sense of fear, negativity, and contrivance that their life has become. How tragic! Yet, we were born free! Can we self-realize this original self, this original freedom again? All people have a desire to be free. But how do we get there? We are so blind. Attached to name and form we are stuck within a pattern that denies any rhythm to our life, any real shout to our life. We may think that because we enjoy certain things and along with thinking that, we are already good people in following the religious practices, and that we need not go any further. Self-satisfaction can take place in which conceit and arrogance appear. In this attitude we are a Devil disguised as a good person.

We become two-dimensional in our way of thinking. Everything follows from this. Our thoughts are as dead because they lack the time-dimension that life itself expresses. Our thoughts seem to be centered around a secularly two-dimensional world as we become scholars to that world – god, bad – right, wrong – moral righteousness, and so forth; all the discriminatory set criteria of our own making.

　"One shout is worth a thousand words of explanation."　　(H. Akegarasu) Here there is a sense of life, organic life, and physical life that pounds my being.

There is a sense of freedom here. The open door, the sun coming through, my mind all lit up. Depressing as the world is at this time, a sense of hope enters. The continuous flow of life does not stop. It kills all the negative stuff. A new day is born, and with it comes a mind that is empty. How simple and how beautiful it is.
    It is like Shakyamuni (c. 563-453 B. C.). Shakyamuni's experience is when he fell into darkness, there came a light. He awoke to a light. He experienced enlightenment. It was not something special. It was just his ordinary mind. He cleared out all the stuff that contributed to his darkness or, it was cleared out for him. Either way, as in "thus comes". The empty sheet says it best. He knew what were the circumstances of the world and the causes of it as he just left it alone. So too, did he leave alone the six steps prior to his enlightenment. They are: gods, humans, fighting spirits, hungry demons, animals, and hell dwellers. All these things were cast aside and transcended. But when the struggle was brought to a climax as when he saw himself as a devil, then finally everything changed when he experienced a new day where there was only the feeling of spacious freedom, and the joy of liberation.
    But imagine all the work he went through to fully realize himself as a free person, emancipated from the mental dungeons of hell. He as a hell dweller was one who carefully watched all the things that traversed in his mind, now in open praise of life itself. The rhythm of life cleared his mind, and he need not look any further than he, himself. This Eternal Life was his inspiration to share it with all others. And so he welcomed them regardless of whom or what they were. And because he welcomed them, they in turn, welcomed him. He became a lowly beggar, along with a begging bowl under his cloak, without any titles or ornaments to wear, just being himself, I as I, nakedly shining. This embracing spirit, which he saw everywhere being manifested, caused him to bow to all things – the world itself. Thus he could worship the world as he saw it, without any need to change it, modify it, or improve it. Indeed, it was the same with him, as he saw no need to merely "improve" himself. He just left it alone. By doing so he became selfless, because he no longer felt the need to attach things to himself. That left him pure without trying to be pure, as he examined himself honestly. The Great Mind that he sensed was already pure, already saving – no need for an external savior to come down from the heavens to save him. He just threw out the useless self when he realized a power beyond himself, a "Mandate of Heaven", as Reverend Kiozawa states, and became at one with the infinite spaciousness of freedom to become this universal person.
    What a quiet joy must have entered his mind after all his struggles left him as nothing but skin and bones, and then his shout: "Oh Avidia!", "Oh Darkness!" He left his seat under the papilla tree never to return to become this world renowned figure of a human being to touch the lives of endless numbers of people throughout the world. We have in Reverend Kiozawa, who actually tried to live the life of the Buddha physically, come to the same point as in the Buddha's case: The self is nothing more than observing the phenomena of life in the oneness of all things.

The way itself is the spirit. Rev. Saito was well aware of the free and independent spirit of his teacher, Rev. Akegarasu. In the following letter, which I quote from Mrs. Toshiko Saito, he expresses his desire to get his teacher's words properly translated. Not only that, but in the process, to inspire us students to express our spirit as well.

"When I encounter the various problems with the translation where the words are inadequate, surprisingly that is where my real friends appear." Here he is referring to us fellow students in the discussion group and especially Joan Sweany his secretary.

"Our struggle is more like a clash of physical body to body rather than of words. When a draft translation is ready, everyone reads it then we see if each person can express his or her understanding in his or her own words. If the translation is not strong enough for you to feel it hitting your physical body, then it is no good. If after reading a passage of the translation, you cannot express Sensei's teaching in your own words, then the English translation was not alive. If it takes a whole life time or even two lifetimes, my hope is that 'The Complete Works of Akegarasu' will be available in English."

Here we can see Rev. Saito's dedication and single mindedness in exposing his teacher's living spirit to his entire readership. In so doing, he came up with his own spirit as well. I remember so often how difficult it was though; how many fiery and intensive sessions we had sometimes. The true spirit that is squiggling with the freshness of life is Akegarasu's true spirit that Rev. Saito not only captured but that which he lived as well. This is the way of the Buddha, the brilliance of the burning spirit, the brilliance of the burning self. This shout that we refer is his shout that when finished became the book entitled: "The Shout Of Buddha". (Published, 1977)

In Buddhism, the Teaching is referred to as the Dharma. It can come in the form of texts called sutras, or it can come from a living person or someone in the past that has lived who manifests the content of these sutras, that is, a dedicated person who breathes life into them. Sutras are by and large doctrinal. By that I mean their intent is act like guides to direct the student towards emancipation. In that sense they comprise the work that must be done in order to reach real freedom. Whether they are in story form or in verse form, or in dealing with a variety of teachings that form the basic content of each sutra, they have in effect formed the basic foundations upon which, in textual form itself, lead us to meditate and self-examine ourselves in terms of Shakyamuni's Teachings. If we are a human being in search of our spirituality, interested in studying Buddhism, we will further it by studying from the sutras, for there is no easy or superficial way to gain one's total emancipation. The shout you hear from Akegarasu, as above, came from his intensive study into the Larger Sutra. But his real impetus and inspiration came directly from his teacher, Rev. Manshi Kiozawa. Of course it came from his own life - his shout was his shout – such as: "Flames of the cremation of the total self are my only enlightenment." What remained was a cool flame as his spirit and life, reborn out of the ashes of self to be at one with the rhythm of life, and with Amida Buddha's unbounded light and life.

The Spiritual Journey

R. Adams   12/13/2015

In back of the self there is the mind. If we can straighten out the mind then we can straighten out the self. That sounds easy enough, but the mind is very elusive, like a slippery fish, squiggling along and always changing this way and that, so we cannot see the mind so easily. That requires a spiritual journey to find out what kinds of things that lurk in the back of our mind that so often cause us the most of our problems. In this spiritual journey where are we to look and what are we to look for? First we must go out and seek a spiritual path. Unless we do that we cannot fix the ignorant self. Here there are no exceptions, as all are in the same boat seeking happiness, but not being able to find real happiness as we attempt to grasp it.

In my case, I wanted to know myself. After years of secular education, I came out with no real understanding of who I really am – it's like having a blind spot that somehow left me dangling. "Who am I?" was left unanswered by all the education that I received. A kind of vacuum exists here that leaves you empty as to what your life really amounts to. Then (in those days) there was a Channel 11 program devoted to Oriental Wisdom in which Zen Buddhism was mentioned, and in which I became intrigued, as I watched every single program. Being naïve, but having a strong instinct, and intuition, the religions I was raised with were too conventional to match the energy and power that I had as a youth. All these teachings that I received simply did not penetrate into my being. I wanted to break out from all the conventional secular and religious systems implanted in my mind and find a new way to think about religion, breaking through all the nice, polite, and sentimental religious modes of thinking, in order to get to the question of, Who am I?

Somehow I happened into Buddhism. I was not born as a Buddhist. So I didn't acquire anything until the need arose in me to find out. Could Buddhism answer my question? I decided to take the journey, a quest to find out. And so I left home.

In the process of learning I have come across many teachings as well as many teachers. But especially when I met my teacher was I able to focus on a person who could guide me through the process of seeking the essential questions of self. Then I could see beyond the clouds of my not knowing. It's not a mechanical step-by-step process, however. Buddhism is not a form of self-therapy, nor does it offer a panacea – a spiritual "crutch" we use to comfort ourselves and support ourselves. Nor will it bless us or pat us on the back, or baby us by telling us how good we are. In that sense it is the most difficult of all religions in the sense that it does not require faith in an external entity outside of ourselves, but instead focuses primarily on the real cause of our problem: self.

I did not know this when I first began seeking into the truth of my life, knowing nothing. Now today I see the One Mind as this subtle self, which flows with the ever-changing nature of life in the simplicity and of the enlightening nature of the spirit. The enlivening spirit of the original mind is the original self shining in all directions.

The Human Spirit   R.A. 10/18/2012

I want to touch the self that embraces the human spirit.

"The self is no other than this: my settling down into this environment, letting naturalness to carry me, riding the unbounded working of myriad phenomena". These are the words by Rev. Manshi Kiozowa (1863-1903) that describe the enlightenment of an awakened person. These words are similar to the way I feel to the flowers that bloom, to the friends I meet, or for that matter, so many things that unbounded life itself brings to me to experience. How joyous then is my feeling to hear these words now that I feel at one with them.

The question of what happens to self after total negation brings to mind one of Rev. Akegarasu's poem-like writings that further describe what Rev. Kiozowa begins. I'm getting into the final paragraphs to focus on just what he means by self as he describes himself as such.

Rev. Akegarasu begins by saying that he has made a terrible mistake in thinking that his thought, experiences, feelings, will, wish, and deeds were his thoughts, experiences, feelings, will, wish, deeds; but since he clung to them he realized that they had became fixed. Realizing his mistake he says the following:

"…. But then who am I? Yes, it is true, that through thought, experience, feeling, will, wish, and deed, I manifest myself, but I also manifest myself when I break out of all of these.

I am not such a limited self to exist apart from others! I alone am most noble. I embrace the cosmos.

What an indescribable, subtle existence I am – I cannot in speaking or writing put down who I am!

I always touch this indescribable self, always follow this indescribable self. Truth is here."

So, this subtle self as described by Rev. Akegarasu (1877-1954), the student of Rev. Kiozowa, described by his contemporaries as the living Buddha, who answers the ancient question of "Who am I?". It reads like a fresh breeze and in doing so makes us feel at one; and that I too, can be this subtle self. Such a jewel that Rev. Akegarasu uses to melt the ice of our hardened and scholarly mind into the flowing waters of life itself. From here what is it that is noble and that which embraces the cosmos? The Tathagata! As a continuous change of life which moves the self into an entirely different dimension. He is this Tathagata moving along with the cosmos – the total universe and this world in particular has such power to come up with this living expression – as it is the One Soul of the universe.

MEMORIAL

Shortly after the teacher's passing away in March 10, 2001, I thought of all the things that he did and all the events that took place. Reverend Gyoko Saito was quite a person. I thought it would be a shame if a book was not made that would record his life's work, both for the contribution he made for the present and future of Buddhism in this country and abroad, and among us who knew him directly, who he influenced by his presence and his teachings.

Here now I still enjoy the warmth of his presence at so many Buddhist retreats, so many of our discussion group sessions, so many working projects at his place, so many events, speeches and activities at the Temple in which over the years a large number of people were involved. Then later his active participation at the Los Angeles main Temple where he was the North American Bishop – all his writings and translations; so much so, that when I put it all together, it is immense. Not to forget, his participation in the Maida Center of Buddhism in which he was one of the main speakers. His various trips to Japan, Hawaii, and even Brazil – all the sessions and places he attended where he was a notable participant and speaker. Ah, if I put it all down it would take many, many pages. But from my point of view and in taking all this into account I admired him as a human being, and I want to focus on the brightness of his life and what that means to me. For beyond words there is something that is communicated that is a direct influence life to life, which has such a living essence to it. It is the core of our life as well as the essence of Buddhism as well. For he was the communicator of Buddhism and Shakyamuni's teachings throughout his life within his own experience and his own feeling. He was primarily a student with an open mind, influencing us to be true students also.

Buddhism is a matter of self-introspection and watchfulness into our own lives into the truth of the teachings as directly as they affect our lives. And in the case of the teacher, till the very end he lived such an active student's life. As the best student he was at the same time the best teacher. Without such sincere studentship one cannot become the best teacher, or as a true human being either. And that was his primary influence on my life that effected a change in my life.

In seeking into his life it is inevitable that I would seek into my own life as well. To be at one with the teacher took my total effort, and as a result of my own aspiration it deepened, which included the teachers he studied from, and also has expanded to include all people.

By visiting all the Buddhas and bodhisattvas you learn. But by seeing oneself as being the last of the unenlightened one's, thus starting from zero with no conceit, you learn the most. Here is where I find Gyoko Saito, the teacher.

Introduction: The Trip to Japan

R. Adams
May 9, 2013

Life is a journey and in this journey we meet with people, and many of these people become our friends. It is through the meeting of people who become our friends that we experience our life.

How fortunate I was then to meet with a true friend. It was through him that I really had a chance to experience my life. I'd like to introduce him to you. His name was Gyoko Saito and as he was a Buddhist minister at a temple here in Chicago (the old temple was torn down several years ago), and his ministerial title was Reverend Gyoko Saito. He came from Japan, born of a farming family not too far from the ocean in Kumamoto-ken, a prefecture which is in the southern part of Japan.

Early in his adulthood as a young man he experienced a great difficulty while attending college that almost took his life. This incident happened between himself and a fellow student who he fell in love with. Because he was so in love with her he wanted to marry her but her parents denied the possibility of such a thing because of the variations between classes that still existed in Japan at that time. So in love, he was driven to desperation on this account. He no longer cared to attend class at the University that he had been attending and even showed no concern over the final exams that were due. Once while meeting with his professor at the train station his professor almost pleaded with him to come back to complete his exams and that he would attempt to intervene on his behalf to rectify the situation with her parents. But alas, to no avail. Meanwhile Gyoko was facing a dead end – his very first love with another person came to a dead end that saw no opening except by ending it all.

Gyoko Saito was at the tipping point when news got out of this possibility to a dear friend of his by the name of Ms. Inada sensei, a teacher in her own right who was also blind. It was she, at the last minute before his attempted suicide by drowning saved him from plunging in. He must seek help, and both she and Rev. Gyosei Ono, head minister of the local temple undertook to convince him to go and listen to a well known minister named Reverend Haya Akegarasu, who had quite a following of Shinshu followers himself and so many beyond. At the time he was one of the administrators of Higashi Hongwanji and Otani Univ., a college for ministerial careers in Jodo Shinshu Buddhism.

So while Rev. Akegarasu was on a speaking tour Mr. Saito decided to attend, and after listening several times became resurrected from a dark period in his life and saw for the first time a light in his life that removed the dark and seemingly impenetrable cloud he lived under.

Listening to Akegarasu changed his life. So much so that he decided to finish his exams at the Univ. of Kumamoto but to leave his prospects as an electrical engineer in order to devote himself to what the teacher had to say as relates to the Dharma Teaching. But in order to do that he would have to enlist as a student at Otani Univ. to become a minister. As he stated it, it wasn't so much to become a minister but that it provided a way to be close to and listen to the teacher's words that really mattered.

Approaching Rev. Akegarasu with his intentions, Rev. Akegarasu told him that to do so he would have to get permission from his parents first.
But his parents objected. After all, being the youngest of several children they put in all their efforts in the hopes of seeing to it that he become an electrical engineer and rise to the top, not to assume the position of just a Buddhist minister. Their refusal was also based upon the fact that they did not know of a Rev. Akegarasu, nor did they realize the extent of their son's transformation upon listening to him. His lowest point was now transformed into his deepest aspiration, of which they had no idea. Once you see the light you head for the light; and in that sense there is no stopping it, you must drive forward with your wish to seek the truth of who you really are. This kind of quest, reaching the deepest part of one's being is unstoppable. This is the truth of our deepest wish. It's like water to the thirsty flower. Once you are ready to listen to the living Dharma a spiritual truth enters that transcends everything else; that is, the deepest aspect of one's soul is stirred, comes alive, and experiences a revival.

During the end of his days at Kumamoto University while in the midst of his difficulty he once asked his professor if he could guarantee him his life. His professor told him that he could not. Internally, Saito in thinking this over must have concluded that in no way could the secular world assure him of anything substantial from this world that would guarantee him of anything much less his life. Beyond position, monetary gain and so forth, what was there to life as his life remained as an open question unresolved by the professor's answer. He must find out. The depth of the teacher's teaching beckoned him forward into an unknowable dimension that attracted him more than any worldly position could have at this time.

Since verbal discussion and attempts at persuasion failed to convince his parents to give him permission, he was driven to take more extreme measures to get their permission. He would go on a hunger strike, which is what he did for several days – just water. His parents grew increasingly worried. His mother put food in front of him, but he refused to eat. Seeing him grow lethargic and weak she finally caved in and they both gave him the permission to become a minister by going to Kyoto to be with the other students who were also studying to become ministers as well.

He was on his own though. Yet I am sure that he bowed to his parents upon leaving them for they only wanted what was best for him.

Once he landed in Kyoto and was enrolled in the classes he ate the frugal students diet of noodles (somen), miso, rice, and dried fish; or tofu, skimono (sour cabbage), spinach and etc.; which because of a skimpy diet that students are not too careful about led him to catching colds or a sore throat which he tried to cure by taking a shot of whiskey some friend provided him! Those were the student days in which he had to learn poverty and frugality by watching every cent. He was living a monk's life!

But he was learning so much, and being close to the teacher made all the difference, so he could put up with all the other things that came his way. On top of that, he also managed to attend Shuichi Maida's seminars, lectures on the Buddha-Dharma held at his place in Nagano City. Rev. Maida was also a student of Rev. Akegarasu and Saito had a great deal of respect for him and so they became close friends. Once when he sat down with Rev. Maida (for that was his honorific title since he was not an ordained minister), Maida told him: "Life is so difficult, isn't it". Though difficult it had meaning and great value for now he was part of the Sangha of fellow listeners and seekers of Shakyamuni's teachings. This by the way is where he met Toshiko which began a warm friendship that ended in their marriage later on upon graduation. She took it upon herself to give him the proper cold medicine to take care of his colds and other things to maintain his health. So now after graduation he was an ordained minister with a new wife and a whole future that lie ahead of him.

If we go fast forward, it was not until some eighteen years later after coming to this country in 1955 did he get a chance to visit with his parents again. It was on the occasion of the World Dobo Convention, held in Kyoto, Japan that was convened in 1973 that gave him this opportunity. A fairly large group of people from the Chicago area attended, myself being one of them. The reason for my going is that this was going to be an almost one month tour of Japan. I prepared a year in advance to attend. My real reason spiritually was to find out from the farmers how they did the nembutsu: Namu Amida Butsu, performed as a quiet chant with hands clasped, head bowed in a humble posture. Even though I had been a parishioner for some ten years and saw so many others doing it I was not very impressed because I thought that these were city people and perhaps their nembutsu was not deep enough, but if I went to Japan to see the real thing, so to speak, I would be more informed as to the true content. Quite naïve' perhaps, but I had to discover it for myself. Studying with the teacher for ten years and now going to Japan? This prospect was so bright!

The depth of the nembutsu is a function of time the teacher once said. The nembutsu is solemn. Because it is solemn it is spiritual. Because it is spiritual it has to do with feeling. Because it has to do with feeling it has nothing to do with logic; one cannot grasp it in terms of conceptualization and reasoning. Therefore it cannot be taught or explained in the way we normally think of in terms of knowledge acquired through a reasoning process. Yet it is the very basis of our deepest spirituality that is directed towards our kneeling before and worshipping all things in the world in the broadest sense without going through a process of discrimination. A process of discrimination would say that since there is both good and bad in the world, then why should I worship the bad along with the good? But this is a result of our relative thinking, not that of worship. Without this worship we have no true realization of religion – except otherwise for the appearance of religious formalities attached to its chanting practices. And since it does not discriminate between the good and the bad, there is no reasoning process involved that would divide things into categories within the feeling of worship. As it is based entirely upon feeling and is not divided into dualistic fragments or abstract words as in our conventional way of thinking, we therefore cannot determine what is good or bad within the context of the solemnity of worship. As that is the case, we can easily understand Jodo Shinshu's c. founder, Shinran Shonin's statement that he does not know at all what is good or bad. He is manifesting here, the very essence of his teacher Honen Shonin and his true understanding of the nembutsu. Indeed, as Shinran stated: "You might as well be known as a cow-stealer then as a mere Nembutsu-practitioner." It takes much time before we begin to realize the difference between merely chanting it as a matter of religious formality, or that which really comes from your total being. As he referred to himself as "A foolish baldheaded one", considering his foolish self as having no real value or merit; yet within the inner power of nembutsu he felt the virtue of oneness with Amida's compassion for all people. So how it is interpreted is very important.

Though I did not know at the time exactly what it was I was seeking, at least I felt the need to get at the "roots" of a tradition that had been going on for centuries and seemed to carry quite a large portion of Japan that embraced it. It moved me to find out its source among the ordinary people as I said who would most likely exemplify it in its purest form. Actually, as far as my teacher Reverend Saito was concerned, he never taught it but manifested it throughout the whole time I knew him, so that I needn't go any further. So the "roots" actually came from him! So in a sense it's like that of the bamboo in which you get down into the roots, cook them, and then taste them – the proof is in the tasting...

.

When he returned to his family in Kumamoto he was given a hero's welcome. By now he had become the head minister of a fairly large temple with three ministers at the old temple here in Chicago after having served as an assistant minister for several years.

Rev. Saito had a personal charm which we could call charisma that attracted many friends, for he loved to make friends and enjoy warm company together with others. So back in his home town many of his buddies from high school and friends from all over remembered him as well as various family members who greeted him with handshakes and hugs. Especially his mother was impressed as I'm sure he intended, with such smiles and ebullience that made her think of her son as successful in America, and also bringing with him a student who had been studying with him for ten years gave her a little extra to go by in her satisfaction. Ha, even he passed out a few cigars to further the celebration! So altogether it was a joyous occasion for everybody. They even rented a banquet hall where it seemed as if half the town showed up for a festive dinner. Jokingly, I may mention that I was dressed in a dark blue polyester suit with the large lapels and bell-bottom trousers – perhaps I looked a little like, you know, Admiral Perry! I remember his mom when she first saw me she peered into my eyes for a while looking up at me – I don't think she had seen a blue-eyed Caucasian before! I guess we were from two different worlds coming together; that is what made the whole trip so unusual wherever I traveled either by myself or with Rev. Saito.

One of the main points, however, was when I met with Ms. Inada sensei (the one who saved him). When both of us met with her in front of her house she stood with hands clasped quietly chanting the nembutsu over and over, stopping only to greet us. Above her head were several sparrows fluttering about which altogether made her look angel-like. When we entered her house she invited us for tea and after a few minutes of chat with Rev. Saito she began to speak with me in English. She began to discuss various existentialists such as Camus, Sartre, and others. I was a little surprised at her knowledge of Western philosophy – I could hardly keep up with her – she was very a well educated and well-rounded person.

This was not merely a trip to a foreign country; it was his way of letting me see the spiritual, social, cultural, and even the anthropological area of reclaimed land near the ocean in southern Japan. So I have to say it was unforgettable because I had such a great guide to show me the way in understanding him and myself. In meeting the people it was becoming my country as well. I'm sure that was his feeling now that I look back.

And then with Ms.Inada I got a sense of the nembutsu that became both visual and physical; in other words, her life was totally devoted to it.

After showing me the town and visiting with various friends we spent an evening at Rev. Ono's temple, the one that I mentioned before. This temple would have belonged to a specific district in which the Saito's lived as a controlling factor at one time dictated by the government, and you would have needed a passport to go from one district to another by way of a wooden paddle bearing your family name inscribed in it (this is the way the civil government could control people so that they would not gather in large numbers to create civil wars and/or upheavals, and etc.) So in a sense this is a family temple belonging to a local district. Well, we spent an evening there which included a dinner and refreshments including rice wine or sake. This was a happy occasion, the majority of participants were women, and in fact I think we were the only two men there (Rev. Ono had passed away). But the result of all this joy was that the women stood up suddenly and started dancing in a kind of O-Bon style of folk dance, humming and singing songs that gave rhythm to their steps and waving arms. I remember the words of Rev. Akegarasu's comment about a lady, who while dancing said: "I will dance my way into the Pure Land".

Now sitting on a bench in my back yard this morning and after all the rains we've had; to see the tomato plants growing, my mind is dancing.

Many Buddhists have complicated ideas about the Pure Land and its meaning, as well as ideas about whether or not the Pure Land will come after we die and so forth. It's like some kind of heaven after death, and so they prepare themselves for it by purifying themselves to becoming good Buddhists like saints so that they will feel comfortable facing their death. The Pure Land and being born into it occurs right here on earth, not in some other-worldly paradise for the convenience of one's expectations.

I only dance when I'm happy. Happiness is the Pure Land – a rhythm of life that flows like the blood in your veins. This organic oneness turns into "onceness" which discards the static, set understanding of dead dualistic concepts into the will and spirit to be together with others who themselves come up with their own physical oneness of life. We can't see this coming from those who examine Buddhism with cold fingers. This is what Rev. Saito communicated and wanted us to see.

When all the artificial layers are removed I am brought by the ordinary emptiness of the Pure Land; empty of the defilements that the mind can conjure up, or derisive thoughts that create set concepts about the Pure Land. I can live in this wondrous world right here on earth, reflecting upon it, as moment to moment life can be seen manifesting it in so many ways.

The Pure Land is what makes Mahayana Buddhism so human. The larger vehicle with Amida Buddha as its focal point and the nembutsu as its devotion was intended for all people to be born into its essence.

Roots of the Bamboo   June 2, 2013

    After staying overnight at Rev. Ono's temple and having breakfast in the morning we left saying goodbye after having experienced a wonderful evening the day before. But before saying goodbye I was presented with a beautiful antique lacquered tea cup holder as a gift from Mrs. Rev. Ono and I remember feeling unworthy of receiving such a gift that I went back to the alter and placed some money near the incense burner – I simply could not accept such a gift simply because I accompanied Rev. Saito – to be treated like an honored guest – then to be given such a gift? This was as a result of the feeling that was generated by participating in the dinner and dance the night before that I think was an outpouring of affection and generosity freely given that still makes an impression on me some forty years later. They must have loved him very much since remembering Rev. Ono as his first teacher from his early days at the temple. This is the feeling of respect coming from this community of sangha.

    In the ordinary world if we dig deep enough we find such treasures. This indeed happened while we were digging for a bamboo roots back in the family's front yard and near the road that leads into their property. I believe that it was one of the uncles of Rev. Saito who upon learning that back in America I had painted bamboo sumei style brush and ink painting but never had seen a real bamboo in my life before, now seeing many of them growing in their natural environment here in Kumamoto, Japan.

    It is true that while studying Zen Buddhism at the time and being influenced by Chinese, Korean as well as Japanese art in which there was such freedom of brush strokes that were displayed without any of the conceptualized art that is so frequently seen in the modern art of the West. Such self-generated art takes none of its inspiration from nature, but rather focuses on concepts and ideas in an attempt to be creative mentally, yet not natural as being at one with nature. Indeed, much of city life is this way based as it is on man, not nature. As a result there is a rift between the natural world and man's world, a kind of disjuncture wherein creativity has a tendency to be artificial based as it is on contrivances and concepts from a secular mentality involved with promoting one's self. It is not to be compared to the naturalness of nature which inspires one to create from its simplicity and beauty.

Spring rain pouring down -
A clematis flower!
Shining like a bright star.

Listen to the spring rain. The benefit of the heavens pouring down on earth, quenching its thirst. A clematis vine is opening with its first flower!

Kyoto was a city of flowers when I arrived in the latter part of March. I stayed with the Frazer's, Dan and Myra. Dan was studying to become a minister at Otani University. Both of them were from Chicago and were students of Rev. Saito from our Thursday evening discussion class of the American Buddhist Association, same as I. This was to be a two week stay that included much sightseeing and things to do. Also, Rev. Saito came into the picture. For instance, he showed me where it was that Shinran Shonin walked down from Mt. Hei and through the park to get to where his teacher Honen had his temple after spending twenty years up there studying Tendai Buddhism. And then there was the Higashi Hongwanji main temple where they had on display the three inch thick ropes made out of human hair that lifted the heavy beams in the construction of this large temple. A woman's long hair was considered a beauty mark and to have it cut off was considered a major sacrifice at that time. To make these long thick ropes would have taken thousands of young women to give up their precious possession. This shows how deep Honen and Shinran's teaching took hold throughout Japan to affect the effort needed in constructing this temple.

But one of the things on the list was to visit the ancient capital city of Nara where there are many temples, but the one most important is called Horyu-ji, a large and old one (A.D. 711), in which Prince Shotoku (572-622), is seated in a kneeling posture with hands clasped in front of a shrouded figure that no one can see because it is covered up. We now know that this figure is that of Bodhisattva Kuan Yin (Ch.) from the Lotus Sutra because the Italian philosopher Phenalosa while teaching philosophy in pre-war Japan had it forcibly removed in the early part of the century. Much later Rev. Akegarasu was to build his own Rosendo, an eight cornered structure in which his teacher, Rev. Kiozowa, was seated on a raised platform and Rev. Akegarasu was seated below in a kneeling posture with hands clasped in a manner of adoration. In all the centuries that have passed since then we see an identical form of feeling, an expression between the teacher and the student that prevails in Buddhism. Such depth of feeling goes beyond thank you or expressions of gratitude as it has the deepest feeling to it.

We said goodbye to Kyoto, the teacher and I, and headed by train to the southern part of Japan, Kumamoto prefecture. I've already discussed how well he was received by his family and friends, but actually our trip began with Kyoto, and now I want discuss in further detail more about my continuing experiences in Kumamoto.

The first thing I noticed when we got off the train at the station was the gruffness of their voices, especially the women who were working at the station – they sounded more like men than ladies. There was a change in dialect it seemed, a more masculine tone of speech, as say in Kyoto, where the dialect spoken is effeminate. These are tough people I thought, but civil strife, battles, and upheavals made it so. For example, they pushed back the ocean with a series of dykes in order to provide more farming space, much the same as the Dutch did in their native Holland. The teacher explained to me how his area at least would be a perfect place for anthropologists to study the native people going all the way back to the earliest settlers who claimed this land, and who pushed back the ocean and were now growing a variety of crops including little pigs or the huge strawberries that I saw being sold in Kyoto. This is the farming culture that sensei is coming from and what it is that made him so unique. So it is a good idea to give a feeling for his ancestral roots since it affected the way he pronounced English, which I liked because it was so crisp, direct, and powerful. And by the way, how it affected my typical college-style English as I began to repeat his words in my mind so that even I began to sound somewhat like him. Such was the strong influence he had on my life, changing my tongue in the way I pronounced words. Now, however, I am comfortable using my own dialect.

If as he told me, Kumamoto created some of Japan's infamous gangsters, yet what I observed was a place that created a spiritual milieu that exposed me to a culture that was simple and direct without smelling of religion. It left an impression on my mind that did not carry big city sophistication but rather came from roots that were buried in the soil and a natural association and feeling for the earth. This is a contributing factor in sensei's direct and organic interpretation of the Buddha-Dharma which is so evident throughout his life, and this is the vital point that so influenced me, and indeed, helped change my life too.

Therefore, whether it was this unique feeling I got from the land and its people, I right away felt at home. It is here where the spiritual down-to- earth Japan revealed and threw light on the historical and family life that the teacher came from that touched me. For buried in that culture of ordinary people shines the exceptional ones who like my teacher exemplify all that this country offers to the world of thought and religion.

*   *   *

On to Nagano, first by train, and then we were picked up by car by Mr. Inoue, a friend of Rev. Nobuo Haneda now living in Berkeley, Ca., who originally came from there. Nagano city sits on a high plateau flanked on one side by high mountains. This is the same city that hosted the winter Olympics in 1998. It also has one of the oldest temples in Japan called the Zen Koji (Good Light) and within it houses one of Japans oldest and largest hand carved Amida Buddha statue and is over six centuries old. The first thing you notice about Nagano is its huge pine trees that resemble our own sequoia trees that grow in Muir Woods State Park just a few miles north from

San Francisco. Then there is an ancient "hotel" or inn that is about as old as the city itself and now is an historical treasure.

The three of us beside the marker of the historical inn.

In the evening we settled down into a more modern hotel. Now an interesting thing happened. Prior to going to bed and sleep, Rev. Saito invited a masseuse to come up and give us a massage. He happened to be blind. No matter, he worked on me first. First he works on one side, then the other. In the first side he got me laughing, on the other side he got me close to crying. Of course, this was in terms of feeling, not in actuality. It was real however, in terms of a realization within me that I was a person with a split-mind. That is, a person whose mind was divided between the spiritual and the secular. This was a physical diagnosis of symptoms that contained a mental problem causing one side to struggle against the other side leading to friction and an unsettled condition. I marvel at how he did it. As the secular world is involved with dualistic logic it cannot be at one with the ever-flowing power beyond self: One is static, and the other is continuously moving. One is non-Buddhist, the other is Buddhist. The fixed self as opposed to the open-ended, non-formed self; doesn't that adequately describe our problem that we can apply to our own lives in so many ways, universally, and with no exception? As such, it does, and Rev. Saito knew this when he invited the masseuse to come up to our room to give me a teaching that prior to this I couldn't see.

Delving clearly into this problem of secular worldliness fostered by greedy desires and embedded within the world of samsara; is the cause behind the suffering of our own *klesas,* or evils of the contriving mind. In dropping one's attachment to the secular world of artifice, stupidity, and contamination, Illusion and delusion along with its attendant profit-and-loss motivation, I can settle down into playfulness of the One Mind, finding my real self within its bosom. Dwelling in "isness" I live a natural person's life.

The awakened person does not abandon the world for some otherworldly existence. But rather, he, in trusting the power within Amida's Primal Vow, is enabled to experience the embracing power of Eternal Life to sweep aside and transcend what is known as *samsara*, the world of birth-and-death while being in it – that is, the world as such. What a creative world this is then! The karmic conditions being dropped, the way to spacious freedom is open for one to live a creative life, and find his happiness there.

Prince Shotoku (cent.), stated emphatically: "This secular world is an illusion". And we, by getting caught in its net, become deluded persons.

The essence of Buddhism is based on the abhorring of the secular world with all its contrivances and ugly discord, along with all its lukewarm promises of doing well and saving people into the illusion of relative and partial happiness's. Instead, we should listen to the squiggling truth within.

Being in the warm bosom of naturalness, I feel perfectly relaxed. I don't need to go out of myself to find happiness, contentment, and peace. I don't need to seek the entertainment that all those personalities of the secular world have to offer in order to relieve the boredom of an otherwise empty life-style. I stay away from them. In other words, I stay away from all the excitement, joking, romanticist, sentimentalist, violence, and horror stuff that appear on T. V. I also push away from the spectator sports of winning and losing that so many people attach to; that is, by transcending that which no longer applies to my life and is irrelevant to it. The age of wisdom is here along with its fallibility. The age of the quiet person is here. It is not what the general public listens to. It is the live-wire life of the Dharma.

* * *

We came to Nagano because Rev. Saito was invited by the Saraguchi's. These were the parents of their daughter, Tomulko, the wife of Rev. Haneda, who spent some time in Chicago and was to show their appreciation for his support and encouragement. As such we were treated like royalty and given a rather lavish dinner by a well-known restaurateur in a private setting along with other friends and family. I remember the huge dog they had behind a fenced off area in the back yard; an Akita, almost twice the size of a wolf, the type that was probably used by ancient hunters for sniffing out bear, dear, and other animals when this area was forested.

From here we went to see Shuichi Maida's place. Since he passed away in 1967 we were met by a Mr. Watanabe, a student of Maida's who then fulfilled the role of caretaker ever since Rev. Maida passed away. This was the second reason why Rev. Saito visited Nagano, to show me the place where Rev. Maida taught, wrote, lectured, and lived.

Shuichi Maida is recognized as one of the most important Buddhist leaders in contemporary Japan. Though not connected to a temple, he was nonetheless an independent person who could therefore feel free to survey the whole of Buddhist texts including the oldest one coming from the Theravada tradition and directly associated with Shakyamuni himself, called: **Face To Face With Shakyamuni** with a commentary on the **Sutta Nipata** by Shuichi Maida (trans. by N. Haneda). It is quite a lengthy work that we have been studying for some twenty years now at B.T.C. He wrote voluminously (12 vols. of books), translated Shinran Shonin's work (Bondo Edition), and conducted over fifty seminars a year and so forth with a list of work that simply amazes those who are familiar with his efforts.

Early on Rev. Saito knew Rev. Maida, attended several of his lectures in around the same time that he was also listening to the teacher to both of them: Reverend Haya Akegarasu, who was most important in both of their lives. Being older and with more experience he looked to Maida for the guidance for his own life as well for the temple back in Chicago. He even invited Rev. Maida to come to the States to help him with the progress of Buddhism in this country, but Maida turned him down stating that he was too occupied with those who needed him in Japan. So they were close friends to the point that when Rev. Maida passed away suddenly in 1967, I remember the speech that Sunday when in heartbroken language Rev. Saito described his relationship with Maida by stating that it felt like he had lost his right arm. So it was like a brother-to-brother relationship....

In thinking of Shuichi Maida and within the depth of his understanding and the relationship he had with his teacher Rev. Akegarasu, who as he stated: "crushed me completely and totally". He gives us the insight into the essence of Jodo Shinshu Buddhism that removes all philosophical and by being seen as wise and knowledgeable? If so, then this knowledge becomes nothing but chunks of ice in one's mind. Here, one is likely to have a big head that is set on the person's tiny legs! Now he can easily fall down by being such an unbalanced individual! Such a smart one wants to appear as a sage, a clever scholarly understanding that causes one to think that he can grasp the Buddha-Dharma with mere head knowledge. After transcending worldly attachments we must return to it to be on our knees worshipping all things in the world as all beings are connected by causes and conditions like the knots that come together in this huge net of life.

Maida's emphasis on "actional intuition" seems to be derived from his first teacher, Dr. Kitaro Nishida, and it means direct perception, direct insight, intuitively. I think this can be related to the "one thought moment" of Shinran Shonin which sounds similar, at least in content. This also relates to the "flash of truth" that Rev. Maida used many times.

Within the freedom of emptiness and non-attachment the spacious skies open into the wide highway of life which is called the Pure Land, and within the Pure Land the experience of life itself within the honest person which allows one to go in any direction without the obstruction of the static and fixed ego. Here one can play, create, and do whatever I wish in harmony with the movement like the river that flows from the mountains to the sea.

The three of them beginning with Manshi Kiozawa (1870-1945), Haya Akegarasu, Shuichi Maida, and then also my teacher Gyoko Saito, form a contemporary lineage, and, within this lineage so many others, as all of us are the sangha who are students of the Buddha-Dharma. But it is these sangha that stand out because of the depth and breadth of their insight.

It is difficult at this time to transmit their full impact to those who have not as yet read them, so by way of brevity I'll give the words of Shinran that applies to them all:

> I take refuge in the inconceivable light,
> I rely upon the Tathagata of immeasurable life.

* * *

Another scene happened when sensei and I traveled a short distance from the city to a nice clean river flowing from the mountains to the valleys downstream where we had lunch in a rather wide river at this point. There was a boardwalk two and a half feet wide and only about two feet above the water. It went straight into the river for about a hundred feet where it ended in a fair-sized dining establishment reminiscent of one of those open thatched houses seen in old Chinese paintings where we had freshly caught fish – no chairs. What a delightful repose within the river itself. Life is so interesting here, in this feeling of having a delicious lunch within the flowing river of life. What a unique and wonderful place found nowhere else.

Opposite to this is the parable attributed to Shan-tao (Ch.613-681) the fifth patriarch on Shinran's list of patriarchs. In it he describes the raging "River of Fire – River of Water"; the two sides of human greed: satiation and anger. The seeker of truth must cross this river on a white path only four inches wide represent the four stages of consciousness: seeing, hearing, speaking, and cognition. While just below the path on one side of the river there are billowing waves of water representing our greed, while right next to it are the raging flames of fire. The waves of water represent our greed, whereas on the other side, fire represents our anger. Meanwhile, the traveler who is on this shore is trying to get away from being pursued by thieves, thugs, evil priests, wild animals, snakes, and biting insects who are chasing after him on the east side of the river of ignorance, evil, and death, and who are all out to get him. If he stays on this side he will most surely die. Yet at the same time, if he tries to cross over to the other shore where there is the Pure Land, he will most surely die also; either by drowning or by burning, as the treacherous flames and billowing waves overlap the narrow path. Then he hears on the shores of the Pure Land, the Buddha who appears and beckons him to cross over, who in a comforting but commanding voice says: "Come to me. Do not fear I will protect you!" Beckoned by the Buddha to cross to the other shore, being pushed by the Buddha on this shore, he gathers the courage to race forward along this narrow path and bravely reaches the other shore of the Pure Land. He made it! So goes the Parable of fire and water.

               Amidst city noises
        a white bush peony blooms –
          capturing me instantly!

As we abandon the secular life-style and transcend the world – this is what leads to birth in the Pure Land, fulfilling one's wish in the land of Nirvana.

All humans want to know who they really are, but it is difficult to see. The teacher who knew me better then I knew myself enabled me to see myself and who I really am so that I may go through and reach the true self. This though, requires a struggle; for it is not so easy, as the final attachment to self has to be shown to us outside of ourselves by the mirror of truth, as shown to us by the teacher or teachers as to the teaching they expose us to.

What it comes down to is are we truly alive, do we really feel the essence of life that fulfills our wish to be truly human, or are we merely storing knowledge for the sake of storing knowledge and somehow expecting to promote oneself into enlightenment as a "know-something" person. Because just below the surface can be a layer hidden from others, a misguided and conceited person who likes to preach to others but who is blind as to their own ignorance. Rev. Kiozowa stated that he'd rather put a stone in his mouth than to preach to others. We get stale when we just borrow truths from others without our own life in it. Truth that comes up as a shout is our self-realization of an organic sense of who we are as living persons who are actually living the teaching rather than merely talking <u>about</u> it.

We forget here of the beginner's mind of an ordinary person, one who sincerely seeks the truth that reverberates into the mind of him.

If not, we are just collecting information and are no longer humble for any real truth to enter – we have a closed mind – finished, complete, arrogant, and conceited. Here we can be misguided, corrupting and defiling the very Buddha-Dharma we seek to promote. In that sense the beginners mind is the real seeker of truth, for seeking the truth in an open-minded way is itself the truth. No matter how much we know about Buddhism amounts to little in the midst of nothingness where the truth appears without any effort from one's self-power position. We have to come up with our very own shout; otherwise we just build up more fixed blocks of conceptualized understanding or collecting materials for one's own self-contained world.

The teacher's job as he described it was to remove our ignorance. Two-dimensional understanding is not the truth. It has no power, it has no life, and it cannot move others, either. One's two-dimensional understanding has deep flaws and errors which are so difficult to see. It also has this ego-attachment out of self-love which means that we will defend it at all costs.

One day we came upon a Shinto shrine. It was quite an outstanding kiosk with several tall shiny red lacquered pillars set atop a raised platform with steps leading up to it. I decided that it was an excellent place to take a picture so I handed Rev. Saito my small camera and asked him to take a picture of me. Fine, but when I got back to Chicago to develop the film the one of me in front of the shrine had my head missing. Knowing the teacher as I did I knew that this was no mere accident, but was intended to show me that my head had grown too large as a result of self-importance, a symptom of those who show signs of themselves as being special, or above others, or having fixed ideas about religion. So he had to clear my head of any number of things, which he did using an expedient means – a camera!

So when we talk about the self it is about being naked as a human being. When all the artificial layers are removed, I am I. A quiet satisfaction comes to me as I think of this trip with the teacher as guide till the very end.

I took the train back to Tokyo by myself where I would meet with him and the others for the trip back home. On the way back I passed through a landscape of rice fields surrounded by some eucalyptus-like trees as the sun was setting. A beautiful scene and a perfect ending to my trip to Japan where I more than fulfilled my wish to see for myself the roots of the nembutsu among those who I came to see as friends and of the sangha.

"Bush Peony"   R.A.

Taking inspiration from Shan-tao's parable of the two rivers, "River of Fire – River of Water" as mentioned before, I have the words: "Come to me: Don't fear, I will protect you!" The Buddha is calling on us to proceed to cross over the treacherous waters of samsara and to come as we are and without hesitation go to the place of Nirvana, the Pure Land. As we proceed our eyes will increasingly be opened to the teachings of the Dharma and thus the narrow path will become wider and wider, until it opens up into a wide highway of life itself. It is here wherein our deepest aspiration as the buds of our yearning will bloom into the bright flowers of who we are as an awakened human being. And the difficulties – even the impossible ones – our travails to cross to the other shore will be well rewarded, going the way of the Buddha.

> The white amaryllis is blooming!
> How beautiful, how beautiful
> –shouting openly, joyfully!

We can think of Dharmakara in the Larger Sutra as that of coming and going: Going to the Pure Land (Land of Bliss) after fulfilling his vows and coming back to the world of samsara, (world of suffering, or the world of birth–and-death) as in the ordinary world, and as that of flat ordinariness. Flat ordinariness has the connotation of no complication. It is in this world where he will fulfill all of his 48 vows, since they require his presence in it. But he cannot stay in the Pure Land. He must come back to the world that we all live in. This shows his compassion and pity for all human beings as they are involved in various kinds of ignorance. Here he comes back as a Bodhisattva in order to mingle with and be at one with the people. Thus he cannot sit on top of the mountain looking down on others in isolation from them; he may do as they do, in order to help them to cross over to the other shore of freedom and emancipation in the land of Amida's infinite spaciousness, and so giving life to the dead.

The Buddha relies on the power beyond the self, that is, he does not rely on the self that has no real substance,. He is as an independent person respecting the independence of all others, which he considers as absolute independence. His independence comes from self-introspection.

The Buddha stays where he's firmly settled, he doesn't compare himself with others through jealousy or envy, nor does he consider himself to be above or below others in a relative way. His way is the best way, just as his mother is the best mother of all the mothers in the world.

The amaryllis that struck me this morning is not just a flower, it is a teacher in the sense that it speaks without speaking, and it opens its life widely to show me the essence of its own life, an unfolding nature of its own existence. How beautifully it shines its own life, and it doesn't need to interfere with anyone else's life either. It just goes its own way nakedly shining, bringing me to it, as if saying "Come to me!"

Using the flower as an example, just as it emerges from its bud, and as it bursts from its sheath, we see a flower that is freshly born. As we look at Buddha's birth shout, they are essentially the same. We too, shared the same experience when we were just born, coming into this world as a bundle of flesh, with a shout so organically alive! The shout of one's birth into the world is like a fresh breeze that enlightens the world!

Freedom of the Infinite   March, 1998 R. A.

One thing that is universal among all human beings is the desire for freedom. But to realize the real or absolute freedom is not so easy. This is so because true freedom has to do with the infinite. Or to put it in another way, it has to do with pure spirit, i.e., the spirit as it touches upon the infinite. Spiritually, we seek the infinite. As finite beings, we are born, we must work, and we will die. But in this life of ours, short as it sometimes seems, there is a need, indeed, a deep aspiration to seek into the infinite nature of existence where true freedom exists. This desire is one of the most spiritual yearnings which transcend all others as a priceless jewel in that it is unbounded.

Reality is our life here and now, whereas the infinite we think of as belonging to another world beyond this one, or beyond reality. Simply stated, reality is everyday life. But the infinite we sometimes imagine as belonging to the other-worldly, something beyond our worldly grasp as we live our life here on Earth. It is something that belongs to God, the Sun, the Moon, and the stars. Here we hear numbers that are infinite. Yet right here on earth we have numbers that are infinite. What's more, we are living amongst them, all these uncountable numbers of organic and inorganic life. Our own bodies are among them – an infinite number of cells, what's more, they are constantly changing. So we are living in the infinite already. Right here as I speak, I am living in the infinite. We don't think of ourselves as constantly changing organically, but we are. It's just that the self does not want to see it that way. We want everything to be permanent, just like our self which we cling to as a fixed identity. And God must be a static entity too. And so too, the Earth stood still, and the sun went around the static Earth, so people believed at one time. Their God created the world as the center of the universe and everything else went around it – so that was God's infinite creation according to the Church. So now we have to clarify the infinite as belonging to an ever-changing reality. Now the infinite, including ourselves, are part of the eternal movement of the universe and are at one with it. This changes the whole picture of the infinite in its relation to our everyday world, doesn't it?

Yet somehow, this permanent, static self that we identify with and cherish prevents us from really opening into the infinite, and once we realize this, then we needn't look any further than ourselves for it. Yet, there is more to it than that, as we shall examine. Buddhism emphasizes the spacious freedom of the infinite by the figure of Amida Buddha, as infinite light and infinite life.

The infinite has to do with freedom, and it has everything to do with reality, or the finite. Indeed, it is because we live in the world of the finite, we can live in the infinite. Dividing one from the other can be rather dualistic as our thinking mind is prone to do. Samsara is Nirvana, and Nirvana is samsara. This simple Zen statement should correct our misunderstanding.

In the Larger Sutra, the spiritual traveler, Dharmakara, sees only one Buddha, Lokesvararaja, who appears before him and who he deeply appreciates as he listens to his Dharma. But as he begins to travel and work out the vows that he has set for himself he begins to see more Buddhas and listen to them; he makes offerings to them, appreciating what he is receiving. The more he listens and is struck by the truth of the Dharma his self decreases, as conversely, the number of Buddhas that he encounters increase – to such a number that it becomes infinite – as uncountable as the sands of the Ganges River! That's infinity for you. And he makes offerings to them all! Countless in number it says. As many as the stars of the universe, I joyously add! The Buddha has this capability – to see all beings as Buddhas, including non-sentient beings as well. This is an amazing transformation, from the dualistically unenlightened to the enlightened through the liberated self at one with the infinite.

Dharmakara becomes Amida Buddha, the eternal light through the shining essence of his being. Light means infinite light: Infinity as manifested through his brightness. Not because he is in touch with God or an otherworldly absolute being, but by his being at one with the Dharma itself, he feels eternal light. This is the essence of Amida Buddha, which we all must become if we are to touch the infinite in our ordinary lives. He, as the constant listener and learner, is discovering more and more, deepening his knowledge and experience. As this occurs, he is experiencing the movement of back and forth, from the finite to the infinite and from the infinite to the finite. He is continuously flowing in real terms which we have a word for: the Tathagatha – or coming and going. This is not done under his own self-power because this "coming and going" has an additional meaning of "thus comes". It is beyond my self-power abilities alone to realize it. This embracing power included in the *coming and going* aspect of the Sanskrit word, tathagatha, is the phrase: "thus comes". This inclusion means that it is beyond ones' own power to control, thus it is the great unknown and unknowable spirit of truth beyond our limited understanding and conventional wisdom.

In his endeavors as the seeker of truth, Dharmakara has been listening to the true Dharma and has been awakened into the true spirit, or *shinjin*. This is the freshness of life, also called "oneness", a term made up by Rev. Saito that I heard from him many years ago as he described the fresh life that we awaken to. So we can say that Dharmakara, discoverer of truth, was experiencing the *oneness* of fresh life in meeting with all other Buddhas, infinite in number. As such, by listening to the Dharma of his own teacher's truth, and being at one with it, he is spiritually transforming the finite into the infinite, as both relative self and the absolute self are inseparable. He bowed deeply to his teacher Lokesvararaja (King of the free life), as he became the bowing Buddha known as the Amida Buddha. This is most important, that of bowing to his teacher. Out of humility and appreciation he put his total being into oneness with the teacher. This enabled him to experience his true spirit, which then became 48 Vows he presented to him.

So when we talk about real freedom, we really have to be the spirit of Dharmakara. When we drop our smallish way of self and become a true listener and learner and that of a desperate seeker, there is a combustion of one's being that comes up as a shout. The student, who is seeking with his total life, is brought to life, born fresh into a clean slate of *shinjin*.

Our biggest impediment towards our own freedom is attachment to self. Here we create a sticky environment, a sticky world for ourselves. Yet, as humans we can't avoid being attached to what we love or what we care for, for it comes naturally with being a human being. But this "clinging" to our limited self- identity is something else. If we don't care for something, then naturally we don't become attached. But when we really care for something our attachment arises. In fact, it sounds inhuman to insist that we should get rid of our attachments altogether. So there are many kinds of attachments. Thus, it may have been that Gautama Buddha was attached to his robes, tattered pieces of discarded cloth sown together as they were, or his begging bowl – symbols attesting to his devotion to poverty and the simple way of life. Simplicity is beauty. But our life becomes complicated, confused, baseless, and dark when we attach to self. That's why we have to become the constant listener and learner towards our own ignorance as regards to the attached shell-of-self. We lose our ability to be straight towards others as well. By overestimating ourselves – stuck on ourselves and our own abilities – we become dishonest towards ourselves and towards others as well. We lack sincerity. We become devious and contrived. We become clever and artful liars. Covered with artificial layers, we lose our ability to see the truth about ourselves, and as such, live in a prison of our own making. And no matter how beautiful we think we have it decorated, it is still our prison of darkness – our little cave of ignorance and death – for there is no light in this cave. No brightness of freedom. No freedom to move freely as we wish, but a kind of blindness which is so deadly to any spiritual life that somehow desires to live in freedom, but can't. The freedom that is only on the surface is negligable.

The whole essence of Buddhism and its Dharma is devoted towards our being liberated into the world of true freedom. Attachment to self is the final attachment, and it is why we cannot attain this liberation so necessary for ourselves to manifest it. We can all have this brightness of being, but so often it is buried by layers of artificiality acquired by the self. I was so fortunate to have met the teacher and teachers who removed, or helped me remove things that I could not see, and they continue to do so by their teaching and example, even after they have passed away. Self clings tenaciously to its own position, either by our trying to be good persons, or by our thinking of us as superior in our understanding as learned persons. Here, we lack the nakedness and humility so necessary for progress into the Dharma. We seek permanence – the self seeks permanence as a kind of entity through self-identity. Unavoidably a thickened and hardened shell is formed, which is self-centered, selfish, and self-serving.

From here, all other static entities are created in our minds, including allies and enemies which conform to our beliefs in a static concept of the absolute which exists externally and to which we cannot actually feel or become. Thus we have an unknowable entity which can bless or punish us according to our good or bad deeds. Some traditionalists include Amida Buddha in much in the same way. There are those who think that Amida Buddha as a kind of savior descending from heaven, filled with compassion for human suffering, and thus grants them their wishes for their reciting the nembutsu. But these are conveniences people use to serve their desires as humans. Being as good people capable of goodness, or thinking of ourselves as sinners – either way, these are all manifestations of the kind of ignorance of self to which we by our own self-power, cannot see. Because of our relative judgments of the good or bad, or the moral and ethical "should and shouldn't", we fall into the little boxes called "judgmental values". Pray as we may to be saved, there is nothing worth saving here; nothing of our relative self is worth saving, rather to be discarded as so much delusion.

Then with this in mind we can go further in our understanding of the true nature of a teaching by which we are emancipated. Of course, it is our self-power which initiates our seeking as we seek for enlightenment, and the first step in that direction is so important. But the more we seek, the more we can get confused and misdirected because we are still reliant on our own abilities to control life – our life. These provisional understandings end in failure because they depend on that which has it basis in the relative self.

The relative self wants to be affirmed, not denied, and here it wants to construct a world based upon what agrees with its understanding so we can go on practicing self-praise and be content with it. We come to the Dharma with naïve but pre-fixed ideas and we expect the Dharma to agree with them. Here, we conceptualize Buddhism into a static system of truths based upon our limited understanding, all according to what we think it is. But our thinking is already tainted and discolored by its very source, the relative self, who is doing all the thinking! We're basing the truth on our own ignorant mind and hardening it until it becomes fixed. The Teacher's job is to crush this hardened shell completely so that we may experience the ultimate freedom that we originally sought to find.

Moreover, we get into all sorts of sundry practices as well, all in the to control our desires so that we can feel pure and good about ourselves. Here we just harden the chains of self-bondage which will not lead us into freedom at all. Like the kind of thinking that leads to calming the self through meditation practices, yoga practices, various other kinds of practices and asceticism. The idea of extinction of self by the self in order to attain ultimate freedom and absolute power is like pouring gasoline on an already raging fire – as what Shakyamuni discovered, when, after taking six steps he declared: "Oh Avidia!", "Oh Darkness!" There are many historical examples of this, these provisional disciplines bound for failure. Shinran Shonin is a perfect example. After spending 20 years on Mt. Hiei involved with moralistic and scholarly practices, he was getting frustrated to break through to freedom, and, that is what led him to come down from the mountain to sit at the feet of a teacher called Honin Shonin, and listen to the true Dharma coming from a living source. Here he felt the true compassion from a living person, who exposed him by way of his own nembutsu which led to him to the truth. Self-power seeking, including all the sundry practices associated with it were taken away by meeting with his teacher, who represented the true compassion in the form of a living person, not an abstract Buddha as separate from himself.

But if we are really sincere, we, despite the difficulty, will awaken to the truth of other-power, or power beyond self. If we become truly humble students, the desire for this eternal truth will deepen until we locate the cause of the problem. We can now progress and see the self, within its shell, as totally useless as we are being hit by life that is constantly changing. Even within our own bodies this is happening. Our blood is constantly flowing; our heart is constantly pumping, for if not, we die. Even on the most elemental and physical level, the static and half-dead mind is not flowing along with the body and is causing us to be sick.

So, we can listen to the truth of Manshi Kiozowa, who exclaimed: "I am as useless as a fan in December." If you understand his life, you can understand this statement more fully and appreciate the real meaning and subsequent impact on our lives of this statement.

Rev. Saito was particularly affected by this statement as it related to his own experience, his own life. In his final farewell speech at B. T. C just before leaving for the Los Angeles Temple he made the confession that in some 26 years of his being at the Chicago Buddhist Temple, he felt being as a "fan in December." Somewhat amazing, considering all that he did and all that he underwent. He really put his total being behind it, you see. Therefore, how can he make such a statement? I was a bit surprised when I first heard him say this at the annual Berkeley retreat in 1999, when the subject of the retreat was Manshi Kiozowa's life. Perhaps he could say that about certain members he felt useless with to the point of giving up, but what is the deeper meaning behind this statement?

I remember us trying to install a huge cold water air conditioner in the rear of the temple – this turned out to be a failure that he even joked about. But he used it to show to us how useless he was like Manshi Kiozawa's confession. I remember visiting him in 1988 in Los Angeles in spring during a religious festival. He opened his speech with these words, quoting from Shinran Shonin: "I will grind my bones to powder and flesh into pieces to listen to the Teaching." He said it so intensely that I'll never forget it.

*   *   *

Now we come to Mr. Fuji and Rev. Saito's talk during the 1999 summer retreat in Berkeley Ca. at the Maida Center of Buddhism, hosted by Rev. Haneda. Being as they were long-time friends, Rev. Saito had a special feeling for Mr. Fujii, and what Rev. Saito felt and what Mr. Fujii felt was towards the end, very much the same. As he began to tell the story to us, his voice was choked with emotion as he held back tears.

He was Ryoichi Fujii, chief editor and founder of the Chicago Shimpo, the only Japanese newspaper here in Chicago. He came here as a Japanese immigrant in the 1931 from Gifu prefecture in Japan. His main reason for coming to this country was to seek an education. He landed in Los Angeles, worked in a physical job and lived in a room with five other immigrants. He was desirous of furthering his education, but had no way until a Christian minister from a local church suggested to him that he complete his High School diploma by way of correspondence school and then go on to college. He received his High School diploma in six years by studying late at night by the light of a small lamp so as not to awaken the others. Then he applied for a free scholarship at Oberin College in Ohio, a Christian college, and graduated from college as well. Then he moved to New York, whereupon he was exposed to post-depression difficulties. About that time communism was gaining favor among the working class as well as some left-wing advocates, who saw in it a possibility of rectification of many of the wrongs being inflicted on the poor and powerless multitudes of working class people by the capitalistic system, immigrants and others who were brought to the level of slaves in their long working hours and deplorable living conditions. So out of sympathy, he joined the communist party by becoming a party member. But as time went on he observed that what the party heads preached and what they practiced were two different things, so he quit. He was an honest seeker who was seeking a resolution to a social problem and human suffering, but he found out that a political solution did not offer the answer.

Meanwhile, back in Japan, he had to do something about his ailing mother. It was always her wish that he become a good Buddhist and study the Buddha-Dharma. That was her main wish for her son who was in America. Now during the time of her greatest need, he felt it was his responsibility to take care of her. But what could he do? He couldn't return to Japan because he was "blacklisted" as a communist, thus he could not obtain a visa. On top of that, she shaved her hair and became a Buddhist nun. This latest event really shook him. Through this action she really expressed her deepest wish. He was neglectful in following her wishes. Now he felt so guilty. But then the war came and completely cut-off all communication. After the war he again tried to set up some communication and locate her whereabouts. He appealed to the Red Cross to find her and see if she were still alive. They reported back to him that she had died from starvation.

As time went on he continued to run the newspaper he established in Chicago, but thoughts of his mother never ended. He felt that he failed her in her wishes. Meanwhile, he was establishing a relationship with Rev. Saito, who by this time became head minister of Chicago Buddhist Temple. I'm not sure, but I think that he submitted some articles for publication (so I hear). So the relationship grew, and as a result Mr. Fuji became such a good friend.

But then was the next blow as he suffered a stroke. Then the stroke worsened. He could not speak, so he had to point to child's alphabet cards to spell out a sentence he wished to say. Rev. Saito visited him in the hospital. At that time, Mr. Fuji spelled out the following words: "Am I being punished?"   Rev. Saito did not know what to say, he felt speechless. Knowing that Rev. Saito was about to leave for Los Angeles to become assistant minister of Los Angeles Betsuin (temple), he then spelled out the following question: "Will you abandon me?" Again, Rev. Saito did not know what to say. He felt completely useless, himself unable to speak. There must have been tears at this time. Unable to say words of comfort or assurance, only one thing appeared: the nembutsu of deep solemnity. That in itself was the answer, the only answer. Mr. Fujii lost his freedom as he was caught by his past karma.

Later, in 1984, when I visited Rev. Saito and his wife in Los Angeles; one evening as I entered the temple apartment where they lived I heard loud crying coming from the bathroom. It was coming from the bottom of his guts, so loud, that I felt I shouldn't stay. I asked Toshiko what was going on. She replied: "Mr. Fuji has passed away". Deeply moved, I went back to my room.

Infinite means boundless – means I am not bounded by anything. But to realize this I realize how useless I am. How useless the relative self is to realise any real freedom other than a freedom that is transitory, likened to the passing of the clouds. Then I come back into the pure and empty mind that opens into the spacious fields of the infinite, the unknown and unknowable infinite. This is the incalculable truth of freedom of the infinite.

The Will and the Spirit
January 8, 2015
R. Adams

 Objectivity and subjectivity work together. Objectivity when it comes to self-examination and subjectivity when it comes to expressing the results of objectivity. The results come up as a shout. My teacher was a perfect example of this. He examined the teaching objectively, and subjectively at the same time. So there was no separation between them. This is a complete picture of the total self, the crucial point being self-examination.

 For instance, the teacher always asked for our opinions after he exposed us to one of Rev. Akegarasu's articles. We were independent persons and he asked us what we thought of a particular article. Here he was expecting us to come up with our own life. That was important to him. That is, from his side, he wanted to know whether or not an article that he and Joan Sweany had just translated had caused a physical reaction within the members of the group to let him know if the translation was successful. On our side, so to speak, we were learning how to approach Akegarasu material with Akegarasu's own feeling within our own subjectivity which came from our physical side. Accordingly, all kinds of thoughts and opinions could be expressed as we individuals had the freedom to do so, not being tied to nor influenced by traditional teachings that could corrupt or influence our approach. So it was like he was giving us Akegarasu's writings to those who had a beginners mind and who were eager to learn. What a vibrant approach to the discussion group he had.

 Even so, since we had our own opinions coming from our own understanding which meant that at times we would disagree with each other. In these disagreements we would discuss or argue over each others' interpretation. Even he had us write out our understanding without signing them, and then have our papers read aloud and we had to guess at which one of us wrote the article and try to identify who wrote it. So from this you can imagine what a lively group we had. Sometimes when it got to a point of heated discussion there was some shouting as an accusation by one member to another due to personality issues. But the critical side of this exposure had us self-examine ourselves in front of others. This is where the objective side of our mind exposed itself to the extent that it enabled us to view ourselves through the eyes of other persons(s) from outside of ourselves.

 As we are isolated we face a greater difficulty to self-examine ourselves that will open us to the truth of what we are; for we are essentially blind to see our own ignorance that we ourselves or others have put there as a result of our not knowing and being able to see ourselves fully. How difficult it is really. We are so accustomed to who we are and we think of it as our permanent identity – like a well worn seat cushion that has our bodily imprint.

In my case I was so fortunate to have a teacher who exposed me to who I am. Sometimes it was done directly and at other times it was through a very subtle method, a "mirror" so to speak, allowing me to see myself as to what I was lacking subjectively to melt the ice of a cold mind. Thus I was exposed to a compassion that was lacking in myself that would make me a human being; that is, soft and yielding, and most of all humble, removing any smartness or arrogance. This was the first thing he had to crack down on. But even here I could sense his compassion for me, a beginner.

The point is that to become a true human being, which was his aim, not just for me but for all others, that brings me to my knees as a manner of speaking, and that touches my being with this feeling being human; is, or belongs to the subjective side of my life that also encompasses the objective side through self-examination. Yet because of the fire within my spirit, I have the will to accomplish what I set out to do.

In all of nature we see that the will and the spirit are as one. Take flowers, as an example. We cannot see the growth of a flower to its blooming without observing the power of both will and spirit come together as a blooming plant that we admire with delight.

The will then, we can ascribe to our being objective and intellectual, and its companion, the spirit, to being a subjective link to our emotions of feeling such as love or hate, like or dislike; empathy or jealousy, anger, selfishness, unselfishness, loneliness, joy, sorrow, hope, and compassion of giving. Together, it is within our organic self, as we think about the natural world of the spirit and will, and within this the wisdom of our understanding.

In Shinshu Pure Land Buddhism, we have the figure of Amida Buddha. Its purpose is two-fold, one of its attributes is that of Infinite Light or Wisdom, and the other is Infinite Life or Compassion. We cannot leave one out without the other; otherwise it is not truly Amida Buddha. Therefore it is clear as to what is our focus is as far as our spiritual life is concerned.

Two legs are furnished by the Name, but the third leg must be furnished by ourselves, that is, our organic self which begins with the physical flesh and blood human being. Then we have to watch our self objectively, coldly, in order to come up with a clear subjective expression that resonates with others in such a way that it creates life which then gushes out as a shout, that is, as the living truth as it just pops up.

True religion then, is not for the laid back individual. Nor is it for those who worship an entity outside of oneself. Truth as truth has an organic feeling to it, not gotten from practices that worship things outside of one. Amida Buddha is as a natural feeling to worship all things in the world.

So when we think of our objective self or subjective will, we have to think of the live spirit and the power of will as our shining essence of self.

Make unto yourself your own light.
Depend on no one else for your brightness.
Seek no external entity, but follow the Dharma
and listen to it carefully – then you shall be free.

Shakyamuni

"Wild Iris" – R.A

When my mind is focused on the flower, I am the flower. How to be free is to be at one with all of life including sentient as well as non-sentient life.

IN PURSUIT OF THE TRUTH

The student-teacher relationship is very important in Buddhism. This is so because the student can focus one's whole attention on a person who embodies the true spirit of a seeker, rather than just gathering information from books or text documents and sutras, as important as these are also. As the learning process involves visualization, the image of the teacher has an organic feeling to it that is important to understand. The organic life of the tathagata is reflected in the teacher as a human being. As Dogen said, it's better not to study Buddhism without a teacher. He himself, traveled miles and miles even to China to find one. Imagine crossing the treacherous China Sea in pursuit of the truth in a small boat in the century, then to go around seeking the right one.

I was extremely fortunate to have met a person who did not allow us to accumulate knowledge merely for the sake of accumulating knowledge and then taking pride in it. He cut us off from such attempts. Here I consider him to be a very rare teacher. In doing so, he prevented us from conceptualizing Buddhism. Head knowledge does not lead to enlightenment. By having such concepts in our head and in clinging to them prevents us from being born into the freshness of life. If we think that we can rely on our secular intellect to give us the spirituality we need in terms of being a human being, we are no closer to the truth in our real humanity, but rather miles away. We are just reinforcing the relative self and thus making it more difficult to proceed. We need to go beyond the secular.

I met a real human being. He was an eager student to learn. Because he was such a dedicated student, we relied on him as the teacher. We are the ones who made him into the teacher because of our trust in him. Yet in his way of thinking he was an open-minded student, indeed, one who was eager to learn from us. The best student makes the best teacher, he once commented. This is the way he approached life, as a student. So when you talk about great teachers, they are primarily students, first of all.

Next, what is the feeling that they have? Because they are learning – their whole life from their own teachers, they have this deep feeling of bowing in front of them. This bowing is known as the nembutsu. Though you may bow to an article written by a teacher because it has made you feel as a humble student, you are indeed, bowing to the person who wrote it. No one bows to a scholarly article, for instance. Indeed, it's the reverse that can happen. Here you see the effect of such knowledge, for there is no nembutsu within it. It doesn't create the same feeling that living words have. Nor can we study the nembutsu any more than you can study life. If it is genuine, it evokes feeling. As humans, we can intuitively tell. All great teachers have this feeling. This determines whether or not they are sincere teachers. It is something beyond our limited understanding that they have that can turn around this limitation and that they can convey to us. In that sense, out of the depth of listening,

I too feel it.

In terms of our spirituality we cannot be true students without being humble and receptive. That's the only way truth enters. It does not enter by way of our smartness or how clever we can put words together. People distance themselves from the truth by their own attitude. So to be a person who is humble and willing to learn is the best way to reach the goal of Buddhism, which is self-realization. One can say from this, that one's enlightenment is based upon how well enough a student one is. Here one's false understanding is completely negated by the truth itself, and it is this that makes us humble. So the end result is that we become the best students, dedicated to learning.

And ultimately, what is it that we are learning? What a foolish person I am. How stupid I am. How attached to the fixed self, the ignorant self. And yet we think that we are deserved, good or smart? It is regrettable in our life that we practice all sorts of evils that are not so good after all. We have a lot to learn from Buddhism; and it is the teacher, who by his compassion, removes these blocks of so-called conventional evil we so often overlook, so that we wake up to who we really are. Here you see the function of the teacher most clearly. We may think that this is some kind of unnecessary business that doesn't apply to oneself; but we are mistaken, for there are no exceptions. And if you've lost your life the teacher will give it to you; if he feels you as a human being, otherwise you will have to wait till you're ready. For we really have to be sincere, otherwise nothing will be able to penetrate as far as our spiritual life is concerned. The essence of the teaching is to remove our self-assertive mind and to be free of it.

It was a stormy day in May, when Rev. Gyoko Saito arrived at the LaSalle Street Station in downtown Chicago in 1956. The rain was coming down in buckets – something he had never seen the likes of in his native Japan. It was a precursor for an unusual career he would have here at the Chicago Buddhist Church on the south side, as it was then called. When it moved to the north side near the lake at 1151 N. Leland, the name changed to Chicago Buddhist Temple. It was an active and growing place, with a large population of Japanese Americans – Issei, Nisei, and Sansei, plus a fair amount of Caucasians, as well. Then there was the younger set, called "Jay Bees", for Junior Buddhists. They were very active and wanted to be involved. This was one of Rev. Saito's new jobs, to take care of them. It was just one of many that he would be given that would keep him more than busy.

But first, he would have to learn English. With his Kumamoto-style Japanese dialect he would have to translate that into refined English – quite a jump! Kumamoto-ken has a somewhat similar dialect to that of our southern states; that is, abrupt, masculine, and direct - so unlike the effeminate style of say, Kyoto.

There are many cute stories about how he and others learned English. Like, if you want to buy some eggs you flap your arms like a chicken!

But Rev. Gyomei Kubose, head minister of the Temple at the time promised in the original contract, that he would have him enrolled at a local college to learn English; but it took him some time before he fulfilled that promise, I don't know how long. Meanwhile, a few Caucasian friends helped him out, including me, but especially that of Joan Sweany, who later became his secretary. But his use of English was an interesting experience. Also, I got introduced to his family, consisting of his wife, Toshiko, a son Shin, and two daughters, Dawn and Maya.

But going back, what brought Rev. Saito to Chicago? What were the circumstances surrounding his coming to America? And further, what is the significance of his coming here? What did he achieve the significance of which we should take special note? Historically, he has the significance of introducing his teacher, Reverend Haya Akegarasu, to the United States. Without him, we may never have heard of Rev. Akegarasu in this country. Though the head minister Reverend Kubose was also a student of Akegarasu, he hardly ever spoke of him. Surprising, considering how important in Japanese Buddhism he was.

So it was through his translations of Rev Akegarasu, which he tested out on us during an eighteen year period that I and a core group of members of the American Buddhist Association participated in that led to his publishing the book, "Shout of Buddha". This was our Thursday evening discussion group meeting, in which we as members were exposed to so many other great teachers as well. Manshi Kiozawa, Shuichi Maeda, and etc. – all of the contemporary Japanese teachers, writers, and philosophers, he exposed us to and we discussed. Indeed, we had to write short papers as to our response as we held "critiques" on each other's understanding. So it was a very proactive and hands on group. We even had bi-yearly retreats consisting of two and a half days at various places, and even once on a large boat of a member, for a relaxed but purposeful discussion.

But when I think about it, his main thrust was his teacher Rev. Akegarasu. I often said that he "milk fed" us on Akegarasu! I said this because he did this rather consistently. For in this he was building a strong desire in us to awaken our deepest aspiration. Without him, we could never have reached this depth. Sensei referred to it as our *deepest wish*. It focuses on who we are as humans. But to reach it requires our single-minded effort. Reverend Akegarasu expressed his total life, his total being, so directly in his own shout. So too, did my teacher. His articles and speeches attest to that. And so I wanted to, just as he was. But it takes time to intensify that desire; this voltage needed to overcome the limited self that is as a barrier over our deepest wish to be fully alive and to express the core of our being through our very own shout. This is what he was really listening for in each of us: the living words like sparks.

Over a period of time, the student becomes attached to the teacher. This is natural, but at the same time a distorted as a form of a relationship, as the teacher exerts such strong influence on the student. Yet there is a danger in this in that a relationship of dependency exists in the mind of the student, in which the student is not going in the direction of true independence, i.e., standing on his own two feet, and expressing his own life. The teacher did not care for us in terms of nurturing us or babying us. And as for his side, he didn't get attached to us either, like some kind of father figure. He was there to expose us to the teaching, for that was his real purpose. So he didn't go in for some kind of easy-going "social Buddhist temple" either, as he focused on what was of real importance to the parishioners. Once, with a smile on his face, he told us, "I am your friendly dictator!" But we didn't mind! He was a real man and we respected him.

True independence does not mean isolation, as coming from the self-centered notion of independence which leaves us as an isolated person. It includes the feeling of interdependence as well, respecting all others as contributors to my life, even essential to it. When I feel my being humble before all others leaves me open to receive them into my life and makes me feel the sense of oneness that transcends a separated existence that otherwise would cause a problem. This feeling has the effect of empting me as the last of the unenlightened ones, confessing that I am the most evil one, as to the fact there is nothing good about me at all – this useless person – an icchantika who must rid himself of the smallish conceited person he is. So even those I consider as the "no good ones", or those I'm angry with, or the misguided ones, can enlighten me because they expose me as to what a good scholar I am in judging others, but have a lack of seeing myself in them; but instead complaining or accusing others, which leads to conceit.

We really have to research our mind here. We really have to have the so-called carpet pulled from under our feet so to speak – from that of a smart guy to that of an awakened and humbled person. In a negative sense, we merely judge and discard, and yet we are subject to delusion ourselves and therefore should be included in our little "no good" list! Are we not overlooking ourselves in the process of not seeing ourselves in others? For in that sense, do we not all breadth the same life? The more we live, the more we find how our surface independence cuts us off from others and can even cause open conflict with others. True independence and interdependence are both part of the same coin, front and back. Further, they are joined by the deep feeling of nembutsu, which is a humble feeling. We cannot live in a spiritual sense without bowing to others. This is very important in our relationships with others. Thus true interdependence and true independence are as one. This is how we attain independence in the real sense, by way of our confession which comes by way of one's thorough self- introspection.

To respect everyone's independent life keeps me healthy in my relationships with others and not to interfere with them. Religion should bring us together and not separate us or let differences divide us. This is a very simple practice of interrelated independence. An interrelated feeling gives me more freedom and space to communicate, while at the same time respecting the independence of each person to live their own life. When we touch and feel the absolute independence of each one of us, we can then feel the One World that I cannot help but worship as in an embracing spirit of eternal life.

Sensei's deepest aspiration was aroused by his teacher, Rev. Akegarasu, who completely changed his outlook on life and with whom he studied for two years with at Otani University while getting his ministerial qualifications. It's not so much that he wanted to become a minister as he stated, but that it would enable him to be close to his teacher who was at that time an administrative head of Higashi Hongwanji. This meant that he would have to become a minister in order to pursue his deepest wish which was to study with his teacher.

The first step that we have to take towards an unknown fulfillment is that of finding out who we really are as an emancipated person. When starting out no one knows the future with all its conditions and/or circumstances, but the first step in the right direction is important so as not to go in the wrong direction. Now he faced the opportunity to come to the United States and to start completely fresh, but first he had to clarify his reasons for coming here.

Then, just before coming, he had a dream. In this dream, like coming from the wish itself – he was before his teacher who was seated erect before the family shrine at Sensei's temple at Kita-Yasuda. Here, in a grave voice, he gave to the young Saito his final words: "Your stated objective for going to America is to spread the teachings of Buddhism, but there's nothing special about that. It has nothing to do with Saito truly becoming Saito. The real foundation from which Buddhism can spread is only this one event; when Saito truly becomes Saito."

When he awoke from the dream he was in tears. Perhaps we cannot fully understand this relationship between himself and the teacher that led him into tears upon hearing his teacher's instructions. This is really a spiritual relationship that such a dream should take place to begin with. Next, the instruction is not so much to spread Buddhism which is treated here as secondary, but rather, to discover who he is. We have to go back to what drove Gyoko to seek out the teacher in the first place to find the significance of his movements later on. I mean there was a real conviction inspired by his past. As it happened, this crisis finally evolved through a chain of events that led him to his teacher, Rev. Haya Akegarasu. Rev. Akegarasu was a very unusual person who himself had such difficulty when he was young. The point is, when you are experiencing a real difficulty that is beyond one's power to resolve, one inherently seeks out a teacher and/or teaching that will guide a person through the difficulty; and if it is a life and death matter, no question about it. Our real life is very important to us as it is the only one we have, and therefore we must get to the bottom of who we are.

At the time, Reverend Haya Akegarasu wrote an article expressing his desire on the part of young ministers that they expose Shinran Shonin's teachings and the nembutsu to foreign lands. At some other time, he clearly defines his own missionary effort by stating: "My only missionary effort is the total cremation of self." and, "We should bury our bones in those lands where we set our feet on."

As Shinran Shonin stated, "The teaching is for me alone." This can be re-phrased and expanded as Shinran would have meant it: The teaching is for me alone because I alone am as a good for nothing foolish person, and as an ignorant one.

Okay, if the teaching is only for me, then....? Enlightenment is awakening to the fact that I am far from being liberated thinking that I am superior to others? Being as such, the worst thing is to be a teacher. Indeed, it is the reverse that occurs: "All others are expedient means towards my own enlightenment." – H. A.

When we first begin we seek enlightenment for ourselves. We are only concerned about ourselves. Here we look for something that is self-benefitting, not realizing that it is self-benefiting only when it is benefitting others. A person who is forgetting himself in the wish to help others is an enlightened person. We cannot be enlightened while still being attached to the smallish self-centered person who cares only for himself. In the kingdom of the first, I am the last. I do not wish to be blessed. I do not wish to seek heaven, nor do I wish to be "saved". Nor do I wish to be virtuous like that of a saint. I just wish to be myself in the freedom of being myself, and if that is helpful to those in need then I am most grateful and happy.

It is only when it comes from the sincere mind, the honest mind within one's shout with living words that pop up that can change things; the creative power that can move people's minds, as it has the power that emanates from an intuition beyond self. It is only by being liberated into the spacious world of freedom wherein I can fulfill my deepest aspiration. Only when I expose myself to the world – with whatever I know or feel – will the truth be reflected back to me by the sincerity of my seeking. After all the work and struggle is exhausted, the fulfillment of all the seeking – in which surprisingly there is no seeking – it just comes!

In the Larger Sutra the tathagata of eternal life begins as, "Thus have I heard". In our life the one who truly hears is the one who steps into the unknown and unknowable life. This is the way of the enlightened person.

So his real reasons were not just to come to this country to teach Buddhism, but to discover the truth in Saito's truly becoming Saito, now applying it to myself as Roger truly becoming Roger. This is what the teacher was looking for in each of us.

In that sense the true nembutsu is for the teacher, who came here with his own life and gave us his life. It was here, in this place and with this feeling, he fulfilled his deepest wish.

Completed, 9/14/15   Roger Adams

Life of the Temple

The Buddhist Temple of Chicago has some significance, both locally and in a wider perspective, worldwide. From its modest beginnings in October 8, 1944 by a few Nisei (2cnd generation Japanese Americans) who wanted to establish a temple for themselves even while the war was going on in the Pacific, to a much wider public that it serves today.

In terms of my life it has a great deal of significance for this is where I met with the teacher, Reverend Gyoko Saito. If it were not for this temple I would have never met with him. Others too, many who have since passed away, would express the same feeling as well. It was filled with so many activities by so many groups related to the temple that it would make up a long list of participants who partook in the life of this temple – some four generations of them – of all nationalities and cultures who have circulated within its walls. Indeed, the building itself got overused and outdated to the point wherein it was decided, due to so many repairs, to tear it down and build a new structure to replace it. This happened in the inauguration of and new temple on May 21, 2006.

But I loved the old place, because that's where I met with so many friends. It was really quite down to earth for simplicity's sake, nothing flashy or imposing about its edifice or its interior. These parishioners became my family as I used to attend Sunday services, especially when the teacher was scheduled to speak. Then with the various festivals and along with Buddhist holidays where we would get together in the basement for luncheon and meet all the people – so many friendly faces – all ages getting together for lunch, so you really got to know them as they got familiar with you. Oh, what a history this temple had in those days. I mingled with Japanese people with no problem. For after all we were all there to listen to the teachings of Buddhism, and you needn't be sophisticated to pick up on the essentials. I practiced along with the rest and found a home for myself so to speak, a familiar place where Buddhism became a reality in the most down to earth realization.

That was the teacher's life too, both within the temple and those he met outside of it who he took note of and included them in his writings.

Dialogue and Nembutsu Gyoko Saito

We all assume that as long as we speak to each other, there must be a speaker and listener; otherwise real conversation will not develop. Whenever we have a discussion in which we do not understand each other, we insult each other by saying "No conversation!" This unconscious saying illustrates the truth of what I mean by dialogue. If we think about our so-called conversations carefully, we realize that in most cases they are one-way speeches in alteration. Between couples, parents and children, friends, teachers and students, acquaintances, or even different nations – so often it is two sets of one-way speeches.

Of course, when we share a common subject and understanding, we may think we are having a dialogue or conversation. We can talk about baseball, or golf, or local gossip, for example. But so often when I talk this way with someone, I feel that I become a garbage can or he does, or if we both do, and we just throw ideas at each other. This kind of sharing is not deep enough to be a real dialogue. Even among people who are very close to each other (husband and wife, parent and child, two dear friends); their daily talking may get no deeper than this. Real dialogue must be a sharing not just of subject matter but of being.

Gautama Buddha must have had many pleasant superficial exchanges with his parents, wife and acquaintances. But perhaps when he left his home it was to seek the real dialogue that could exist not only with them but with all persons and all beings.

This desire to have real dialogue, not just sharing of superficialities, always begins by opening up a world of trouble. When I become aware that my speech is a one-way speech, that I hear one-way speeches from others, my world becomes a very lonely one. Out of that loneliness, I may try to force agreement from others on matters that are deeply important to me. And when I cannot get agreement, as a result of my dissatisfaction, my conflict begins. I begin to imagine that my one-way street is a two-way street, and at the same time I desperately live the life of protest and fighting, and finally I try to live the strong life of "might makes right."

But this is not the way that Gautama Buddha went to seek real dialogue. After six years of asceticism he sat on a spot (since called the Diamond Throne) under the Bhodhi tree, and in his honesty opened up the true dialogue. This was, according to the Eternal Life Sutra, the life of listening to the life of all beings as identical with his own life. Gautama Buddha could not be fully satisfied with the dichotomy of listener and speaker, but awakened to the dialogue of listening.

Being a minister for many years, I am in the position to listen to the members' life struggles and to discuss with them how to solve their problems. In a true sense always I am looking for a real conversation.

And this real conversation does not even need words. Whoever it is that shares his life, suffering and joy, it becomes my life of struggle, suffering, and joy. When a member felt such pain and sorrow on losing his wife, I received an indescribable communication just by looking into his eyes. That is the real world of dialogue.

Shinran asked, "What is true dialogue?" and answered: "All the worldly dialogues are false. Nembutsu is the only true dialogue." That was his reaffirmation of Gautama Buddha's original experience when he discovered the true dialogue. When he was sitting in front of an audience of 12,000, the Buddha did not need to say one word. It was unnecessary for him to speak out, because all of the audience communicated with him and he touched their lives, so he sat quietly with an august face, shining with joy. To celebrate Gautama Buddha's birth is to be born into such a world of the shining life of his life.

So it is the case that we must become true listeners. Then when we feel the need to speak and communicate with another person, not in terms of a dichomized position, but in the true feeling of oneness. Even though the other person may disagree with me or may be himself disagreeable I have to see to it where exactly is he coming from. Since we all have our own minds and therefore no two people see things exactly the same way there may be a dispute that comes about as to things we see differently. Yet as I feel a nembutsu of respect towards others then I can have a true conversation of which is as vital to my life as a dialogue.

First I must go behind differences to find similarities. The thing I need to feel is that we are both human and, not only do we breath the same air, but that we share the same eternal life together; that is, we both come from the same source. We should listen carefully to find out if we can have a true dialogue rather than biker or fight over one another's position.

People who fight with others invariably fight over a position that is obstinately fixed and irresolvable. They remain fixed and are afraid or unable – because of their ego – to move within a flexible state of mind. Instead they cleverly try to maneuver things around, manipulate the facts to suit their own advantage. Such a person seeks to win, no matter what. To them life is like a hockey game in which all tactics are okay to beat out and crush their opponent. Such people make it impossible to have a true dialogue with because it has reached the level of "might makes right". The nembutsu that Rev. Saito says is the only way to have a true dialogue.

(R. A.)

THE FACE
Gyoko Saito

When I was in high school in Japan, we had a very stiff and dignified teacher of mathematics who had a deep crease in his forehead. The rumor among students was that when he was a student at Tohoku University in northern Japan, he never had time to enjoy the skiing which is so popular in the north, because he was too busy studying mathematics. Because of that deep crease, most of the students believed in that rumor.

When I first came to the United States, I felt great loneliness because I could not speak English. The deaf-mute cannot speak because he cannot hear. Because I could not understand others' speech in English, I felt like a mute. But my inability to understand English did not mean that I didn't understand people. Just as when in high school my friends and I read a long personal history out of the deep crease in our teacher's forehead, so now I could understand people's faces even though I couldn't understand their English.

Somehow, a face reveals the unconcealable truth. People think they can hide everything, but so long as they show their faces to others, the truth is always revealed there.

Every Sunday we have been chanting the sutra called Tan Butsu Ge, which begins KO GEN GI GI: "...what a radiant face he has, like the peaks of the Himalaya mountains! What brightness in that shining face which cannot be compared to any light..." I do not know any statement since the beginning of human history that so praised the truth appearing on the face. The sutra says that even the brightness of the sun cannot compare with the brightness of the face; if the two were compared the sun would be dark as black ink. If we don't understand this statement then we do not understand Buddhism at all.

Shinran picked The Great Eternal Life Sutra (The Larger Sutra) from many, many sutras, as the real essence of Gautama Buddha's teachings. He didn't try to justify his assertion with logic. He just said: When Gautama was meditating, his face was so radiant that his student Ananda interrupted him with: "Why do you have such a radiant face?" That beginning of the sutra is itself the reason that Shinran called it the greatest sutra.

Some moderns, with their scientific mentality, may comment that it is ridiculous to say a human face shines out more than the sun. Such a person is a fool. He is to be pitied. He could never have had that experience of seeing his lover's face so bright that its own details were lost in its shining.

One has lost his humanity who cannot understand the brightness of a baby's smile, which melts the rigid coldness of the adult mind. This is my simple and concrete proof, from our own experience, that Shinran's statement about the Eternal Life Sutra is true.

Perhaps you are still not convinced. You think that it is ridiculous to say that Gautama's face is brighter than the sun. Let me explain more. A person must be emotionally defective if the loss of a loved one doesn't make him experience despair for the brightening future of his own life. When he loses a lover, a person has his own life thrown into utter darkness. The poet has said, not even the light of the sun can penetrate the darkness of the mind in such loneliness and sorrow.

Ananda was one of Gautama Buddha's oldest disciples and had been with him a long time. Yet suddenly he was astonished to discover that Gautama Buddha's face was so radiant. This shows that Ananda's insight had grown deeper. (But Gautama Buddha wanted to make sure: "Did you come up with this question yourself, or did someone else tell you to ask it?")

Everyone in the world enjoys seeing actors on the stage. But since the beginning of history, comedians have been pessimists! A human being who doesn't live up to their inner life is like a comedian living this double life. His face is fixed like a Noh mask.

But if even such a person touches the true light, then he sees his own nature. To meet the teacher is to find out the double-faced nature of one's own life, and then to die to such a life. The person who laughs continually, as if he had a nervous tic, and never shows sorrow on his face, as if he were wearing a mask, never lives the inner truth.

Die to all that life. This is the beginning of Buddhism. By touching the light, we start to see ourselves, and at first we really feel: How terrible to show our faces in front of people. But when we really awaken, we can see the individual life history on everyone's face, and always the true self is revealed through the individual face.

I realize now that the difficulty I had communicating in English was not the real trouble. The real trouble lay in not knowing the true face. Ananda discovered the radiant face of Gautama Buddha, the brightness of the teacher's face, which was such that it made even the sun dark.

The answer to Ananda's question, "Why do you have such a radiant face?" was this: "I am looking at all the Enlightened Ones, instead of preaching to an audience. Not only all the people, but the trees, the stones..." To see people and all of being in that way is the whole secret of why Gautama Buddha's face was so radiant.

To meet, Buddha to Buddha, means to discover such a reverent being within oneself. To pay respect to one's own reverent being: this is the essence of Nembutsu. And this is what is manifested in the face of Gautama Buddha, the shining one, which drew Ananda's attention to it.

From <u>Meditations on Death and Birth</u>
Gyko Saito (published by Joan Sweany)

September 17, 2015
R. A.

Even though I cannot see my face right now I know that it is smiling. I'm enjoying the emptiness of this morning's awakening after working so late last night on my project well into the night, having a good dinner, and having a good sleep, and being delighted with the results, most positive.

The light itself is the radiance, the flame that is the spirit that greets the morning. As soon as I wake up, make coffee; I can't wait to get out into the porch and greet the day. Because of this "greeting", so to speak, and with an empty mind, I cannot help but smile. Why am I so happy – like everything is so bright? I never explained or reasoned it out, I just feel this brightness. And I know that it shows in the face because I can feel myself as smiling. I just throw open my mind to some unknowable brightness that has no reason other than I am fully alive and soaking up the atmosphere of the life going on all around me. (This I feel is the Dharma's light, because I've been focusing on the Buddha-Dharma.)

The fire that burns in the universe is the flame that burns within me which melts the cold mind that is reflected in the face. How welcome and delightful is this light that penetrates the universe. Not only the world but the universe itself is this light, this life that is ever moving; the absolute infinity within me whereas I am at one with it. How joyous, how solemn is its movement; its brightness overwhelms the world, and is the cause of all things. This is our true worship, for the praise of this flame, this light, for it pervades the world. Thus we should worship this ever-moving essence called <u>mujo</u>, the Tathagata of continuous change, as all things in the world come of it. So too, I am at one with this shining light, the flesh and blood that organically far exceeds the brightness of the sun, as was reflected in the face of Gautama Buddha.

Joan L. Sweany

ST. JOSEPH — Joan Louise Sweany, beloved sister and aunt, was born on July 6, 1926, in Chicago, and died Oct. 31, 2001, in St. Joseph, where she resided since 1993.

Miss Sweany received her undergraduate degree in 1948 from Pomona College in California, where she graduated Phi Beta Cappa. She earned her master's degree in 1959 from the University of Chicago, and became a professor of English at Roosevelt University in Chicago. She went on to teach at City Colleges in Chicago, and later wrote computer programs to teach English with the Plato Project. She also studied medical technology and Japanese.

SWEANY

Miss Sweany was a Buddhist, and was active with the Buddhist Temple of Chicago, where she was awarded special recognition for contributing many hours to the writing and editing of their bulletin over the years.

With her mentor, the Rev. Gyoko Saito, she helped to translate and publish a volume of writings by Japanese Buddhist teacher Haya Akegarasu, called "The Shout of Buddha."

She donated hundreds of hours as a volunteer at the St. Joseph Public Library, where many came to know her as a resource for literary questions of all kinds. She was also a passionate advocate for peace and justice.

◆ ❖ ◆

Dear Mrs. Toshiko Saito, November 9, 2001

Joan Sweeny's funeral was a beautiful event befitting the years of work she did in translating and disseminating many, many Buddhist related materials throughout her active life in Buddhism for over fifty years, ever since she met Reverend Saito and helped him with so much of it, without which we would not have what we have today. She was a dedicated student of the Teaching as well as its translator. She devoted her life to this effort, and I for one, have so much material because of her helping Reverend Saito. The two of them: we could not read so many important articles related to the Buddhist teaching without their concerted effort.

In looking back, I was so fortunate in being her friend for all those years. I visited her many times in St. Joseph after she moved there in 1993. She lived very frugally, focusing all her attention on editing and privately publishing small booklets on the various authors – Kiozowa, Akegarasu, Maida, Saito, Santoka, and so many others that both she and Rev. Saito translated together earlier. And she disseminated these to all who were her Dharma friends – including three sutras – all these very important translations, I have.

She went to St. Jo, Mich. to retire, but instead, she worked, and worked. Towards the latter part of this time she became sick. I went through her sickness with her, as both both mentally and physically she was quite sick. During that time I did everything I could to cheer her up. I wrote articles I sent her, along with phone calls and so forth as we kept in close contact. And I did actually cheer her up. From the very beginning we were such good friends. She even referred to me as her "younger brother".

Now she, like Reverend Saito, are gone; two very important people. Still, beyond the tears, life must go on. They are alive. In my mind they live. The saying that "Death is but another word for life." for a dear friend is like saying that they are reborn, as these two individuals become the light of both sadness and brightness in my life. How much I miss them.

Roger

Tears flowed at her funeral, unstoppable tears, as I read one of her favorite articles, Reverend Akegarasu's "The Solitary Pine". She was this solitary figure, so generous with her time in helping others - I can't help it.

She once told me that she was not a nun. No, she was more than that, she was likened to that of a bodhisattva, one who with untiring effort and selfless determination endures the difficulty of helping others. She went to St. Joseph Michigan to be with her family, her sister and nieces to be what she knew was to be the sunset of her years. Occupying a two room tiny apartment – living independently – not asking for anything but love from them, and her sister.... A few potatoes, some carrots, a few string beans and some tomatoes were all she had for our lunch at one time when I visited her in the summer. Her bedroom/living room served as a study room where papers were scattered here and there, proof of her dedication.

Oh Joan, you are with me now and forever in my life. We went through so many sessions with our teacher, both indoors and outdoors, even putting out the "Artist of Life Festival", a three day event at the temple in which you taught us how to be actors on stage: without you - no way. Yes, you became my older sister; as I was to you, your younger brother.

She led an interesting life, and contributed to all our happiness through her depth of feeling and in all her efforts, incurring our deepest respect.

Good morning!

This morning as the sun comes up I am greeted by three large amaryllis blossoms. My mind is of cheer and happiness in witnessing this event.

Watered by the rain, then brought inside before the cold of the winter. Now it blooms – like birth – I can't help being born too. How beautiful as I'm taken away!

THE AMARYLLIS IS DANCING

"The Amaryllis is Dancing"   R. A.

Birth of the New Year   R. Adams
1/1/14

After all the dancing last night, and being with numerous friends, I awoke in the morning with the feeling of warmth and happiness. The falling snow cheers me also and it seems to add to the warmth. Then after coffee I went to water the plants when I noticed that the Christmas cactus had sent up its first bud – it too, has its own shout which I interpret as joyous, as if it too, welcomes the New Year. No more than a quarter inch – but there it is – soon it will be ready to bloom! This plant was almost dead, when seeing how miserable this plant was I decided to get it to the emergency room right away and transplant it into fresh potting soil and try to save it. Picking it up from its old habitat it pulled away from its old roots that were completely rotted out. Could it possibly survive? I didn't know, but I went ahead and transplanted it anyway with the hopes that it would survive and bloom as it had done in the past. That was three weeks ago. I had to watch it, water and fertilize seeing whether or not it could survive.

Small things you may say, but there is an element here of embracing life that is given to us and that which we receive that applies to all of life, and in which we feel the sense of gratitude. There is no brightness in our life without this sense of gratitude; for we are receiving something which is beyond our power as it is connected to the embracing nature of life itself. It concerns our body and mind, which has to do within a life spiritually, lived, that allows us to communicate with others openly, that is, with a welcoming feeling.

"Live your life to the fullest or die." said Reverend Kiozowa. As I live my life to the fullest, life is given to me. Life is a gift that one receives and can't help it, by the same means is the desire to give life: this is the oneness of coming and going itself within the effort to live fully with one's total life.

So there is hope – not the kind that we expect in return for some object we have in mind, a kind of hope based on expectancy, but simply the kind of hope that gives life to the dead, as in the case of the Christmas cactus. There are times when I feel lonely and I don't know if this is good or bad or what to do about it. Yet it is important to my life, for it makes me want to be with others. For without others as friends and yearning for them I cannot live.

Last night it came out as a shout; being with friends, dancing the whole night through. With so many styles of dance, everything from jumping up and down to the spontaneous flexing of bodies in rhythmical proportion to the rhythm of the band. Then to the final countdown: 4 – 3 – 2 – 1 — Happy New Year! Everyone is shouting and making noise blowing horns, popping balloons to the music of "Old Lang Sine". Now up with the New Year's song with everyone singing to the top of their lungs – how happy we were to be together. Unimaginable, to be with others the whole year and now the climax of all our efforts to greet each other and to welcome a new year and to be reborn in it.

All of the past is turned into fertilizer as freshly born we enter into the joy of the transforming from the old self, and leaving it behind, to greet the fresh self.

I guess the snow is over now and from the west the sun is beginning to shine through all this lake effect snow we've had – up to fourteen inches. The car is buried in it as piles of wind driven snow will have to be removed from it and the yard, alley, and sidewalks. I'm in a much more sober mood than I was a day ago when I shared with others the brightness of New Year's Eve. This has given me an introspective side of a new year. A little time helps to cool down the frothy bubbles and introduces another side of New Year's from an article written by the teacher from Chapel Talks between the periods of 1966 – 1978.

Where I found New Year's by Gyoko T. Saito

When I was living in Japan I remember a New Year's custom from the time I was very young. They would ring a gong one hundred and eight times. The listener was supposed to think of 108 desires, and the sound of the gong would drive them out of his or her life, one by one, so that he was completely free of them by the time the gong had stopped. New Year's was celebrated in this way by getting rid of the old life. I did not begin to understand this custom until sometime after I had come to America.

At first I thought that way of celebrating New Year's was different here than in Japan. People would go to the movies or have parties or watch T. V. and drink together, and all of a sudden at midnight everyone would yell "Happy New Year!" and blow horns and ring bells. It seemed very different from the solemn Japanese gong.

But only at first, as gradually I began to see that in spite of the difference in custom the same thing was happening: People were getting rid of the old and introducing the new with a celebration, whether solemn or gay, with much excitement and festivity.

It was not until a few years ago that I really came to understand the Japanese custom, however. It was just before New Year's, and I was cleaning up the temple, when a member and his son dropped in. I thought they wanted to speak to me, but no, they had come to clean up the temple. So I went on with what I was doing. A few minutes later I noticed that they had chosen the washrooms to clean. This was very unusual: no one likes to clean washrooms. They did a very thorough job, working for several hours and cleaning every corner, and then they went home. A small happening, but it opened my eyes. I began to see that there is a way of welcoming the New Year quite different from the solemn ceremonies or light hearted parties. The man and his son did a routine and not a very enjoyable job, and they did it carefully and thoroughly. It is a job that has to be done every week of the year: there was nothing special or fancy about this job – it was life as such, as it must be lived from day to day.

The washroom is not a place that anybody enjoys having to clean. But unless we keep it clean we cannot endure using it for long. And we cannot clean it for once and for all; it will need cleaning again in a short time. We cannot get rid of the dirt for good.

So with the 108 desires that the gong symbolizes. We cannot get rid of them for good; we can only become aware that they are in us – we can only become of ourselves.

If we listen to the 108 sounds of the gong and are reminded of what we are, with all our desires, we will come to know ourselves better. And it doesn't matter if we listen to bells rather than gongs, or listen to nothing at all but just clean the washroom. What is important is that we do not ignore or forget what we are.

Awareness of what we are makes our life new. In fact, the 108 sounds symbolize the unlimited and ever-changing life itself. There are, in fact, no such 108 desires, so to speak; but that our ever-changing life itself becomes conceptualized as desires. It is then that we become victims of our experience, our judgments of good or bad or pleasant and unpleasant; but when we determine to see ourselves, to face our unpleasant selves, to face the darkest part of ourselves, and then we find out the most important, most useful, and ever vibrating life as such.

January 1967

R. A.

So true it is that when all the crazy celebrations which go on for New Year's Eve; we inevitably have to come home to face ourselves as to what we are. His article points us in this direction. Do we come home only to be the same old self that we are supposed to get rid of? Likely, yes. Unless we come to the Buddha-Dharma and listen carefully; the only real change that will occur in our life will not occur and we will once again settle for a comfortable, secure, and pleasant life-style that we will most certainly take for granted and fall into a kind of lazy "repose-ism". Here we will not be given life but rather, a life of mere existence, along with the fatalistic idea of self-survival. Without the brightness to our life that comes when we stand up and say: I want to live, I can live! Such a shout comes from the bottom of our guts that pushes aside all hesitation and is forward seeking to discovery what I really am as a fully alive human being.

Right now this is what New Year's means to me. The realization that unless I cleanse myself of all the dirt that has accumulated over the past year and start living life within the freshness of this very moment of transition from the old to the new I will not be up-to-date with this present New Year as it is happening right now in this place. This gives me the fresh air to breathe in and the old air to breathe out as it is happening within my body. Follow the rhythm of the body. Listen carefully for it is the organic truth. With this truth we can see and feel the body – this feeling the freshness within one's own mind as it is at one with the body and feeling its delight.

Did we celebrate New Year's for nothing? Were we just acting like spectators watching the craziness of others? Or did we put our whole life into it; because if we didn't we will not be granted our life, the flame that burns up the old and creates the new, cleansing the dirt and evils thereof, represented by New Year's.

Just as important as the friends we meet are the words we use to communicate with them, so we cannot overlook them. Indeed, the words we use are just as important as our friends, for they convey the feeling that creates friends. Even if we use no words at all our wordless communication can be just as strong as we become as listeners. In that case an empty sheet translates into the empty mind as it awaits just the right time to speak. It carries with it the wordlessness we care not to use to touch other people's lives.

Words that are like hot sparks create life, but they come from a voltage alive with sparks. Warm words create warmth and understanding. Introspective words create depth and a feeling of solemnity. Words that create beauty and vibrancy are like a blank canvas upon which words are composed that create one's expression like that of an artist's brush. So altogether then, the fulfillment of my life is dependent on how deep is the understanding and use of words as applies to the teachings I've heard. Words that convey the truth are the truth.

On this empty canvas then, comes the word *arigato*, a word that the teacher has chosen to demonstrate how difficult it is to live. In an article written by him we see how he digs into an expression that I'm sure has the nembutsu behind it. Important, because it is the very core of our whole vocabulary and shows how our spiritual life affects the words we use.

(R. A.) 1/3/14

To Difficult to Live: I Am Grateful   by Gyoko T. Saito

The Japanese word *arigato* is a strange one. It is a customary expression of thanks: "I am grateful." But its literal meaning is "too difficult to exist." How can gratitude come out the feeling that it is too difficult to live?

Of course we often use the word *arigato* thoughtlessly, without considering its deep meaning. But occasionally something happens that makes us aware. About three doors down away from the temple there is an old people's home. This particular home has many people who have just come back from mental hospitals. One woman who lives there walks by the temple every day and stands in front of it for some time. She is about sixty years old, with a very quiet expression on her face. But she is always moving her mouth a little; I assume she is talking to herself. And I can't help wondering about her past life and what kind of life she has had, to make her like this. Even though she has transcended the chaotic world of normal human life, she has such an atmosphere around her of the pitiful human life. What she says to herself, moving her mouth a little, may be an endless complaining about a particular person in her life. Or perhaps it is a murmuring about the unforgettable grief she has. Maybe she is grumbling her distrust of all human beings. I feel sure of only one thing: she is living within herself, without any relationship to anyone in the entire world.

Looking deeply into my life, I wonder how much I am essentially different from this old woman. We are both born into the same world of confusion, with the same mind, the same human life. "Born alone, die alone, come alone and go alone." I too live alone, without thinking of others, feeling that I live by myself and grumbling by myself, complaining about life.

Into such a life of the mind, the feeling of *arigato* gushes up: difficult to live. If that is all, if I feel only this way, perhaps I am no different than this old woman. But *arigato* implies more, it implies "difficult to live without ..." – without your kindness, without your criticism, without everything that you are. This "you" is everybody and everything. And the gratitude includes acceptance of all things received – all difficulties, of whatever kind.

This is the important and difficult point. Being what I am is *fukashigi*, unimaginable. Logically I too should end up as insane. This feeling of *fukashigi* is an abyss across which we leap from *arigato*, difficult to exist, to *arigato*, I am grateful.

This recognition, this leap is beyond all logic. But the Tathagata's teachings and the teachers' teaching make it clear. *Arigato* gushes up as thankfulness because of the teachings of the tathagata and the teachers of all human beings and sentient beings including the old woman. When we recognize "difficult to exist without..." then gratitude arises in the depths of our being.

I know of no words that express *arigato* as well as a poem by Shinran. "We must express thanks for the Tathagatha's teaching, even if we must crush our bodies into powder in doing so. We must express thanks for the teaching of the teachers even if our gratitude is the crushing of our bones." Why did Shinran express gratitude as he did? He is the one who most deeply recognized how difficult it is to live without the guidance of the teaching, who knew the chaotic condition of our life and was yet able to move across the unimaginable abyss to the most profound gratitude.

--December 1966

R. A.

In mentioning as he does Shinran's profound gratitude, I'm thinking that it is for his own teacher Honen Shonin. The catalyst for our suffering brings us to the nembutsu upon hearing the teacher's teaching. The nembutsu moves us to bow, both body and mind, as it is the essence of spirituality that allows us to cross over the abyss; this impossible leap from our sickness to our awakening occurs when I feel the depths of the teacher's teaching. I have this solemn feeling that even goes beyond expressions of gratitude that touches the depths of my being.

I have nothing but gratitude for this article, indeed, for the teachers life itself, the one who wrote it, and the reason I placed it at the end of this section.

I know how difficult Rev. Saito's life was at times. Things were not so easy at the temples, both in Chicago and then in Los Angeles. Some people oppose things that do not go their way thus causing trouble. So yes, he faced these "abyss's" every so often that he had to jump over and he did this with gratitude.

From the Eternal Life Sutra (The Larger Sutra)

How do we recognize as to what we are? Do I see myself as the most evil one? We have to go through the three gates to find out. The three gates more or less correspond to the three births. First there is the <u>Necessary Gate</u> which links us to a focal point which is Amida Buddha. Next is the <u>True Gate</u> which Rev. Saito describes as the Vanishing Point. The third gate is the <u>Wide Vow Gate,</u> the "Gateless Gate". (Rev. Saito's term: Scorching Point). So we have the three gates that every truth-seeker must go through according to Shinran. (The two notes were inserted by me) – R. A.

San   Gan   Tennyu (Spin)   Enter

SAN GAN TENNYU   **by Gyoko Saito**

(Recently a friend of mine heard me discuss the <u>San Gan Tennyu,</u> the Three Gates, or three stages that any truth-seeker must go through, according to Shinran. He asked me for further clarification. Shinran Shonin selected, out of Hozo Bosatsu's (Dharmakara) Forty-Eight Vows, the 19th, 20th, and 18th, in that order, as symbolizing the three stages of his own while seeking the Dharma journey. During the lectures in Hawaii last summer I came up with three images in order to explain the <u>San Gan Tennyu</u>.)

As background, from the larger view, we should see the image of the Focal Point (<u>chu shin ten</u>), as the focal point of the Absolute Circle. As you know, Amida Buddha is the Nameless and Formless; the modern expression for this is the Absolute, so here I will use the image of the Absolute circle as Amida Buddha. Naturally we cannot talk about the Nameless and Formless: Absolute is Absolute. Yet we can talk about a point as the center of the formless, nameless circle. As described in the Eternal Life Sutra (The Larger Sutra), Dharmakara is the focal point. Corresponding to this focal point, any point on the circle could be the focal point, because an Absolute Circle is never enclosed. (A circle with a limited scope can have only one center but if its rim is at infinity then it has an infinite number of centers.) So in the true sense, the spirit of Dharmakara is the spirit of everybody. The Eternal Life Sutra explains this point.

But to realize this in oneself fully, one must go through the stages of the three Vows. The vanishing Point (sho ten...) is an image I came up with to show the meaning and direction of the Nineteenth Vow (Necessary Gate). Any human being has a finite enclosed circle of self, which represents one's experiences, thoughts, and other contents of ordinary human life. The center of such a circle is the concept of "I". The ordinary concept "I" represents the finite circle or the finite range of human life experience.

The direction of the self is self-expression in terms of enlarging the circle: more experience, more money, more reputation, more power, more self-righteousness, and so on. But by meeting with the Teacher and the Teachings of the Dharma we realize that self-expansion will never clarify the most essential question that everyone will come up with, that bumps us against the absolute wall of "Who am I?" consciously or unconsciously.

The importance of the Nineteenth Vow is to give one's whole life direction a 180 degree turn, from seeking self-expansion to seeking "Who am I?" So finally what we are aiming at in this direction is to find the vanishing point of the so-called "I." Instead of enlarging the finite circle, we find the circle reduced into nothingness in terms of how evil I am, how stupid I am, how ignorant I am.

In the case of the Zen experience of No Self, all the Theravada and Mahayana Buddhist <u>shodomon</u> (holy-way gate) try to reduce the "I" content in terms of finding out No Self. It is the Necessary Gate for any seeker to enter. Otherwise – as regards suffering – confusion, doubts, uncertainty, anxiety keep arising.

The importance of the Necessary Gate has been greatly neglected in the traditional Jodo Shin sect. It was almost taken for granted that we are already at or past the Nineteenth Gate, we already realize it, and so on.

But Reverend Kiozowa was the one who spent the forty one years of his total life showing how important and how difficult it is to realize the real vanishing point.

Now the Nineteenth Vow, in order to realize the true Vanishing Point, leads us into the Twentieth Vow, or True Gate. In dictionary terms, passing through this gate is impossible.

For Honen Shonin the final contradiction, the final struggle, took him from the age of nine, at the time of his father's death, to the age of forty three. For Reverend Kiozowa, the struggle took him from the age of twenty five till one week before his death at forty one.

The whole point of going from the Twentieth Vow (True Gate) to the

Eighteenth Vow, that in Hawaii I called the Gateless Gate. When we realize it, we are already in it. I there came up with what I call the Scorching point (sho ten ...), or shout of total being. So essentially I talked about of the Necessary Gate, the movement through the stage of the True Gate, and the vanishing point which became the scorching point.

(Editor's note: It was Shinran's final recognition of his inability to perform any good works on the basis of all his self efforts that had failed – and then having the good fortune of meeting Honen Shonin, his teacher, that for him was both the "scorching point" and the very point of his turn around and entry into the True Gate of emancipation. Accepting the fact he as a foolish one; Shinran, now free of self-power delusion, is what Rev. Saito is looking at along with several others that are mentioned here. This deep confession is what he refers to as the "scorching point".)

As you know, in Shinran Shonin's understanding of the Three Vows, San Gan Tennyu, there are two meanings, ken as the "front" meaning and on as the "back" meaning. According to ken, the truth seeker must go through three stages and the beginning involves self-effort. But according to on, when you realize it, none of these three stages is achieved by self effort.

If I describe this in Shinran Shonin's words in the Keshindo, at the time he wrote the last pages of the Kyo Gyo Shin Sho, he stated: "When I met Honen Shonin at the age of 29, I was instantly in the Eighteenth Vow." Reverend Maida, just before he died at the age of 61, looking back on his total life, said that he shouted the same thing: "When I met Reverend Akegarasu at the age of 19, everything was already said then."

Prior to Shinran's final statement in the Kyo Gyo Shin Sho, he explains San Gan Tennyu, the three stages of life. These are really stages of deepening. They are very difficult to trace back year by year in the case of Shinran's life, because there is no record except for the very limited materials (monjo) written by Esshini, and Shinran's own writings.
Therefore I thought of tracing back Shinran's deepening process in terms of the life processes of Rev. Akegarasu and Rev. Maida, and come up with their clear-cut strength in terms of how they realized the vanishing point that turned into the scorching point.

Only when we experience the vanishing point as they did, will we reach the scorching point. The Shout of Buddha is nothing but a manifestation of that scorching point, that is, of the dynamic and powerful Nembutsu. The whole book is nothing but the contents of the Nembutsu itself. The simplest statement is "Namu Amida Butsu" but that whole book is Namu Amida Butsu itself. That I summarized in the image of the scorching point.

(Note: The book The Shout of Buddha that he is referring to was translated by him and Joan Sweany (his secretary) was published in 1977 and contained many of the most important writings of his teacher Reverend Haya Akegarasu; and, by the way, we of the American Buddhist Association discussed in many of the pages by way of feedback in our discussion group.)

The scorching point is not just a mere shout but, but because of the focal point (Hozo Bosatsu or Dharmakara), it is the innermost deepest self which represents Amida Buddha – Nameless and Formless, the Absolute calling on us. In other words, Gautama Buddha (or Shakyamuni), the real Teacher, is pushing us from behind.

Don't be afraid to experience the Vanishing point. Amida Buddha, as the focal point, is telling us: "That's Not the Vanishing point that is the focal point!" When you realize it, the Nembutsu gushes out: That is the vanishing point. And in the final analysis no vanishing point or focal point but only the scorching point remains.

(Note: Here, the scorching point is revealed as "The total cremation of self is my only enlightenment" – (H.A.), whereupon the past stages are but the materials used as fuel that contribute to the flames that enlighten and are the light of the universe itself.)

Last time ... I described the vanishing point, scorching point, and the focal point to explain the San Gan Tennyu of Shinran's life – but that was more or less an outline. Now, based on what I said the last time, I want to look at the life of Reverend Akegarasu so the skeleton will become flesh and blood.

At the age of 16 Akegarasu met his Teacher, Reverend Kiyozawa. This relationship deepened so that Akegarasu, from the age of 23 to that of 26, to the last day of Kiyozawa's 41 years of life, lived together with him at the Kokodo in Tokyo. Those three years are very important in Akegarasu's development and the deepening of his understanding. And, as a follower of Shinran Shonin, Shinran's Tannisho was particularly important to him because of the meeting of these two men, the Tannisho gained new life and started to take on its own life in Japan, and later, the rest of the world.

But the main thing is that during this period Akegarasu experienced the vanishing point. According to Maida, "During that time of three years,

Reverend Kiozowa really crushed him and completely took everything away from him." Indeed it was the vanishing point that Shinran talks about, the recognition of how evil I am. This was Shinran's experience. Now Reverend Akegarasu must reach the next stage; but because of this experience the later incident deepened the vanishing point in him.

For the next ten years he was profoundly influential in the revival movement of Shinshu teachings in Japan and active in the publishing of his magazine Sei Shin Kai. Then came the deepening process of the vanishing point. He was 36.

While, during my trip to Hawaii visit, I was struggling with the vanishing point, scorching point, and focal point, I made a trip to Hilo Betsuin (main temple) on the "Big Island". Rinban Kondo welcomed me and put me up in the guest room. It was really fukashigi – inconceivable – the scroll that I found hanging there. What timing!

It was Rev. Ruikotsu Matani's haigwa, a simple drawing with a saying. The drawing was one peach, a very lively peach. The saying was: "A hundred peaches spoil and one peach remains unspoiled." To tell the truth, I had trouble reading it, so I asked Rinban (Bishop) Kondo. He gave me the correct reading and said, "This scroll belonged to my late father and he treasured it greatly, so I brought it to the United States and am keeping it as a real treasure." I didn't realize it then, but this has become my treasure too; because Reverend Matani played a very important role in the life of Reverend Akegarasu.

Reverend Matani was the student of the very famous Pure Land teacher Gojun Shichiri; but he was not a minister, at least not that we know. He discarded his identity and became publisher of Chu-gai-nippo, the only religious newspaper then in Japan. He knew all the important leaders in Buddhism, Shinto, Christianity, and various new sects. In his mind he was in his own way seeking Buddhism. "A hundred peaches spoil": all the religious leaders he met were spoiled in some way. Some peaches were good on the surface but are eaten through by worms; some have a perfect shape but no taste; some have a perfect color but are bitter. He wrote his dissatisfactions in the newspaper anonymously. In a sense this newspaper was scandal sheet, though in his own mind he was looking for a true religious leader. The harder he looked, the more he found that no one practiced what they preached.

Then he had found that Kiozowa and his followers were truly practicing a religious revival movement. And then he heard that Akegarasu had betrayed it. When the scandal about Akegarasu broke, Akegarasu became the strongest symbol of these decadent religious leaders and their movements for him. So Matani took action: he attacked Akegarasu with all his might and made sure that he killed him completely. The scandal was totally out of proportion to the facts. He buried Akegarasu completely. He did it thoroughly.

Indeed, Reverend Akegarasu remained in his own country temple for six years after the scandal broke. He recovered, revived completely, by himself. That was a real surprise for Reverend Matani. He was sure that he had terminated Reverend Akegarasu's life – but he survived, revived. "One peach remains unspoiled."

During that crucial period he wrote many articles: I published these in Shout of Buddha. We know that this was his crucial period of change from the vanishing point to the scorching point. To understand that turning, we need to understand just one significant statement of Akegarasu himself: "The flames of the total cremation of my being are my only enlightenment."

> This one peach is manifested as the Shout of Buddha that I published. Indeed, for Akegarasu the shout is not the ordinary shout that we know of but resonates with the undying truth of the life of Gautama the Buddha and Shinran, and yet the shout of all of us that we have not really touched yet.
>
> Honen wrote his <u>Senjaku</u>–<u>hongan</u> <u>nembutsu</u>–<u>shu</u> at the request of Zenjo Hiromutsu. The crucial essence of shinshu, or the deepest meaning of nembutsu is contained in it. Those who see this text can understand it easily. It is indeed the rarest and most superior text. It is the highest and deepest treasure–literature. – Shinran quoted at the beginning of the "The Crucial Essence of Shinshu."

As far as Shinran is concerned this quotation, given at the beginning of Maida's article is the focal point. Through the ninety years of Shinran's life, he really received the totality of life in such a manner as he says here: the crucial essence of Shinshu, or the deepest meaning of nembutsu, is contained in it.

This at once raises the question for each and every one of us. How do I see the focal point of my teacher's teaching? How do I touch the focal point of the teaching in everyday life?

For Shinran, Honen was not just a vague being who wrote many articles, many ways to explain the truth of Buddhism. Through the ninety years of Shinran's life, he proved the focal point of Honen's teaching. It is very clear. Even though there are many different ways that we can focus our attention on the teaching of Shinran, Rev. Maida is the one who clearly pointed out the focal point of Shinran's teaching, as Shinran did for Honen's.

Where did Reverend Maida's crystal clear understanding come from? He says that it came from his teacher, Reverend Akegarasu. Here again: there are thousands and thousands of disciples of Reverend Akegarasu and 78 years of his life: he manifested his life in hundreds of books and uncountable numbers of public lectures. But through the 61 years of Maida's life he gave the crystal clear awareness of Reverend Akegarasu's central teaching as "I am the most evil one."

Reverend Maida crystallized his understanding with his total life, into one phrase which is also the manifestation of Reverend Akegarasu's own crystal clear awareness of his own life. Reverend Maida is really pinpointing here what the focal point is. It is ikkusu, "the one phrase." If this one phrase is not the crystallization of the total teaching and the total life, then it is not the focal point at all. So this "one phrase" is everything. The way to select the one phrase is through the total life of the disciple. This is the correspondence between the nembutsu of the disciple and the nembutsu of the teacher.

The focal point is Dharmakara, Hozo Bosatsu (as Amida Buddha). I guess this needs a lot of explanation. To avoid vagueness I will start with the facts of Reverend Maida's life.

The historical person Shuichi Maida met the historical person Haya Akegarasu on this earth at a particular place at a particular time. The historical encounter of two persons is accidental, no matter what anyone says. But the way the two of them developed the crystal-clear understanding of the depths of the teaching made their encounter inevitable.

Through that inevitable encounter, the teaching of Reverend Akegarasu became the focal point for Reverend Maida. This focal point is the focal point of the Dharmakara. The depths of the feeling about the inevitability of The Encounter can be manifested in the "one phrase," just as in the feeling of the "five kalpas of contemplation only for Shinran" (i. e., "The teaching is for me alone.") which Shinran expressed. Thus the "one phrase" that Reverend Maida stressed here has such an important meaning. Reverend Maida throws everything he's got into the explanation of this, in the first section of "The Crucial Essence of Shinshu." This is the unique presentation of Reverend Maida's focal point.

Later on he thoroughly develops the concept of "simplicity" (<u>kanso</u>) in this manner: awareness must be the simplest, the most precise and crystal clear. Later on, this turns into <u>ichinen</u> – single-minded, One Mind, One Thought – the word is hard to translate because it has all these meanings.

At end of his first section, Maida suddenly brings up Dr. Nishida as the target. You know that Dr. Nishida was Maida's teacher; in the whole 61 years of his life, Maida was so involved with him that he couldn't eliminate him. So Dr. Nishida is really Reverend Maida himself.

The point Maida is trying to make by bringing up Nishida is to clarify his own vanishing point. Maida put himself on the operating table and, using the sharpest scalpel, opened up the deepest darkness of his life in a bloody way. So here we have to put ourselves on the same operating table: otherwise we cannot understand the vanishing point either.

For him the word "scholar" means "the total inability to be cured." Do you know who the scholars are? Once the words good/bad or right/wrong pop up and threaten one's own life, any person will turn into a scholar. If someone accuses me: "You are wrong!" I will become a "scholar.", and this "I" is everybody, young or old, educated or uneducated, of any race. Anyone will come up with a unique logic in such a complicated manner, to defend and expand his life.

As it so happens, Dr. Nishida symbolizes this fact in our lives. Maida gives his characteristic in one word: h<u>a</u>nsa—roundabout, detailed, ever-entangling, never-ending explanation after explanation. I have talked about this characteristic as the finite or limited circle of forever enlarging the self. By meeting with the teacher as the focal point, we come to the awareness of our round-aboutness and scholar nature.

So now you know that Reverend Akegarasu's Vanishing Point - "I am the most evil one" – became the focal point for Reverend Maida. When Reverend Maida himself realized his own vanishing point, then that vanishing point turned into the scorching point. It is rather difficult to comprehend this transition without any concrete explanation. The following example of Helen Keller will clarify these three turning points.

I don't know if you saw the December (1974) T.V. production of the "Miracle Worker" – I got to see the last half of it. Even though you may know the story, I will review it briefly, in case someone doesn't. The child Helen, because she was blind and deaf, and unable to speak, and was like an animal. The movie shows how her teacher Miss Sullivan brought her to the point where she recognized the meaning of sign-language letters – words, and entered the human world. To do this Miss Sullivan first had to fight Helen's parents, to have complete control over her teaching. The parents set a limit to the time she could have Helen alone with her; when Helen returned to them she again went out of control. But Miss Sullivan forced her to go to the pump to get water to clean up the mess she had made. That is when Helen suddenly got the connection between the letters w-a-t-e-r and the water she felt. The <u>ikkusu</u> (the one phrase) that we talked about is water in the case of Helen Keller.

The (19th Vow) or Gate, the Necessary Gate, means the selection of the problem. For Helen's father it was just a matter of discipline; if she behaved just a little like a human being, had table manners, and didn't show wildness – that was good enough for him. For the mother, the mother's love was good enough. For Miss Sullivan, her teacher, the sign language was the only way. If Helen could get the meaning of the words she could become a human being. To select THE problem is the essence of the 19th Vow.
(Note: The 19th Vow has to do with the innermost desire to be in his land, along with performing meritorious deeds; "….who sincerely

aspire to be born there, shall, upon their death, see me appear before them, along with a multitude of sages." This is the first provisional stage.)

To make the Necessary Gate THE Necessary Gate, Miss Sullivan had to gamble her total life. She had to fight with Helen's parents before she could actually fight with Helen. Always, in Buddhism, how difficult it is to cut off the on ai no jo affection of blind love between parents and child. This is the hardest thing to cut off: and if not cut off, there is no Necessary Gate.

In Helen's case, it wasn't her fight but her teacher's fight on her behalf. That is almost a miracle. For if her fight had failed, can you imagine, there would have been no Helen Keller.

As a Bodhisattva, Miss Sullivan compromised, agreed to a time limitation, so she could convince Helen's parents and she partially succeeded. But she knew that a real confrontation would come sooner or later. Because she was convinced that sign language was the only way to Helen's enlightenment, she used all possible methods and taught Helen.

So there were three attitudes towards the Necessary Gate. For Helen's mother, only affection, no one can deny it. For her father, discipline: no one can deny it. And then there was her teacher's way. Within the limited affection of the individual, one will never, never reach the truth.

That's the reason why Shinran said SHO DO (no JIHI), affection, has limitations. No matter how much Helen's parents love her, that love has limitations, so she will never become a complete individual. Only the nembutsu has the complete, thorough affection. Even in this Vow, the Necessary Gate, it is very true. Only the understanding of the meaning of the mujyo no "sign language" is the thorough affection which will make Helen a complete human being.

But such a limited circle of being as Helen and I cannot understand that. In order to realize that truth, the teacher's function is so important, so vital. Absolutely, the zen chishiki is needed at the Necessary Gate. So Miss Sullivan fought against the shodo no jihi (parental affection) demonstrated by her parents – how ironic.

Now we come to the 20th Vow, the True Gate, and the Vanishing Point. (Note: This is called by Shinran as the second provisional gate, the so-called religious gate, yet not the final gate.) Now Miss Sullivan knows only nembutsu, only sign language, as a way: but in order to reach Helen she will have to become a devil. That is, she came to realize that she must become an absolute disciplinarian – or absolutely evil – in order to save Helen. In order to reach Helen she will have to crush the Helen who was so firmly fixed in one way, not even on a conscious level. If Helen tries to understand the meaning of sign language of what she knows at this point, she will never succeed.

The struggle is so vicious that Helen's parents could not face it. But Miss Sullivan knew that it was the only way. That is the difficulty of reaching the Vanishing Point.

The essential characteristic of the Vow is doubt. Even the teacher has this doubt: Is this useful, gambling my total life for this kid? Many times this doubt struck Miss Sullivan. The harder she fought against Helen's parents, the bigger and deeper this doubt became. She had to exhaust all the known methods: sign language, isolating her from her parents, and so on. The most <u>hansa</u> or roundabout life appears at this point. And in a sense Miss Sullivan had just given up, when the right moment came.

Then the final 18th Vow, the Gateless Gate, appears. When Miss Sullivan's wish become an equally vicious devil itself and finally crushes Helen, then something non-organic w-a-t-e-r suddenly becomes organic water, the manifestation of life itself. Then for the first time Helen understands the shout of water as the shout "I am the most evil one." This is the first time she shows appreciation to her teacher. (Note: By actually sticking her hands in water; she, for the first time, discovers the organic living truth behind the word WATER.)

When Helen shouted WATER! This water is exactly the nembutsu that Shinran is talking about; it is what Reverend Maida tells us about Akegarasu's shout "I am the most evil one". Through the three stages we realize the difficulty of self-awakening is so evident. First of all it must be thoroughly one's own awakening. Truth must be organic truth, not static – that's why it is so hard. <u>Mujyo no shinri</u>, the living truth, is organic. In order to catch it, the self must be broken. The hard shell of self must be broken. The hard shell of self was the problem for Helen Keller, not just the triple difficulty of no sight, no hearing, and no speech.

Helen Keller as a child had no eyes to see with, no ears to hear with, and no tongue to speak with. But inchantika (impossible to be cured) as I am, I have double this triple suffering: I have this notion that since I have eyes I can see the truth and can understand it. Yet the reality is that though I look on the truth with my own eyes I cannot see it. So it is too with hearing and speaking. Here I deeply realize the meaning of inchantika. "No roots" means no hope of realizing the truth. So the teacher here is crucial.

And here too we have to clearly understand the meaning of nembutsu. How in the world can we become equivalent to Buddha by recognizing the nembutsu? It seems very mysterious. But Helen Keller's life clearly shows us that since w-a-t-e-r became water the whole world opened up and she became a human being. It is precisely the same with us. If we CAN once utter Namu Amida Butsu – Reverend Akegarasu's I am the most evil one!" – then this will happen.

* * *

We translate <u>mujyo</u> as continuous change: let's look at its opposite: the fixed, hardened being in which the lively life is immobilized. As I said before, to have freedom we must experience the infinite circle – but our being is that of the finite circle. Let's analyze the hardening process of this finite-circle being. The core hardens; then the whole being becomes – openly or subtlety – alienated from the rest of the world. Every encounter with circumstances becomes a hindrance, an obstacle. And the hardened core of "I" senses: I have no freedom, no flexibility; I am the same as dead.

For some reason, this core starts the process of cancerization and alienation. Cancerization starts at the very first moment the "I" hits an obstacle. This fact is well known to us: otherwise we could not understand why we take such crazy actions to eliminate circumstances. All such actions are based on this cancerization, the unusual, unexpected, sudden growth of the core called "I". Alienation is sudden withdrawal from a dynamic living relation to the rest of the world so that this finite circle is as if fossilized.

Helen Keller did not develop this cancerization and alienation of self because of her naïve honesty, though the formation of the self-concept was the same as everyone's. Because she lacked the sense of seeing and hearing, she did not develop the verbalized, sophisticated defense system which we cannot capture with fixed ideas, fixed mind. The more sophistication there is in one's life, the harder it is to reach. That's why Reverend Maida kept stressing that the truth cannot be grasped by scholars but only by ordinary people.

Maida speaks of the "freedom of evil." In order to go further into this, let's look at our traditional understanding of shuku-go, "past karma." As soon as most Jodo Shinshu followers hear this term, a definite notion comes up in their minds. There is an almost fatalistic feeling: what I am today is the result of past karma. Or, at most, we should accept our past karma and what we are and then transcend it.

But this misses the boat by a million miles. That's why Maida uses such a strong phrase: "freedom of evil." What an extraordinary statement he came up with!

Let's examine our basic attitudes toward karma, particularly toward past karma. When we hit an unsolvable problem in this very moment in present life, we may react: "What have I done to deserve this painful life? Why do I deserve this life?"

Recently the son of one of our temple friends passed away. He was only 20 years old, a good athlete, a straight-A student, a considerate, kind, friendly person. Out of a blue sky the parents had a phone call that their son was in the university hospital in Bloomington, in southern Illinois. There were not adequate facilities there, so he was transferred to a Chicago hospital.

But still, a couple of days later he died, as the result of a liver disease. The parents could not take it – that is very natural. Always the question remains: why did this have to happen?

The classical presentation of this problem is the story of Idaike in the Meditation Sutra. She raised the question, "What did I do in my past life to deserve this?" when their son Ajase killed his father (the king) and imprisoned his mother Idaike (the queen) so that he could be the king.

With our very basic mental patterns, we try to figure out our life in very simple cause-and-effect equations. But no matter how sophisticated the equations become, no matter how emotionally written up, they are still equations: simply because of that cause, life should go this way. Who is it that uses these equations? I do. But in this operation I never question the operator who is "I".

We say there is only one way to escape from this painful calculating: we must accept with resignation. By accepting – we say – we shift our focus from the past to the future; and we hope that in the future we may transcend this hopeless situation, or powerlessly say that time will heal it.

Either way, present life is understood either by looking for a future of pink dreams or by giving up the past life negatively. Shuku-go (past karma) has been a key word in pre-programming the minds of Jodo Shinshu followers. "In your previous life you did something wrong, so there is trouble in your present life. Accept it. By accepting it, you will transcend it." What a pitiful attitude!

As long as we have such a past life that can't be given up, such deep wounds, it will keep popping up in our present life. Something that we never lived out fully, burned up fully, in our past life, will keep sending up smoke.

But we try to get hold of an intellectual understanding of the cause of the past and try to figure out our present life. We say that the past life is controlling the present life, and make excuses for ourselves for the past. And we never live 100%.

Shuku-go, in fact, has nothing to do with the above attitude towards the past. It is instead like the shout "WATER!" that came out of Helen Keller – the deepest sense of feeling for life itself, the most sensitive understanding and reverence of life.

Our life is a dynamic, organic one, an endless huge net in time and space. But I start thinking about myself as a single knot in this immense net; and, because of the difficulty of this present life, I try to figure out the relationship with all the knots. Complexity, round-about understanding of life, begins here.

In my last article I quoted Reverend Akegarasu's most important one phrase: "I am the most evil one." As soon as the word evil (aku) occurs, all of us have certain reactional attitudes towards it. So let me clarify. For

Reverend Maida the only evil is when one does not know what the truth is; for Reverend Akegarasu the only evil is when one does not know what mujyo is (continuous change). In Akegarasu's struggle, from the vanishing point through the scorching point, there came the recognition that he could not know what the truth is, he could not know what mujyo is, by any conceivable effort on his own: "I am the most evil one."

When the self-centered, self-powered, calculating jiriki attitude is broken completely, then suddenly you feel such an organic life relationship. That is the truth of shukugo. So Reverend Maida says that his teacher called himself as a devil:

> ...because he was a common person with deluded ideas ... a restless and unconcentrated mind in which there is no logic and order. Human existence or human life is produced by causes and conditions (which are) limitless and unfanthomable and cannot be grasped by the finite wisdom or intellect of human beings.
>
> Men pretend to themselves that they can regulate their own living, and in living concentrate on the center of themselves, but their life is actually in the reciprocal relationships of the unfathomable causes and conditions of the infinite world. It is simply moving around as so-called karma. Hence Shinran's confession, "If a certain action-condition arises, I could take any action." This statement tersely explains that a human being is an existence with deluded ideas.

In other words, the proclamation is very true that "my evil deeds are not my deeds." This is the freedom of evil. Then the organic huge net becomes suddenly a lively one! It was such a complicated round-about life, but suddenly you feel such lively relationships!

This is the point I have been meditating on. This is the raw material – a lot to cultivate. One thing: I am sure that when we understand the true meaning of shuku-go, we will understand Shinran.

(This selection of articles was sent to me by Joan Sweany before she passed away along with other articles that appeared in the B. T. C. Bulletin from 1966 through 1981. I'm sure she would be happy to see them introduced again.)

GREED, ANGER, AND IGNORANCE   April 5, 2014
R. Adams

Human beings are nothing but filled with desires. Desires define the human being. Among the strongest of our desires is greed. But greed does not come alone, it is accompanied by anger and ignorance, thus we have the three poisons of greed, anger, and ignorance. Greed and lust compose the main selfish desires we have to face as humans, as well as the total negative aspect of what we can expect if we don't examine ourselves carefully. The original self, the natural self, or self as such, comes up as greed. If we cannot get what the object of our greed desires then we get angry. From here our anger turns into ignorance. But ignorance does not stay as ignorance for it moves back into greed because this is our basic condition as humans. Since as humans we can't escape the fact that we have desires because we are made up of desires to begin with, therefore greed will be ever present in our selfish state of mind. There is no use disputing the fact that we are selfish, even when doing seemingly unselfish things. The fact remains that it is part of the circle within the dialect of human desires that carries with it our emotions. As we cannot deny that we have emotions, anger is one of them linked to greed.

Our greed therefore, turns into the emotion of anger when it no longer satisfies our control over others. People do not want to be controlled. If so, they fight back or rebel thus negating our control over them. As we are negated we get angry. Anger as an emotion becomes our ignorance. From here, ignorance crushes against ignorance. We are then returned back to greed as a natural condition of our being human. If we do not learn our lesson from this we will repeat the whole process again and again like a ring that never ends – no beginning, no ending.

What is important in all this is to realize that we are nothing but a chunk of greed, anger, and ignorance. That in fact, we are deluded into thinking that within our desire for the things of this world we are displaying our greedy behavior that must end in anger and ignorance. We ourselves are the cause of our own ignorance which will be our own suffering, agitation, and despair. However, when we thoroughly awaken ourselves through self-introspection, we will see how worthless the self is, reach emptiness, and throw the whole greedy self into the garbage can and become naked to experience the joy of being free of greedy desires.

To see oneself outside of oneself, is the thing. How difficult to see it.

As ignorance crushes against ignorance because it has nowhere else to go it sparks a light that comes up as wisdom. Through this wisdom we come up with our own confession of how ignorant and useless I am.

We must discover who or what we are. Already we know that we are human beings. We also know that we have many kinds and types of desires within the makeup of our being human. But until we carefully examine ourselves in relation to all these desires we will be ignorant of who or what we are as humans. Mahayana Buddhism is the Teaching that allows us to recognize the reason why we are human by focusing on our self as greed, anger, and ignorance of blindness, stupidity, and foolishness.

Here I will use Shuichi Maida's own words:

"... Life discovers itself as ignorance, or, rather, the human being discovers himself as ignorance. And this is the awareness of Mahayana Buddhism or the awareness in Mahayana Buddhism. This is the very reason that Buddhism is the teaching of awareness. Where else can you discover this kind of awareness? I say that this is the most essential contribution of Buddhism to world thought. Besides Buddhism, no teaching has said that awareness is only to grasp oneself as ignorance. For example, what in the history of western philosophy proves that to discover oneself is to find out simply that one is greed, anger, and ignorance? The awareness of human life is the discovery of oneself as this chunk of greed, anger, and ignorance: this is the essence of Mahayana Buddhism."

In discovering myself as nothing but a product of my desires with varying results, makes my mind feel settled. In the understanding that there is an occasion wherein the liability for greed, anger and ignorance occur – facing it squarely – there must be a confession. I've just had my dinner so I've satisfied my desire to eat and therefore feel kind of rosy. So when I witness so much suffering that greed, anger, and ignorance plays on peoples' lives I am saddened into shaking my head. So many evils come from greed; some very serious, like those shown on T.V., daily.

Through self-realization comes this freedom from ignorance, as ignorance loses its support found in greed and anger. It is taken away along with the cause and effect karma that makes it exist. The awakened state of nothingness is like a flash of light that occupies nowhere, not even those with heavy burdens of *klesas*, karmic evils, are made to exist.

Oh emptiness! The bottomless reality of life opens into such awareness.

"To be aware of the human being as a chunk of greed, anger, and ignorance, is to throw away one's whole being. This is confession: and this confession is the nucleus of Mahayana Buddhism. Aside from this there will be no Mahayana Buddhism, nor any kind of religion, nor any kind of salvation. Confession itself is enlightenment; aside from that there will be no enlightenment."

We see from this that greed, anger, and ignorance can be transcended.

Notes on "Late Summer's Delight" 10/2/2012 R. A.

    While waiting for the Sutra discussion class to begin and having a coffee break in the rear of the Temple's annex building while sitting on an old picnic table, I was struck by what I saw. What I saw was a flower shooting up about five feet tall, whose origins and/or name I did not know, but which right away struck me as a perfect symbol that in its shining essence represented the independent seeker. Along with that, there was a large group of vines draping over a seven foot fence – a trumpet vine, upon which were blooming some trumpet flowers. Ah, here was the beginning inspiration for a painting that began to germinate in my mind. Where it was to take me I did not know, but surely a way could be found to come up with a sufficient composition to manifest and express what I was feeling.

"Late Summer's Delight" Acrylic 48"x48" –R.A.

First, I had a table – but what was I going to put on this table? Then I began to think of the table itself. It was a piece of outdoor furniture saved from when they tore down the old temple so it had plenty of age behind it. Being well weathered, with knots and all showing made me think of the long, long, age of Buddhism and the Dharma itself, traveling through so many countries and so forth, for some twenty five hundred and fifty plus years from its origins in India. As to what to put on the table, somehow the idea of apples came to my mind. Okay, now I have apples; but then, how many, and in what context? That's when the idea of the seven Patriarchs of Shinshu Buddhism came up as listed by Shinran, and they are: Nargarjuna (2-3rd cent.), Vasubandu (4th cent.), Donran (476-542), Doshaku (562-645), Shan-tao' (613-681), Genshin (942-1017), Honen (1133-1212), and so I decided to have at least seven apples. Then another thought came to mind and I came up with the idea of including the contemporary or "modern Patriarchs", i.e., 20th and 21st cent. teachers, which would be chronologically: Rev. Manshi Kiozowa, his student, Rev, Haya Akegarasu, and his student, Shuichi Maida; and lastly, my teacher, Rev. Gyoko Saito, who was also a student of Akegarasu. So now we have eleven apples. But as long as I'm going this way, why not include Shinran Shonin (1173-1262), who was the one who listed the first seven, and certainly by now, should be considered as a Patriarch of Shinshu Buddhism? Then there is Prince Shotoku (572-622), who in modern times at least, gained familiarity among the Japanese, therefore should also be included. He is the earliest one since Buddhism entered Japan in the 6th century and who influenced modern Japanese thinking with his 17 Article Constitution, again coming from the roots of the Pure Land tradition. (Here I have submitted an updated version of the term: Patriarch). So now we have thirteen apples, all who most deserve to be included in and around the basket.

All these apples, but how to organize them – Ah, a basket – put them into a basket! But I have to find a big enough basket to contain all these apples (not just a big pile of apples). Then on one of my daily walks I happened to see one just large enough in a re-sale shop window – it was perfect! Now the large basket reminded me of the *Larger Sutra on Amitayus* [The Sutra on the Buddha of Infinite Life], which also carries the connotation of that of a larger basket. This is the famous sutra that all other sutras lead up to, and really represents what could be called one of the main pillars of the Pure Land tradition because it touches upon Darmakara's becoming Amida Buddha, the main focus of this Sutra which is behind the largest sect in Japan known as the Jodo Shinshu sect of Pure Land Buddhism where the teacher taught and where I attended.

Now a Buddhist theme begins to emerge, one that will carry me towards the ultimate completion of the composition and meaning of the painting. I realized, however, that the background or atmosphere where the original inspiration took place was not suitable for what the subject deserved, so I was in a quandary over where the main subject would take place. Then I caught it, while noticing the red succulents in full bloom in my own backyard, the stone path curving around the evergreens and so forth; that this would be a perfect setting for the table and the apples, so why not?

So, starting with the unknown flower, or "unnamed flower" representing the person who desires to be free as his deepest wish; who also desires to speak with his own voice as an independent person. There is no true freedom without the practicer's wish to seek the truth within him and come up with the truth as he realizes it. The spirit that touches him is that of life itself, as the will of the spirit wherever it goes; but realizing this also means listening and learning from my predecessors who have come before me. These teachers open my mind as to my ignorance or unawareness. I am indebted to them for all the teachings I have received through the years. I am through them, listening, learning, and examining myself as it applies to me.

Now in the painting the "nameless flower" has four blooms so I thought of <u>The Four Noble Truths.</u>
1. (My) Life is suffering and agitation.
2. (My) Self is the cause of my suffering because of my desires, cravings and delusions.
3. There is a Path that I must take for the transcendence and cessation of my suffering.
4. The path that I must begin with is <u>The Noble Eightfold Path.</u>

Here the Teaching provides guidance, and these guidance's form a path consisting of eight directives. As the Path itself suggests a system of thought Shakyamuni may not have listed them. Originally Theravada, they became part of the Mahayana Buddhist tradition, also in terms of the "middle way" as guides intended to direct us toward eventual attainment. These are self-power initiatives that form the necessary gate to direct us properly. Let's list them: Right view, right thought, right speech, right conduct, right livelihood, right effort, right mindfulness, and right meditation. All these move us forward towards emancipation. For instance, meditation refers to self-examination as well as getting into an atmosphere of nirvana.

Then there are the <u>Six Paramitas</u> of giving, morality, listening, perseverance, meditation, and wisdom that are listed in the Larger Sutra.

ETERNAL LIFE April 14, 2014
R. Adams

    All things are made to exist by the power of eternal life. As humans we came into this world by its inconceivable and embracing power.

    This morning shortly after I awoke, I went to water the plants in one of the bedrooms when I was met by a surprise:
> The white amaryllis is blooming!
> How beautiful, how beautiful!

These are the words that came out of my mouth, which came out as a shout. Later I began to meditate on what it was that made me, almost suconsciously, exclaim my oneness of being born along with an amaryllis flower! This is the manifestation of the eternal life that closed the gap between me and two huge pure white blooms that so captured me that I ceased to exist as a separate person observing the life of another living being. A flower that's wish is so powerful that it broke out of its sheath, and near death as a plant to bloom and shine its essence as a flower.

    Mind you, I had no hope for this plant. For years it had been struggling to survive in its pot having used up its entire nutrient. Just a few half-dead leaves are all that remained of this fading thing. Seeing it in such poverty I decided to at least give it some fertilizer just to keep it alive, feeling guilty over the fact that I was unable to take care of it properly, having no time. Boy, did it revive! Now after all hopes were gone it rewards and surprises me with such beautiful pure white flowers. By giving to it, it gave back to me! This embracing spirit came as pure joy.

    Oh, how can I say it – I am beckoned into the life of this white flower, become its essence, or, is it eternal life that made this event happen along with a feeling of being at one with it? As a human being I am allowed to exist by being at one with an unknowable power beyond self called eternal life. You too, all of us, no matter what our position – for eternal life has no position – you too, are made to exist by the same power. No matter how much we may think we know, how much wealth or power one can wield, it all comes to nothing besides what is it that enables us to live.

    Those who think they know something; so smart, conceited, and feeling self-important, are fortifying their blindness. Come down to it, we are oblivious like an inchantika, wandering around this way and that way. Yet how simple it is, in seeing the beauty of a flower as it fulfills its own wish to bloom so quietly, so exquisitely, and so nobly. Here, I too share its life. Then how could I realize it? It was out of the embracing power given to me by Eternal Life that made me see Eternal Life.

The core of our existence is to be at one with Eternal Life, the Tathagata. As that is the case, how can we not help others to attain the same realization? The aspiration for me now becomes the aspiration for all beings regardless of whom or what they are. Keeping this in mind, when we realize it and are awakened to it, the confining aspects of discrimination are blown aside with the realization that we are all at one and on the same boat sailing across the ocean of birth-and-death and the swirling tides of samsara to emancipation in the tranquil shores of Nirvana.

Amida Buddha is this symbol of Eternal Life. And the Nembutsu is our confession and praise of this eternal life. Amida Tathagata as it is called exists within us just as is the pure white flower that blooms within the mind of one who is awakened to receive it. These are the virtues given by the Buddha of Infinite Light and Life. As these virtues are given to us, so shall we give them to others. As we give unto others so shall we receive in kind. This is the fruit, or the fruition that completes the cycle of self-benefitting within benefitting others.

Therefore the statement, "All others are expedient means towards my own enlightenment", for which I cannot go forward without learning from others. Learning from others is at the same time learning about oneself. The core of our true religion is based on my assuming the lowest level of where I place myself – by lower I mean empty of conceit. It is within this core that gushes up as a shout that comes up as the very essence of our being that manifests life itself. This is what is given by the infinite power of eternal life. This is what is means by its directing of virtues to us.

The Teaching then, the only one that is alive and fully functioning by moving us – pops up without my control – and that is what is meant by helping others. Otherwise there is a dualistic separation between the speaker and the listener which so often happens in the secular context. The secular world is bounded by dualities all stored in the head that is known as head knowledge in the form of conceptualized knowledge. This is what scholars and philosophers do. But the teachings of the Buddha-Dharma do not stand on dualistic intercourse at all but of, "One within the many and the many within the one", as the One Mind.

This sudden happening, this reason that goes beyond our reasoning, is what Shinran Shonin understood as giving unto others the virtues beyond reasoning. Many traditionalists cannot get over this fact and so they go on preaching Amidism in the form of a religious practice which marginalizes the true meaning of Amida Buddha. Thus we have the concept of, "The Buddha goes to the Pure Land, and comes back to the world of samsara". The Pure Land is simply the honest mind, the pure mind, not as a physical or geographical place.

The world of samsara is the everyday world, the secular world, and the real world that we deal with and experience in our daily life. It is also the world in which our desires arise. We have so many desires that we want fulfilled. Some have to do with practical necessities. Others are organic. Yet others have to do with our greedy desires. When our greedy desires go into action they become our passions. Driven by our self-love and egoistic attachments to ourselves they express our ignorance in all directions and in confused ways. As a result we become deluded beings, incapable of seeing into the nature of the misdirected and lack of knowledge of what constitutes the real and firm truth. Lack of understanding of what is the fundamental truth within our being as well as outside of it we are led into the world of birth-and-death, the world of arising and perishing in an endless cycle of happiness and sorrow as well as our expectations that fail (arising and perishing). So often we are like the proverbial bull being pulled by a nose ring into things that wastes our precious time. Self- examining into this we can get a good look as to what our human condition appears as. Here we need help, for in a certain sense we are sick because we ourselves are blinded and cut-off by not knowing what we do. Indeed, if we truly realized it, we ourselves could cure ourselves. But amidst all our cravings and seemingly unending desires we cannot see ourselves clearly enough to be able to see the very cause of our suffering to get behind it to pull out the rotten tooth which causes our suffering.

The Buddha took pity on our suffering, entered the world as a Bodhisattva and acted as a doctor. Without this help I would have lived my life in vain, perhaps even have become insane. In all the years of struggle and seeking, by listening and following the true path is my deepest satisfaction. I now live in quiet joy and happiness of having listened to the true teachings of the Buddha-Dharma in discovering my life within its embrace; and, seeing others in difficulty wish to give life within the same embrace that helped me to discover my life. These are the virtues given by Amida Buddha's Vow towards all sentient beings to realize their true spirit within life itself.

But in all I went through there was an underlying spirit encouraged by my teacher to keep my mind focused on the Dharma as a true direction for my life. The virtues given to me by the teacher, to look deeper into the truth, discover what I am, and to be an awakening person who keeps on discovering the truth. How unbelievably fortunate I've been. To have heard the truth, sought it within my own life and now verify it by listening and helping others. By doing so I am deepening *shinjin*, the sudden flash, opening to ever more spaciousness within the freedom I now enjoy.

Once we realize that all of us are supported by Eternal Life, and in fact, owe our existence to Eternal Life – why then must we fight, argue, and hate others? Why must we cling to our smallish judgments of good and bad – but rather hug each other. Why can't we be naked, nakedly shining, instead of clinging to our decorations, and the things we use to decorate ourselves, by self enhancing ourselves in the process. The artificiality of all the layers we carry around to impress others must be removed. All that we have acquired by our relative way of thinking, so dualistic, will be removed as so much will now seem insignificant, useless and without meaning or substance before the light of Amida's wisdom that comes from Eternal Life. We must touch upon this life and awaken to it, in order to realize our total self-recognition.

This is my happiness and joy, no different as when I met with the amaryllis that bloomed and immediately became at one with its essence. Then from here we can realize that all of us have the potential to awaken to eternal light with which to share with one another in this brightness.

> Rotten leaves and frozen soil – springs' rebirth – and
> fresh shoots pop up everywhere!

This year as usual there is a family gathering on Easter Sunday. Some fourteen people attended and we had a wonderful dinner along with many activities, much conversation, and a child looking for Easter eggs hidden around bushes and trees, playing some guessing games (women on one side, men on the other – with the men winning this time), and with everyone in a festive and happy mood. Winter, it seemed, finally let up and we were enjoying temperatures in the upper 70's, as everyone was outside happy as bunnies. I decided to take a walk in the forested area around from the house. I always enjoy the silence of the tall pines, the quietude and peace of nature as I walked around the path that surrounds this large area. I saw the ground covered with leaves from the fall and everywhere life was shooting up from the ground.

After all, life is very ordinary and I was among ordinary people, and who, because of all the years of being within a family that knows me from early childhood. So I am relaxed, friendly, and care for them.

But the earth is getting busy, and in responding to the warm and bright sun all kinds of life is breaking the grip of winter and springing up. I'm at one with this new and fresh growth, so even though it's the ordinary world that I'm living in I just can't sit still. Feeling my mind dancing – its spring!

Seeing is acting and acting is seeing. This is called actional intuition. Now the question is how do we see? Hearing the teachings of Shakyamuni allow us to see. Thus seeing is hearing, and hearing is seeing.

Being allowed to see, I feel the shining light. The essence of Buddhism is the gratitude we have toward the teachers who allow us to see.

SONG OF THE FLAME   Shuichi Maida

    In our Ishikawa Prefecture in Japan we have two great modern-day thinkers. One is Dr. Kitaro Nishida, the other is Reverend Akegarasu. I was fortunate to know these great teachers and learn from them. I am deeply grateful that I was fortunate enough to receive the Teaching from them. Dr. Nishida taught me while I was studying in the department of philosophy at the University of Kyoto, and Reverend Akegarasu is still teaching me by reprimanding me.
….I would like to talk about what kind of teaching I have been receiving from Reverend Akegarasu. He is 76 years old this year. Throughout his whole life, what kind of teaching has he been giving me? What is the world that he wants to communicate? Up to now he has written over a hundred books. Within the large volumes of his books I would like to discover the world that my teacher describes. According to my understanding of my teacher I can find this out from his main collection of three books (<u>Kosei no Sanbusaku</u>), which are <u>Kosei no Zengo</u>, <u>Dokuritsusha no Sengen</u>, and <u>Zenshin suru Mono</u>. I would like to select one statement from <u>Dokuritsusha no Sengen</u> (Declaration of the Independent Man):
    "The total cremation of myself is my only enlightenment." – H.A.
    To burn up, to be cremated totally: then there is this flame that comes out of the burning self. This flame is the only enlightenment; that is what the teacher is saying. I definitely think that this statement of Reverend Akegarasu reflects his whole life, and explains the essence of his thoughts. This is my understanding of my teacher's whole life. But am I right or not? That we shall have to check...
    First I must explain the teacher's statement. He is saying that the total self is extinguished. Not only is a part of the self negated and extinguished, but the total self, completely is extinguished. This is very important. It is the key point to understanding this statement, that there is no longer any self, so to speak. That is the very reason why the teacher emphasized <u>total</u>. If I describe this more thoroughly, then it is not the partial negation of oneself by introspecting oneself, saying "I am no good" or "I have this or that shortcoming." If that is so, then the self still remains as an entity that complains about a self. Instead, when the teacher says "Total," he throws himself away as a whole. He throws away the whole self including that self which judges "good" and "bad."
….Suppose you have a toothache. The tooth is only part of the body, but you suffer as a whole individual when you have a toothache. No one will

laughingly say to himself "Hey, My tooth is suffering!" You feel pain and struggle as a whole being. This is to same as to say that when a part of a being is contaminated, the whole being is contaminated. Partial contamination is total contamination. This is the very reason the teacher throws away himself as a whole. The teacher never thinks about himself as something capable and useful. He throws away himself completely as a useless one, the "stick-in-the-mud" one. He never imagines that he himself is capable of doing something good for the world. Without regret, he throws himself away and dumps himself into the cemetery.

Such a being as I have no value living in this world: I must burn myself up. "Total cremation of myself" is my teacher's world of confession. Awareness of myself as a hell-dweller: This is my Teacher's awareness as the chief of the evil one's, a wasted human being that is useless to the world and makes trouble for other people. This is such a thorough confession of his life: that this entire "I" should not live. A body decays but my Teacher found he himself decaying even though living; that is to say, a living dead body. He is saying, "Such a decayed one should burn up and purify the world." Nothing remains in my Teacher's statement of any notion or of any self-conceited notion about his own ability or brains.

Once Napoleon said, "In my dictionary, there is no such word as <u>impossible</u>," but in my Teacher's dictionary, there is only the word impossible. Rev. Akegarasu is the teacher who completely lost hope about his own ability and about his own self.

Total cremation of oneself is the shout of the Teacher's despair. No one will understand the Absolute who does not crush himself against the cliff of impossibility and despair. Despair is the gateway to religion. If we really honestly, seriously look into ourselves then all of us will feel such despair….

When we have given ourselves up as thoroughly useless and helpless, when our total being as a living corpse has been carried to the cemetery for cremation and burned, then a flame will emanate from this burning corpse. Comparing this decayed corpse with the flame that emanates from it, we must remark how beautiful that flame is. But the fuel for this beautiful flame is just the dirty self! … There are many flames in this world. But this flame that consumes our self is the strongest and most joyful thoroughgoing flame. Truly, this beauty, this climax, reaches into our very guts. Even while being burned up, we want to praise and adore the beauty of the flame.

This is such a strange thing! But even though it is strange we do experience it in our lives. For example, we say, "Even though he is my enemy, he is admirable." Even if we are defeated by an enemy, if the way he defeats us is remarkable, then we forget our defeat and praise his victory. Falling in love is another example. When we are completely enchanted by another we lose ourselves completely and praise the other. Falling in love means having our life completely taken away by the other. This is complete defeat: but it is a joyful defeat. In a sense, it is the same as saying that the flame which destroys our dirty self completely is a beautiful, terribly joyous, and solemn flame.

Then what is the essence of this fire that burns us up? Here I can't help recalling the ancient Greek philosopher Heraclites, who said that the essence of the universe is fire. He said, "The universe never remains in the same form, but at every moment it is continually changing." He said that all beings change. Thus to say that the essence of the world is fire is to say that everything changes. He used fire as a symbol of what we call mujo (change). And thinking of Heraclitus I can't help being reminded of Akegarasu's "flames of cremation of the total self."….

And the stream of the world's changes washes away that self which is always, "I am good I am bad I am dependable I am undependable." You will be inundated by this torrent of mujo. This flame is the torrent of the eternal life of the universe itself. But being seen in the reflection of mujo, which is the absolute image of the universe and the torrent of life itself, we are aware that our self is limited and relative. This is the very reason why the Teacher speaks of the cremation of the total self. If I may rephrase what he said, it means that one is aware of the true aspect of self when illuminated by the light of wisdom, the light of the flame, the light of truth.

"Flames of cremation" means flames of the universe itself, not the small flames that petty individuals can make out of half-used charcoal! The flame is the light of the eternal universe and the wisdom of Tathagata as the light of the world. By the flame, Reverend Akegarasu meant eternal light and eternal life. This flame symbolizes both life and wisdom.

When he said, "cremation of the total being" he implied cremation by the flame of mujo of the universe, not the little flame that we ourselves make. That is to say, to be aware of one's limited, relative self in light of mujo. This is the true meaning of the cremation of the total self. Therefore the flame of the cremation is entirely that of Other Power, the fire of the Tathagata, not my fire. By meeting the truth of the Tathagata's light and wisdom, we become aware of ourselves as negligible, small, and useless.

As I have said, the cremation of the total self is Akegarasu's confession. This is not a confession that he makes but a confession that cannot help gushing out, under the light of the Tathagata's wisdom. Because there is fire, we are burned up. The fire comes first; the cremation follows. Thus Reverend Akegarasu, forgetting himself, praised the wisdom and the life of the Tathagata, the wisdom of the fire that thoroughly consumes our so-limited selves. There is only this mass of flame. Besides this mass of burning, nothing else exists.

This is exactly like Heraclites' way of understanding life. The real being is only fire. In other words, the way of understanding life as mujo is the only way of understanding life. And this is the only wisdom of Buddhism.

My Teacher praises only this mujo. The Teacher's confession of self is praise of the Tathagata. And the praise of the flame is the cremation of one's self. Confession is praise and praise is confession. And this means the same as the words of Zendo Daishi, "Every uttering of the Nembutsu is confession."

Reverend Akegarasu praises the fire of the universe by forgetting himself. The existence of this fire itself is the essence of his total being. Buddhism teaches "no self" here. Here the Teacher is not trying to stress "no self". Here the Teacher acknowledges, recognizes, praises only the existence of the flame in which he discovers himself, having already forgotten himself, and lives in an unlimited life of emancipation.

The flames of the universe that burn up the totality of self are the voice of wisdom that echoes throughout the whole universe. I see the Teacher listening into this voice of wisdom: it is like a beautiful symphony that is being played by the universe itself. I can't help calling this "the song of the flame." In expressing it more rationally: The enlightenment of my Teacher came only when he recognized mujo as the true Dharma of the world.

> From "Suchness", an A.B.A. Pub.
> Translated by Reverend Saito
> and Joan Sweany.

> The clean burning flame
> Is like the symphony of light
> That lights up the world.
>   -R. A.

ABOUT NATURE
Haya Akegarasu

I've been reading the article, "From the Future World," which you wrote for me. I was quite interested in your deep understanding of Shinran Shonin's, <u>Collections of a Foolish Baldheaded Man</u>, especially the section "Comparison of the Inner and Outer Teachings." Your presentation of the relationship between inner and outer has given me such guidance that I'm deeply grateful to you.

This article with its profound thoughts and the flower on my desk give me the same feelings. There is no better or worse between these flowers; one blossoms on the plant, the other in a person. Both are beautiful, aren't they?

In your article you said that the world of nature speaks now and manifests everything of itself in the two-dimensional world. In that, I don't agree with you.

I cannot see the red camellias on my desk as two-dimensional! Of course I often listen to two-dimensional discussions, which have no time dimension, no depth – those discussions carved by so-called scholars using their knife of the small wisdoms' of clever people. Two-dimensional things are dead things. To have the time dimension is to have life.

The scarlet camellia opens the red mouth of her petals and lets me see her shining white spirit. To me she radiates and lives with great power.

You surround yourself with a two-dimensional nature. That is why you call nature two-dimensional. But I am in that nature which has depth of the time dimension and shines with its own life, and so I live as nature itself. Are you saying there is no will or inevitability in this? Don't you see here the great shining will and great inevitability?

Do you really think that nature has no wishes? Next to my desk stands a pot of white quince, ready to flower. Buds have such a bursting-out force! They must have an immensely strong wish; otherwise they could not open with such power. The true wishing power that I touch here – great nature's wish flowing naturally into every bud of quince – is entirely different from the kind of artificial wishes that we have – wanting to do this or that or the other thing.

Don't tell me that you want to discourse on the true meaning of "Dharma itself" and the "manifestation of the Dharma," on the meaning of the static and dynamic! I don't understand these small itemized points that scholars are always constructing. Like great nature itself, I shine with hope; I dance with life as such. Don't ask me why: I don't know why. But everything I see is living and dancing. I deeply pity those smart people who use their own paltry understanding of nature to kill nature and then bury themselves in its cold dead body.

"Modern naturalists" are thus. They see nature as flat and static: they see it mechanically. Don't tell me that your understanding of nature is the same as theirs!

You said: "Once we have departed from the breasts of Great nature," and so on. How can I depart from the breasts of great nature? – I have difficulty understanding this. Yes, I suppose that if I am playing with concepts, then nature and life may meet and part or part and meet. But living nature does not exist aside from me, nor does my living self exist aside from nature. Where is this nature that has departed from me? Stars twinkling, roar of the wind, unfolding of flowers, birds singing, animals running, people talking – all are nature and all are myself, aren't they? Where is this nature aside from my own living? Where is this "manifestation of the Dharma" aside from my living?

Don't tell me you are thinking of a nature that exists in opposition to your life. Such a life, such a nature are not true, do not exist. Do you think you are alive but plants are dead? And don't you understand that iron and stone are living, too? Don't you see that our country is moving? Don't you see and hear? The world floods with life.

I don't understand what you said in your article about leaving nature or going back to nature. There is only nature itself; there is only myself. There is no leaving. There is no going back.

You ask me to roar like a lion in front of the general public. Yes, it's true that this general public will cry and laugh and sing and dance to my words and sentences. But these people are only a manifestation of my own life. Surrounded by this general public, in the midst of this general public, I alone am the noble one. In the Lotus Sutra you will recall that the great audience of Gautama Buddha was conjured up out of his own wisdom.

Not all of those who talk about Dharmakara are themselves Dharmakara, storehouse of the Teaching. Without talking about the Dharma, think about it. Oneself is the storehouse of the Dharma.

I was reborn where my wish to be saved was crushed. At that point I became like the wish of great nature itself. I hope that you too will be reborn by destruction of this whole human characteristic; that is, your last wish of "wanting to be saved" should be crushed completely. My friend, the way is so near you. It is so simple. It is not reasoning. It is not something you can discuss in your discourses on the Dharmakara.

This morning I walked two miles through the snow to one village and this afternoon I went three miles to another village to receive the great teachings of Shinran Shonin and Honen Shonin with my audiences. I'm so tired! I ate supper and took a bath and now I am writing to you. But I've suddenly become so sleepy that I'm going to crawl into a warm bed. Don't you see the power of great nature's wish overflowing my body as sleep?

    Let's bury reason and then bury the reason that would bury reason. Ah natural man! Ah foolish bald-headed man! When I'm thirsty, I drink. When I'm hungry, I eat. It's so simple! In such simplicity I dance with great nature itself. Now don't you see and hear this manifestation of the power of the wish of Dharmakara? …. But I've written too much. What the heck! I want to shout: it's a dead struggle! It's dead because it stinks of theology and the scholarship of Shinshu Buddhism – I hate it. Let's burn this letter and warm our hands. My friend be healthy, be strong!

                                From "Shout of Buddha" 1977
                                Trans. by Gyoko Saito & Joan Sweany

---

                                        April 24, 2014
                                                R. A.

This article really touched my life. After reading it I became very solemn, in fact, fell silent and speechless. During this time I did some serious introspection and found, that yes, I was seeing into the very depth that came from Akegarasu's understanding. So deeply he describes what he means by "great nature" and how it applies to our life. "In such simplicity I dance with great nature itself." Or in wanting to crawl into a warm bed, he says to his friend "Don't you see the power of great nature's wish overflowing my body as sleep?"

    Ah natural man. He takes eternal life and brings it down to earth as great nature's wish. He too is examining himself and just as he gets into Dharmakara's wish he sees himself just beginning to get into religious theology and scholarship of Shinshu Buddhism as he says "What the heck!" and dismisses it with the remark: …"it's a dead struggle!" … I hate it. Let's burn this letter and warm our hands."

    Nowhere in literature, religious or otherwise, can I find anything that can come even close to his teaching that manifests natures' true wish that allows us to deepen our understanding of what it is to live within the truly organic threshold of life itself. The time dimension that he brings out is itself that of the tathagata. The "storehouse of knowledge" that he states represents Dharmakara (the main character in the Larger Sutra), and his becoming Amida Buddha as infinite wisdom/compassion within us.

FROM DEATH TO LIFE　　　　　　　　　　　　　　　January 27, 2014
　　　　　　　　　　　　　　　　　　　　　　　　　　　　R. A.

    This morning I feel nothing but brightness. Nothing stops the progress of my forward seeking as I'm surrounded by such wonderful articles that have contributed and inspired me to go forward expressing my feeling from such wonderful teachings I've received. Looking at this empty sheet of paper I cannot sit still but want to go forward expressing my own life.

    Outside it is bitterly cold, one of the coldest on record (or almost) with temperatures as low as -17 degrees below zero and wind chills at -25 and -40 degrees below zero along with such accumulating wind driven piles of snow – br-rr-rr! Yet, from inside I'm warm as it seems that all this cold just adds to my cheerful mood. Like the freezing temperatures outside gives rise to a fresh feeling inside.

    The sun is shining brilliantly. And with the sun, the world, and myself are all part of this movement of life, even to the snow that is sparkling outside. And, since there are no blockages I'm tasting infinity being at one as such. It is indeed, infinite light. Like the light of the sun shining off of the sparkling snow, all moving within a clear sky.

    Usually we talk about freedom that is relative, that is, depending on circumstances, whether or not we are free becomes bounded by our ability to be able to move our bodies or whether our mind gets stuck or not on something, and etc. But spacious freedom has no boundaries and is coming from the one who is open to receive it. It's like rain, the rain that waters the world and keeps it alive – or like the snow outside that freezes the world so that we can feel the re-birth of spring. Freedom involves movement and contrast that produces life. So infinite freedom involves infinite light, and infinite light is wisdom. Wisdom as the Great Mind as we come across Amida Buddha. The creation of Amida Buddha in Buddhism came from those who lived in this freedom which they then called the Wisdom of Amida Buddha. So they were themselves Amida Buddha. They were reflecting on who they were and gave it a name. This is the process upon Shakyamuni's original intent. From here came the story of Dharmakara as seen in the Larger Sutra.

    I have to live the life of Dharmakara. The struggle that it takes is between death and life. It is not an easy path. There is no easily marked road. Since it is my own life to begin with no one has gone before me. But I do have guides, and these guides, by living their own life point the way, therefore I'm not totally alone that I would otherwise be. The light within is reflected by the teachers who come before me, as are those who are contemporary; even on a daily basis of those who I meet greet me.

This way as new insights come – new creation comes! An endless progression forward and that is where the life is.

The Christmas cactus is booming, once thought dead. And the Amaryllis is sending up a strong shoot, another one I thought was dead. From death to life, that's the progress of our growth. I know they want to bloom; they want to show their shining essence. In the same sense all humans want to bloom, and they too would want to show their shining essence. But in the case of humans so many get unfortunately diverted from their essential wish and fall into darkness, pettiness or mere mundane things because they have no idea. By clinging to our surface self we can experience a kind of living death where there is no real movement; where our spiritual life is all dried up, non- existent, or rotten. Experiencing our "death" while still alive is no easy matter for us, we have to struggle and work for our own salvation. No external power will save us. Depending on an external power is useless; when in fact, the only power we need lies within ourselves. Swimming on the surface of the ocean as we do, and experiencing all kinds of disturbing, turbulent, confusing currents there, we cannot possibly get to its depths without our seeking a living peace in our lives within the calm, deep movement in the depths of the ocean of peace.

When we hear the words "Come to me", it is the Buddha that is calling us. And, because we want to live in the same world as the Buddha, we listen. In the case of Reverend Akegarasu, he sees in the flower the essential wish of all people to come to the life that is manifested in his orchid plants that provides this truth. What is this open invitation that sparks our attention, and turns our so-called living death into a rebirth.

FOR ORCHIDS
Haya Akegarasu

Since you take no interest in plants, you probably pay no attention to orchids. But perhaps you remember, from your visit here last October, that I had many covered glass bowls of these plants lined up along the south wall of my library. Among them is a magnificent specimen with vigorous leaves which is called ho-sai. It is a native of Formosa. When I visited Nagasaki in May of last year, your close friend Mr. K. granted my wish and gave me a cutting from his ho-sai. As the plant had sprouted and grown up in a warm country, I was worried, after bringing it to northern Japan, about what the winter's weather might do to it. So throughout the year I took especially good care of it. As a result it grew into a very healthy plant. Finally it developed vigorous new buds, first three and now six. A month ago I heard from Mr. K. that his ho-sai was in flower. This made me check my own ho-sai carefully but at that time it gave no sign that it was about to have flowers. That was a month ago.

Today another plant, my Cypripedium insigne, was ready to flower, so I brought it into the room and happened to set it down next to the ho-sai. In doing so, I glanced at the ho-sai. It had a bud two inches long. In crazy delight I shouted to myself, "A flower - the ho-sai has a flower!" I remembered the beautiful image of the ho-sai flowers last April in Shizuoka – violet-colored flowers.

I had given up expecting that these orchids could possibly produce flowers. So when I suddenly saw the ho-sai ready to flower, my delight was beyond comprehension. This is something you'll never understand – my friend, I am immersed in this joy. I went downstairs to my mother and wife. My mind was filled with joy, and dancing.

Today there was a special memorial service among my village friends. I was given a chance to speak, and did so, but somehow I had only cheerful feelings inside. Then this evening I was trying to write an article I had promised you and came to my library to work. My wife, after bringing the lamp into the library, carried the bowl of ho-sai to my desk. "Look!" she said, "There are two flowers." Delight flew up at my heart at this. When my mother entered the room, my mother repeated the news: "Mother, there are two flowers!" My mother, who has weak eyes, started peering into the bowl, and my wife tried to take the candle out of the lamp to increase the amount of light. Suddenly the candle set fire to the paper lamp shade: the paper flared up and burned. Ashes gently floated up to the transom and the picture of Reverend Kiozowa.

So both my mother and wife left to go downstairs. Now I'm sitting alone: On my desk are the ho-sai and a single red rose. The west sea is roaring steadily along the shore line, but there is no wind – a quiet night. And quietly I think many thoughts. None is stronger than my joy for the orchid that I tended last year that finally produced buds. I imagine the buds will open into flowers by, perhaps, March. After they open fully, there should be one month of fragrance. And so, for a hundred days, I shall care for them and watch growing flowers, and enjoy them.

By the year's end, I don't have enough money, and since during the year I have neglected many things, these things now pursue me, and the money troubles pursue me too, and I become irritated. But even in the midst of that feeling, how much I enjoy the flowering of the orchids! It is an important event.

What an easy-going person I am! When I think of my friends and then of the world, my mind becomes disturbed. Then I look at the orchids, so vigorous yet so quiet, which do not fight with other life, and I am reminded of the feeling of deep meditation. I feel that the life of the orchids lets me slip into a state of Nirvana. These orchids teach me, guide me, more than people's words or articles. The orchid has no philosophy, literature, no religion – or if so then she is herself is philosophy, literature, and religion. She doesn't discuss, doesn't draw conclusions, doesn't preach, but lives her own natural life very cheerfully. In her there are no countries, no societies. Her buds cluster together in harmony among her roots. But the orchid does not force me to follow her, and I have no wish to follow her, either. The orchid taught me this: Her life is straight forward: she makes a sincere effort to live in her own way without looking at the lives of others. This life of hers touches me very deeply. This is why I am attracted to her life, and why she teaches me the way. And the thing that has impressed me the most: She has a special character not seen in other plants – she herself manifests tranquility in solitude, effort, hope.

On the eighth day of this month I left home and went to Nagoya…. Then on the twenty first I returned home. During this time I heard frank opinions from many friends.

Yes, I love friends. And because I have a longing to see them, I got together with them whenever I went on my trip. Whenever a friend of mine discusses and thinks about his life as his own art, I respect him, but whenever he just tries to impose his thoughts on others, I become deeply opposed to him, and I fight him strongly. Among friends I feel that something is communicated without discussion or thought, study, or action.

Orchids have no thoughts – not even experiences – no study, faith, or morality. So orchids will say, "Welcome!" and "All right!" to everyone and open their arms to embrace everyone, saying "Come to me!"

For a long time I have done no writing. Now, having a pen in my hands again and trying to write something, I seem to persist in making excuses or preaching, even though I don't intend to, and can't set down my life as it is. This is too bad for me.

It's getting late now. The lamp is burning ever so quietly. The charcoal is just becoming a white ash. The burning candle lights up the charcoal which is turning to ashes. Even from here the light is bright, and I can feel the heat. Now I put the pen aside. Now I shall crawl into a warm bed. Goodnight, my friend.

(*This Nirvana-like scene that he opens with towards the end of his article gives me the same feeling. How beautifully he expresses his* oneness with the orchid, the ho-sai. I cannot help but feel the same way, as I too am drawn into a state of Nirvana. And here, it is the orchid itself which is drawing us into such tranquility, solitude, effort, and hope. He sees the effort of the orchid to grow and bloom through his own effort. It is the effort to come up with his very own life: "This is too bad for me." he confesses. Then there is a kind of cremation scene in the words: "The burning candle lights up the charcoal which is turning to ashes." His being is like that of the burning candle, seeing the dying embers of the charcoal, similar to that of making excuses or preaching. Then at this point he lights up the charcoal with the candle. The dead stuff turns into ashes....

This is very subtly expressed, and unless you know what to look for it can escape your attention. So with no preaching he lets his friend know the essence of the teaching he received from the orchid that he describes so well. In that sense, through the orchid, he's giving his friend the Dharma of organic life that his friend, who has no interest in plants, sorely needs and which includes his opposition to a controlling person as stated.

Now he has completed his writing; and satisfied, he crawls into a warm bed. He has self-realized himself subjectively in the orchid as himself; both living their respective lives straightforwardly, both in tranquility, effort, and hope. Both he and the orchid are born into the same world, the world of Nirvana. This is the Teaching I got from him and his ho-sai.

He interprets the orchid as if it is saying: "Come to me!" The one who sees this is Akegarasu himself. I cannot describe anything more beautiful. The Nirvana being expressed here is the tranquility of nature herself as manifested by his ho-sai.) - R. A.

THE GLOWING JEWEL OF HOPE

R. Adams
January 29, 2014

In this cold hard winter, hope is like a fresh spring of water that gushes forth that provides the light and life that pushes me forward. And in this hope, even though the snow is whipping horizontally, driven by strong winds of a blizzard, I am kept warm (viewing it through a window). And within this warmth there is a brightness which is the joy as the motion and the snow go together in a state of "onceness." This is the rhythm of life that I'm participating in that pushes all else aside, this huge universe where I now sit admiring the snow and all its lively patterns.

Nothing of substance is accomplished without difficulty, and it is this hope that provides the light that allows us to overcome and break through these difficulties. So we first should be willing to go through the difficulties.

Now, this quick episode has passed and I shall continue on with my fast walk filled with such hope. My hope is to understand the Teachers' teaching thoroughly and to come up with my own life and to be able to express it clearly and distinctly. At times, it is difficult to put into words.

So later this evening, while reading some of Reverend Akegarasu's writings when by accident I came across an article by him on this same topic. Surprisingly, when I read it I found certain similarities – amazing! Now when I read it I find this kind of in-depth oneness. He spoke of a flower, his ho-sai orchid for instance, as having this hope, and I've seen it in my own plants; whether indoors or outdoors, and identified it with the spirit of life as well, and so I've been meditating on it for some time. A kind of perception and feeling that I saw in life, yet so illusive and quietly manifesting itself; deeply moving the human mind to discover this living essence as the very spirit that turns a negative into a positive. What I needed to do is to put into words what makes me aware that in the world of nature we all share the same spirit, and are moved by the same hope that nature shows every time we step into it, as we are open to receive it.

By virtue of its own light, alone, and without any attachments this hope exists in all things. That's why it is so important for us to realize it, and not to waste our valuable time on cheap, easy hopes that have no real value. The hopes that people generally have are the ones that are of dreams and desires. These kinds of hopes are relative in their proportions, like those of winning the lottery, or hoping for a "better life", and all that the secular world has to offer in the way of hopeful expectations. But when our hopes and expectations fail we will experience the truth. We are on shaky ground here, and have not as yet experienced the deep and penetrating hope that is the light. It is this light within one's own being. The Great Hope, that turns the difficulties and struggles we seek within the truth, the very living core within myself, where the fresh spring gushes forth that transforms our objectivity into subjectivity that turn negative darkness into positive light. It is within this light that I live. The flame, so to speak, is fueled by the negative karma it transcends. Thus negatives do turn into positives: And these positives are the spirit, the flame itself, the truth of which is for me to discover within my own life. The more input, the more output; till the voltage comes alive enough with the sparks of transcendence. What a lively life I want to live. So this hope is always here within, kicking me to go onward.

SHINING HOPE   Haya Akegarasu

   My soul burns with hope and shines with hope. All things are fuel for it; all things shine with it. I stride forward on this way of hope – my life blood leaps up.
   The flame and light of hope burn strong, too strong for fame and wealth to stifle or poverty to quench. Men call me a heretic, dangerous, immoral – all manner of abusive names – cut off their friendship, damming me, even from all sides hurl threats at me. All this I accept crying, but I accept it all as fuel: The flame and light of hope burn brighter, and shine out of darkness like the blazing sun.
   It's a dark uncertain future that is cast by expectations and experience. So throw it all away and dash naked into the way of hope itself. Then the future brightens and shines.
   Everyday life is like an inexpressibly fascinating new movie, which can't be guessed at ahead of time. In it I find myself dancing, crying, laughing, shouting, singing, suffering, enjoying. And from an inner core, all this fans the flame of hope still larger.
   My hope is neither the result of expectation nor expectation of results. The way of hope is great nature itself, transcending cause and effect. Hope is light and life. Listen to this hope speaking from out of my soul:
   "Come now, with intense and honest mind. I will protect you. Do not fear the decent into fire and water. Do not fear any evil."
   Let's advance, shattering all difficulties. Let's go onward, following the way of hope as such.

                          From: "Shout of Buddha"
                          Trans.: Gyoko Saito & J. Sweany

Sunday Morning Awakening   R. Adams
                                               February 2, 2014

   "It's not the way of enlightenment to suffer." These are the only words I need from Haya Akegarasu to begin the day with. From these words alone I will compose this article. I do not know where it is going, but I can begin with my own words and follow straight through.
   The fresh snow is covering the trees, and the sun is brilliantly shining. It is this peace, tranquility, and freshness – my mind is lit up. This is the way of enlightenment: This joyous union with life itself.
   Being with friends last night – what a cheerful crowd! Singing while we were dancing, joking and laughing, and just being together in good

company along with lively music from a three piece band who put their heart into the music that made the event memorable. These are rare chances to be in such an atmosphere, and I look forward to be together in such a group with music devoted to the "upper age" – an active group – where the oldest are the youngest! Ha! I'm one of them – first person on the floor, and yes, the one most alive who feels the rhythm of the body. Upward and downward, sliding along, arms in fast movement, body gyrating, gracefully gesturing; all in all, like a lion on the dance floor creating his own territory, or moving sensitively like a butterfly, while going from here to there! "Buddhism in action" my Teacher would have said. Yes, so many friends are created this way as we dance together in so many styles. Dead styles, live styles; their unique styles show their life.

    Of course, not everyone can dance, nor care to, depending on how they respond to the music, and/or if they have a partner, and etc. But those who do get up to at least participate have an advantage of loosening up their bones, loosening up their muscles, and most of all, getting in rhythm with their bodies which is most important in order to get rid of the static self-conscious ways that are the cause of our stiffness. Actually, I don't do it for any reason like therapy or aerobic exercise. I jump on into the floor, or into the crowd that is already dancing, and since I don't have any self-consciousness to worry about, I travel along the rhythms that come from an unknown source that just keeps occurring at a one-thought-moment at a time that carries me along with a feeling of such freedom. This feeling of freedom which has no object other than a rhythmical movement is selfless. The fervor in this simplicity comes within actional intuition as a dance within within the fluidity of endless space. It is the life-movement within, not just sloppily playing around. I am serious yet playful with the steps, insofar as listening to every beat, every step in tune with the music of the band regardless of almost every kind of music imaginable as long as my feet begin tapping, and my body begins moving, experiencing the great will of nature which can't be thought up or formulated in advance.

    "The truth that does not touch the flesh is not the truth." More words from Akegarasu, quoting from Nietzsche. As for myself, the truth won't let me go as I am finding it everywhere – inside, outside, here, there, everywhere – just look, listen and be aware of it. That's the same as the dancing I was referring to. While the way of enlightenment is not to suffer, it is to be aware into the core of one's being; for that is where the truth gushes out freely and spontaneously. The one-thought moment is so important here: not to drag along a lot of dead weight in terms of past karma - brought about by our attachments. We suffer from the effects of this karma in our waking life and even in our sleeping life. Worse than that, we will be unable to listen and partake in the true rhythm of life, the feeling of infinity that carries the whole world with it, as in my mind that is dancing, or: "I will dance my way into the Pure Land". The unpredictable dance is coming from the unknowable life which is at this very moment and which is the truth that is so joyous and interesting, never boring or dead. The shining light, the burning flame consumes the suffering of the static mind and produces the pure clean light within one's naked self.

To purify the world means one's self that is quietly and brightly shining. As I see the world the world will exist, regardless of what hellishness exists there, misfortunes exist there; for non-attachment lets the world do as it wishes from an uncountable number of karma's of which I have no control over or does anyone else. So the infinity present in the Dharma of life transcends all worldly karma's to reveal the soul of the world as it is.

It is a process of deepening – the emptier, the more fullness and well-roundedness. Not trying to grab hold: the possession-less life leads to the fulfillment of life and the real riches; real treasures come of it, such as a simple flower that upon blooming opens our eyes to life as it is.

Now the Christmas cactus is blooming profusely. How delicate, how pure and virtuous with no artificiality. This power of life, this solemnity, is our life. We can be as is this flower, as all flowers are if we really look and self-examine ourselves. The transforming nature of life is what removes past karma's. It is not necessary to live in the darkness of our past karma, but open our life to the freshness that listening to nature gives us. We are that nature. We shouldn't separate ourselves from the very core of our being which is within the harmony with the Great Mind of nature itself. This is the real world of "no-possession" which means getting rid of our clinging to things that are unnatural and artificial and enjoying the simplicity that is the essence of our creative life. Then we can join along with nature as nature changes continuously; without hesitation, thinking and reservation, revealing our true and natural instinct to be at one with nature. The whole point of being a natural person is answered here.

We have the words of Reverend Manshi Kiozowa: "The self is no other than this: my settling down into this environment, letting naturalness to carry me, riding the unbounded working of myriad phenomena."

He was very relaxed when he wrote this; but it so relaxes me at this late hour into the night as it warms me, and causes me to smile.

(Listening to the Dharma also means listening to Reverend Akegarasu who embodied the Buddha-Dharma. In this particular article taken from "The Shout of Buddha", a book that Reverend Gyoko Saito and Joan Sweany (as editor) translated and published in 1977, that I found accidently while looking for some things, I was struck by such a beautiful translation they did in so far it is as if Rev. Akegarasu were speaking to me directly; and as such became a focal point that I kept meditating on adding to the compilation of his articles for this book. Therefore I will insert it here as it has awakened in me a power of Reverend Akegarasu's life to leave me speechless before this person who really strikes into my being. He was seen as a living Buddha by his contemporaries. He was the teacher to my teacher, Reverend. Saito, who introduced him to us discussion group member's back in 1963). - R.A.

MIND OF EMBRACING ALL THINGS

(H. A.)

Reading an early passage of the Kegon Sutra, I came across a poem by the Ho-E Bodhisattva which made me want cry out, "How wonderful!" Here it is: from subject and object,

> Be free from subject and object
> Get away from dirtiness and cleanliness.
> Sometimes entangled and sometimes not
> I forget all relative knowledge:
> My real wish is to enjoy all things with people.

This poem expresses so clearly what I am thinking these days that I use it to explain my feelings to everyone I meet.

Subject or object, myself or someone else, individualism or socialism, egotism or altruism - forget about such relative knowledge, be freed from it! Right or wrong, good or bad, beauty or ugliness - don't cling to that either. Forget about ignorance or enlightenment! Simply enjoy your life with people – this is the spirit of Gautama Buddha, isn't it? I'm glad that Shoran Shonin said, "When we enter the inconceivable Other Power, we realize that the Reason without Reason does exist," and again, "I cannot judge what right and wrong is, and I don't know at all what is good and bad." I hate to hear about the fights or clashes between two different faiths. I don't care about these things. Somehow I just long for people. I hate to be separated from people by the quarrels of ism or dogma or faith, and what is more, I hate to be separated from other people by profit and loss.

I don't care whether I win or lose, lose or win. I just long for the life burning inside of me. I just adore people, in whom there is life.

I don't care about, isms, thoughts, or faiths, I just long for people. I throw everything else away. I simply want people.

It makes me miserable when close brothers are separated by anything. Why can't they be their own naked selves? Why can't longing people embrace each other?

I love myself more than my isms, thoughts or faiths. And because I love myself so I long for people. I am not asserting that my way is Love-isim or Compassionate-Thinking-ism! Somehow I just can't keep myself in a little box of ism, thought or faith.

I must admit that I am timid. Because I am timid, I can't endure my loneliness. I want to enjoy everything with people.

> I go to the ocean of the great mind.
> I go to the mind of great power.

Once I hated people because they lived a lie; once I saw them as devils. Once I lamented because there was no one who cared about me. But now I long for them, even when they are devils and liars, even when they are evil. I don't care, I can't help it – I adore them! They breathe the same air that I do, even when they hate me, cheat me, and make me suffer.

I am so filled with the thirst to adore people that there is no room in me for judging whether a person is good or bad, beautiful or ugly, right or wrong. This is not the result of something I reasoned out, such as that I live by being loved or loving. Regardless of any ism, thought, or faith, I cannot be separated from people because of that.

My spirit shines with the mind-of-embracing-people. Without reason or discussion, I just want to hug everyone! My missionary work is nothing but a confession of this mind.

The Garden of Life
R. Adams 5/20/2013

My first white peony has opened – what a delight! Oh, and the first daylily, too! The face of absolute life shines in the garden. There is nothing in between myself and the universal One which inherently includes the many.

We need a name for it; a universal truth that applies to all life. We need a name that brings us to a garden of life. Amida Buddha is such a name. A name, a symbol, and an essence that we can communicate and bow to; a name that will form our innermost aspiration expressed as in the nembutsu: Namu Amida Butsu, or bowing in oneness with Amida Buddha's limitless light or wisdom, and limitless life, or compassion. A true expression of universal life, it has within its short expression of wisdom first and then compassion. For without wisdom compassion will have no focus as relates to life itself.

But compassion comes to us as a double-edged sword: It gives us life, but it also can kill us, that is, take away our most cherished attachments. Indeed, it can leave us with nothing – making us possession-less as naked human beings: All that we've acquired that is taken away by a power we've no control over. This is true compassion when we finally come down to who we really are.

The Innermost Aspiration of compassion is awakened in us when we are aware of the Tathagata of limitless life that limitless wisdom allows us to see.it.

Buddhism always speaks in terms of the universal truth, just as our very first original shout that we all expressed loudly. Life comes first, and then comes the words to express it. In this case the life and the shout are at the moment of birth.

The Jodo Shinshu founder, Shinran Shonin, (1173 – 1262) expresses this oneness in his own words; as his feeling is in his compassion deeply expressed in this poem. Here too, when we speak of what is noble as in the Buddha's birth shout, as it came out of a compassion that he felt while being in such darkness.

The Innermost Aspiration of compassion:
Is like the great earth, for it sustains the birth of all things.
Is like the great waters, for it washes away all blind passions.
Is like the great fire, for it burns the firewood of all deluded views.
Is like the great wind, for it goes everywhere in the world and is without hindrance.

So for Shinran, having given up his dependence on self-power after he met his teacher Honen, he relied on other power, or the essence that he describes above. He identifies, and is at one with the inconceivable power expressed within the feeling of nembutsu, and experiences the light and life which allow him to come up with such a universal and profound expression.

What is it that supports us and gives us life? It is the inconceivable eternal life. This eternal life has a will and a spirit that manifests itself everywhere. From the flowers in the garden to the trees in the forest – the whole world!

We can bow to it out of reverence for the fact that there is a power beyond man, indeed, a power beyond our limited self-seated ignorance and confusion in which there is no solution. Here we have reached a point in our lives that can become critical, and while we cannot see it clearly by ourselves we can seek into the teachings of the Dharma in order to be at one with the essence of this eternal light and life. It is life itself that attracts us, and in fact, beckons us, calling us to listen as we reflect upon ourselves. The deeper we go in our reflection the more is our wish to be at one with an embracing life. Here we don't need to just chant the nembutsu; we can deepen it by seeking a true dialogue with others.

As we listen, even when our limited understanding is being refuted, we feel a sense of being lightened as a result of the burden of one's ignorance is removed. It is our fixed ego and conceit that is being negated. Absolute negation is absolute affirmation. This is a process of transformation that must take place if we are to understand, be humbled, and fully appreciate the compassion that is being given to us and is embracing us.

So actually, not even the words, but just the feeling itself is incorporated into our being by our deepest aspiration. Thus the very seeking of the truth resides in one's self-examination. We must not believe that by using the words alone with a bit of humility we can therefore over-estimate and be satisfied based on a partial understanding. The true Dharma is not easy to understand so long as a person languishes in self-satisfaction. This is a common mistake. Instead, we should be seeking like all others in the sangha, because the more we seek the deeper becomes our aspiration – on and on – as we become at one with Amida's light in a one-thought moment of continuous change. Amida's wisdom means life itself which includes the whole world as it is. We must experience this self-realization within our own lives in order to complete the process of fulfillment.

What enters our mind and enlightens us is hope, a hope the nature of which cannot be found in the relative sense, but that which simply wells up within me – which miraculously transforms a blockage from a negative into a positive. The problem thus becomes no-problem by totally relying on the power beyond the self. This insight brings us into the freshness of the original self; the honest pure self is what burns up all the evils that are mentioned in the poem. We come across the most fundamental mind clearing aspects of our life. This is the essence and meaning of the deepest aspiration of compassion in Shinran's poem. The nembutsu of confession is the compassion that converts useless stuff into fresh life: Spontainious life happens and the truth comes to life without my seeking.

Suffering Of Break-Through Haya Akegarasu
(From "Shout of Buddha")

It is not the way of enlightenment to suppress oneself and suffer. It is the way of enlightenment to let go completely and taste suffering by fighting through all difficulties.

So many people in this world let themselves be squashed down by other people's feelings, and suffer from this, and struggle. We have to escape from such a cowardly way of life – always having to guess at which way some other person is going to breath.

Why do you hesitate? What are you afraid of? Why not do it more that totally?

Someone might attack you, you say? Someone might persecute you? Then why don't you accept the attack and the persecution? Even though we must cry and suffer, let's go on our own way. Isn't that the most powerful way?

It's hard to go on enduring negative and passive suffering, but it's a challenge to take the suffering that comes from a positive attitude. With that, we can accept the attack of others and the suffering that comes from it, and even though we must cry out with suffering, once we have accepted this challenge we cannot help smiling. Such suffering is the suffering of break-through.

Go forward continuously. Suffer continuously. Break continuously. Struggle continuously. This is where indescribable joy exists, doesn't it?

R. A.

How true to life is this article by Reverend Akegarasu, for I have a friend who was in exactly the same position as Akegarasu describes. She worked as a seamstress/tailor for one of the largest and most respected stores located on Michigan Ave. here in Chicago. She was put under the thumb by both her department manager as well as her supervisor. Because she was an honest worker who after so many years of service had gained a reputation for her professional abilities as well as friendliness towards store customers (as she was sometimes called by name to do work for them) she was targeted by her jealous superiors who turned their attention on her and attacked her for all kinds of things which were false, contrived, and ugly in the attempt to get her fired. For five long years this suffering and struggle went on to defend her against their attempts to write her up under fictitious charges that they created for her.

Since I've known her for some time, and especially during the five year period in which I observed all she was going through to keep her job,

I too got involved with her problems – so serious – that it caused me to suffer alongside her since I had to write up rebuttals or responses to their various mischievous and downright phony charges against her.

Then too, since she was well paid for her long-time service to the company and all the various things that go with it, there is no doubt that this large company had a policy of hiring cheaper workers on call-up to save themselves money in a highly competitive retail market. This is common practice among various retailers in this market. And in the secular world where profit and loss bottom-line positions can make or break a company based on profits for their investors, and so forth.

So for all these reasons she was put on the "chopping-block" so to speak, repeatedly. Except in this case it became highly personal attacks. Some even quit because of this attitude that affected them as well, but she, with such perseverance, stayed on. There were times when even she wanted to quit, but she gathered the strength, the will and the spirit, to continue to persevere and to fight on.

I often told her that the supervisor's knife that was pointed at her would someday be pointed in the opposite direction, and instead be turned around by the supervisor's own deviousness back unto herself and would be the death of her instead of the victim she intended it for. And sure enough that is what happened. Amazingly, her supervisor was fired!

In her conceited position as thinking that she held a position with the power over others, she thought that she was superior over others, and in particular over my friend, an immigrant from Poland who was not good at English and therefore more vulnerable than others as a perfect target for both the manager and the supervisor to exercise their collective powers.

But as I acted as her "lawyer" and advisor, so to speak, and the fact that I was deeply moved by the way that they treated her, I wrote rebuttals that even the most educated of their managers had to respect. As a result, I, along with her dogged effort eventually turned their collective knives around that so badly affected their own reputations as non-other than liars and manipulators of a system that favored them, not the honest worker and strong person fighting for her own life.

This is what the article by Akegarasu says and means. It was just yesterday that I came upon this article while looking for other things. How ironically now, that it comes to pass that exactly fits in with Akegarasu's own experience prompting him to write about it. I too, was put under the thumb by my supervisors when I was employed. It was because of this experience that I began to see the secular world as it is. There are smiles now as having transcended it with a victory!

The Kingdom of the First

Haya Akegarasu
(From "The Shout Of Buddha")

(When I look at my body I see only one body, I don't see two bodies. Likewise, when I see into the mind that is within this body, I sense that there is only one mind, I don't sense that there are two minds. For if there are I can describe myself as dysfunctional in need of a doctor, or so much better yet, immediately in need of the Dharma that will direct me to the proper source that will take care of my dysfunctional position.

In this case I will direct people to Reverend Haya Akegarasu who in this article will resolve the problem so many people face as having a split-mind, a dichotomized mind, and a dualistic mind that is due to the way we so often think in terms of dualistic logic based on our conventional way of thinking, which we then utilize when we think of our religious, spiritual and ordinary life. This is so common when we think of religion aside from the one mind, and start to divide the mind into two parts.

It is in the way he treats this subject that so fascinates me that I decided to include it here at this time following his article on "Breakthrough", for it illustrates our basic problem that everyone has in breaking through the way we treat the secular life and the spiritual life, as well as the false self and the true self, the relative self and the absolute self. For instance, how can the relative self figure out the absolute self? It is here where he comes up with a series of remarks ending with his "In the kingdom of the first." This kingdom will be a manifestation of our own life.
– R. A.

Trans. by G. Saito and J. Sweany

*If a person divides himself into a "true self" and a "false self" I'd say he's living a superstitious life.

　*Philosophers analyze "ich sebst" or "I" as a relative or absolute by attaching pronouns to it. They say "absolute I" or "absolute self" or "We must find out the absolute self by leaving the relative self" or "We must find out the great self instead of clinging to the small self." It seems to me that such a philosopher never understands himself.

*To talk about leaving the relative self and going to the absolute self – that's nonsense. Once you say "absolute self" then where does the "relative self" exist? If you say "One must leave the "relative self" then there is no such an absolute self either. It is playing with ideas to say,

"Cut off all your desires and go to Nirvana," or "Leave the relative self and go to Nirvana," or "Leave the relative self and become the absolute self."

*Modern philosophers are moved by Kant's "Ding an Sich" ("the thing as such") are merely playing with concepts which never touch real life. It is interesting to hear Nietzsche's comment that any thought which does not touch flesh is hollow.

*I think there is life only when human thought is manifested through the flesh. If thoughts are not like this, then they are mere concepts, and anyone who thinks they point to a spiritual life or a holy life is either a Sunday school goody-goody or a fool or a liar.

*One of my friends said, "In the depths of my life the mind of love – is moving, and I must respect it." In my mind I see only hateful and cheap things, so I live without worrying about whether I survive or not. I have no ideas for self reform. I am good enough, I as I, for eternity. I don't want to become a Buddha which is separated from my being or any other Special One separated from my being. I am satisfied being what I am. Even though I negate myself, I am a great affirmer of myself! I have no wish to become a Buddha aside from myself. I want to live as I am, eternally.

*Of all things, I like a baby the most: a chunk of naked being. When I discover myself in this life I feel the deepest satisfaction of my being.

*One who thoroughly finds out his way, truly, will gain such confidence of "I am the absolute first!" In the world of the first one, there is no such small conflict of winning or being defeated. So in the kingdom of the first one there is no such a word as oppression, nor any such a phrase as "being first." If such a life of oppression or such a life of "being first" exists in the kingdom of one's life, one has not yet found the true life.

*In the kingdom of the first, there is none of that loneliness which comes with comparing oneself with others. In this kingdom all are independent; and that independence is absolute independence. Such a person never fights with others or asks anything from them; he is aware of the power of independence.

*The first one is never caught by the material and phenomena of the objective world. He acts with fulfilled subjectivity, so he is not half-starved but richly satisfied. The first one is never oppressed by others' actions or criticisms. He doesn't occupy anything but his own subjective world.

*The first one is not oppressed by evil nor by good; because he has no cheap standard of what good and evil is.

*The first one has such a mind of tranquility! What we call such a spiritual atmosphere of Nirvana. It's true that sometimes he cries – and laughs, also. Yet always a very tranquil mind flows through his laughter and tears.

　*The first one occupies life and death, without ever being controlled by life and death. He lives the eternal life.
*For him, anyone who has no awareness of the first one is a dead person. So he tries to give life to that dead person. This is his work. His job is to make <u>each</u> person aware that <u>that</u> person is the first one.
*In the country of the first one, there is no new or old. His kingdom is always new, yet old. And the youngest person is the oldest one!

　There is much to be reminded of here. First, there is his emphasis on subjectivity. It is his subjectivity that determines the outcome of the debate over false self and absolute self, in which he emphatically denies. He sees everything in terms of <u>one</u>. He sees no need for the mind to be divided into two separate entities, the false one and the true one. He sees no need for us to get involved with any entity aside from himself – the Buddha, or the Special Person. All these assertions, ideas and concepts are but artificial implants upon our naked being, which he compares to that of a baby as a "chunk of naked being".

　This is an article that one can read over and over as I get deeper into its content; a seeming inexhaustible source of teaching comes out of it. So many things are discussed that have to be translated and entered into our life, like never being caught by the material and phenomena of the objective world which I compare to the secular world. Or how we are oppressed by our own ego-based desire to be the first one which leads to one's feeling of superiority over others in the contest of "Who's the best".

　His "I am the absolute first", is not engaged in the smallish conflict over winning and losing – indeed, it is the most sincere feeling of absolute certainty that can be described in the world of the first one. This is the Buddha that is within the very content of no-separation.　　　　　　　　　　　　–R. A.

"Eternity"
Watercolor

In Such Praise

R. Adams
12/3/2014

I awoke this morning thinking of the power of independence. This thought came to me after going over Reverend Akegarasu's article entitled "Kingdom of the First" yesterday. After listening to him intensively, I was left with just this phrase in the morning. I was struck with a sense of joy as the sun was streaming through the windows and the partly opened door. Soon I started to write for some unknowable reason except for the fact that my mind was happy!

But if an article doesn't touch my physical being what good is it? After reading an article, I decided that dead stuff along with the article should be thrown out. But now fresh thoughts just came up after a review, and so....

The power of independence is no matter what others say or do, I will go my own way, eternally. Such freedom exists here. The joy overcomes all things, as I sense this brightness; the essence of my being that just came alive. The brightness of the sun as it streams through the windows and the open door and into a highway of no end. Light occurs here in this moment-to-moment life. Praise the light that turns darkness into life.

The independence of all beings, the oneness of all things; I am I is being at one with my life, and in going my own way freely in this freshness. Here I am good enough eternally.

All my predecessors: Haya Akegarasu, my teacher Gyoko Saito, and all others, like Maida, Kiozawa, Shinran, who took away my limited personality, while guiding me so I could join with them in such praise.

Oh those who have not as yet found their way, come to the teaching that allows us to be at one with the Buddha of infinite light and life, and the liveliness that is found here.

So much time we waste with all sorts of nonsense. What substance is there to our lives from all this frivolous going nowhere sort of life? The secular world seems tied to this idea of pleasure and entertainment in a response to the fear of survival in the world of profit-and-loss. As we cling to the secular world we forfeit our true independence which then becomes covered over by layers of stupidity and foolishness in which we get lost. We must abhor the secular world that exists on so much wasting of our precious time. "I see nothing but ugliness, so the future is assured for me." – (H. Akegarasu) I'm sure he's taking a cold look at the secular world. Then into this small space will unfold into such spaciousness. The ordinary flat life comes alive. True independence and freedom in the kingdom of the first is our true destination, when we've arrived at the other shore of one's own "kingdom of the first." One's very own confession leads to this kingdom.

The Beauty of Twigs (A Subtitle) — R. Adams 12/4/14

What a subtle joy there is now. It is winter and all the foliage has dried up. No sun. As I sit viewing this dried up foliage my mind is of nothingness – Oh Empty! Emptiness is the essence of Nirvana. My mind is still warm, despite the cold. And in this warmth I feel the union with all things. I think of the wondrousness of nature, as my mind feels natural. It is this quietly natural place where I view the depth of winter; feeling this oneness with all things and finding peace within all things. In winter life settles down into an atmosphere of peace and quiet. Viewing this, my mind has the sense of tranquility, for I am alive quietly respecting the dried-up foliage that winter has put to rest. Strange how beautiful dried up foliage and twigs can be as they stand straight and strong. I am happy in this ordinary scene, listening and following the way of natural life.

Be in peace. Make it a lively and eternal peace. Spring, summer, fall, or winter, it doesn't matter all the seasonal changes. For the mind creates everything including our perception of life. So beauty or ugliness depends on how we view things. But when our mind settles down into simplicity, everything becomes beautiful, and then we see how ugly the agitation, violence, and stupidity that takes place under the influence of secularism that so often make us shake our head in revulsion. So too, our peace must go beyond the peace found between wars and conflict. Let's transcend the so-called worldly, unstable, and fragile peace, and seek the true peace and tranquility found in the atmosphere of Nirvana.

Evening Pond

Preparation for Birth and Birth　　　　　　　　　January 15, 2013
　　　　　　　　　　　　　　　　　　　　　　　　　　　　R. A.

　　Winter is the best time to study and New Year's is the best time to get born, wouldn't you say? Every season at the stroke of midnight we're supposed to throw out the old year and with a celebratory display of loud noises, shouting and cheering, and welcome in the new year with a great deal of happiness in jumping up and down, horn blowing and dancing allows us to go crazy for a while. Yet the idea of throwing out the old and bringing in the new is interesting and refreshing. So often people can carry around the same old stuff year after year that they never get rid of; old hatreds, old attachments – everything stale, hardened and musty – even we can smell of it. Are we then even capable of celebrating the fresh New Year? We get stinky when we don't get born. Indeed, every day we really need to get born to avoid our own smelliness. A shower may clean our body but not necessarily our mind, which also contains practical matters. That takes something else. Although a hot shower along with a clean body increases the circulation and cleanses the mind refreshingly.

　　Hatred gets us nowhere and smelliness makes us lose friends. I want to live clear and clean and so I follow the way. The way I'm speaking of here is to get born every day. It's not a matter of my practicing something. It just happens every time I wake up in the morning after a good night's sleep, so it is quite natural. At this time life is most pure, and the spirit of life most direct, and, having an uncluttered mind I fall in quite naturally into the rhythms that come to me taking place in a blank or empty slate before me. It is the birth of a new day. Something indescribable within me is born that lights up my day and has substance to it that allows me to introspect what I've done and where I'm going, and in going in the proper direction. Also, this inspires getting fresh ideas for the day. Here there are the carryovers of accomplishing my real wish in the way of progress for this book which is my greatest aspiration at this time. Anything that brings out this progress of creation is my joy. Creating something of real value that contributes to the direction I'm thinking of, which is in the direction of going the way in the spirit of my predecessors, is the progress of going forward. This is what I describe as a re-birth each morning when I awake. Within this freshness that I seek throughout the day; like right now, as I throw out the old stale stuff and bring in the new – or giving life to the old by finding new ways of expression. Being freshly born is the main impetus of the day, as well this moment-to-moment life that brings life to the squiggling truth. With freshness comes birth, as only birth can happen when we are freshly born! So in that sense, the beauty of re-birth is when I am most alive.

Upon the Third Birth   May 15, 2014
                                                                                                    R. A.

    We experienced our first birth when we were just born. Our birth came with a shout – Waa! Right away we came out as a fleshy self into our mother's arms. Being embraced by our mother's love and with eyes wide open we experienced what it means to be totally naked taking in all that we could see in this fresh world, being surrounded by smiling human beings that we did not know. In fact, we knew nothing, said nothing, studied nothing, and wrote nothing. Complete nothingness attended our birth. In that sense we were like Neanderthal man. But soon we would be taught how to be civilized, first by our mother and father and then by society in the form of an educational process. For the first three to five years we would be given a direction by our mother as to the formation of our character and personality by her wishes for us. This very early direction given to us by our parents will give us a uniqueness that will more or less define us.

    Our second birth happens when we reach puberty or as a teenager. Our powers are beginning to grow. Our experiences within the family begin to move out into an ever-expanding world. On top of that there is the desire to seek our own identity. This leads us to test out our powers. This is very natural. We want to be independent from our parents and from society which we see as restrictions to our freedom as we want to be and do what we want to do. As we are confined we want to break out and because of this become rebellious and even disobedient. We have such power of energy at this time we can lose control because of our over-estimation and the limits of our powers which can lead us into trouble. In short we want to establish our own kingdom. Herein the trouble and confusion begins as we bump into other kingdoms that may or may not be friendly to us. We want to test out our powers by defeating others so that we can feel superior, the real king of our kingdom. Here is where our conflict with others begins, and we begin to suffer the results of our self-identity which is getting more fixed. The focal point in all of this is that of seeing us in a self-centered world.

    On the other side of this difficulty is that we are learning so much and being as students who are growing and expanding our world to such a great degree! There is such freshness about learning and having fun with friends, attending High School "socials" where you could dance and meet with the opposite sex wherein girls and boys would form relationships with each other and fall in love perhaps. So much learning and at such a fast pace that you couldn't stop even if you wanted to. High school, then college; so many experiences that made it so interesting involving our lives at the time. So yes, we can say that this is our second birth

But do we know who we really are? We have a name, and we have an identity attached to our name. So we exist because we are living and are alive, but what kind of life are we living; in the end, where is it all going?

Throughout our so-called second birth; it was categorized mainly by our pursuit of who we are in terms of acquiring a name and identity for ourselves. This acquiring of a name is largely self-power driven. Being as it is coming from our self-power it is naturally limited in so many ways. That is to say, it is limited by its attachment to our relative self, focused on the smallish circle of experience with its limited core of self-centeredness which has no real substance other than the passing winds of circumstance which puts us in the path of samsara, or birth-and-death.

Then too, what has our educational system given us? While it attempts to prepare us in order to make a living in the secular world it gives us nothing in terms of our spiritual life. It attempts to draw us into the system of a secular life-style; i.e., a dualistically interpreted way of set thinking in terms of a subject and object. It postulates theories about life that are bounded by stasis or the static understanding of life. This applies to religion as well, in which you have a static, dualistic God concept preached on the basis of man and his beliefs as an external absolute outside of himself. These fixed beliefs create many of the problems going on in the world today wherein people fight continuously.

We cannot experience our third birth if we are hampered by such external and delusional misunderstandings that have no basis in the actual fact of living life going on in nature, in our bodies, and in an understanding of what constitutes true religion. We should live far from the secular world as it is based on a shaky and even whimsical foundation of the relative self which it promotes, leading us astray.

Something must die for re-birth to occur. The missing space must be filled in by us as to our discovery of <u>what</u> we are. This results, or should result in one's own confession – being exposed to the truth of, "I am the most evil person." Not the person I thought I was, but rather, a person who has deluded ideas, and is far from the living truth.

My third birth happened when I no longer cared to be saved. I no longer cared to be enlightened out of self-enhancement. This is the transforming life of the person who is fully emancipated into ordinariness, liberated from thinking that he is some kind of special person. I felt my third birth when I met with the teacher who changed my life. Through him I had a focal point braught about by my deepest respect, the aspiration to be just like him.

YOUNG GRASSES

The snow has disappeared. In the garden the fallen leaves of last autumn are exposed now, like old corpses – so dirty! Through the dirty decayed leaves, a multitude of young growing things is pushing upward. It's almost as if these young plants are saying, "I have waited until this moment to arrive. I was filled with power so I pushed my way upward." Looking at them, how can I sit still? – Spring has come!

Either the warmth of spring draws them out, or the grasses' own powerful wish bursts out; either they are called by spring and grow up, or seeking the spring they grow up – I don't care which. Any reasoning will do. But the warm spring has come and the green grasses are spilling out in buds.

Spring is alive not only on the earth but in the earth as well – spring has fulfilled itself to the very tip of the grasses' roots. There is no room in me to name a relationship between the two: whether one seeks the other or the other calls the one.

> The grasses, simply, are single-minded. They concentrate on breaking through everything, so they just burst out. That's the power of spring.

From the roots of the chrysanthemum, buds of the chrysanthemum develop. From the roots of the peony, buds of the peony come up. Tulip bulbs do not give rise to hyacinth flowers, nor do flowers of the tulip develop from hyacinth bulbs. Isn't it funny that they never get mixed up! They have no rules or ideals but they aren't capricious and they do not make mistakes. Each pays no attention to the other's world but honestly puts its whole effort into its own way. I deeply respect these little growing things: I put my hands together in reverence. Honestly, courageously, strongly, in the intensity of every moment, never resting – such a real life wish manifests itself in these grasses very clearly, doesn't it? Something – that mysterious power that goes beyond the ability to reason – is manifested so naively in these young grasses. I can't help bowing my head in respect.

Grasses are so tranquil and serene. They keep silence. Their whole body is filled with power. Their growth is a long wide tongue that covers the whole world.

You never catch grasses making noise. They never reject others, nor advertise themselves. Grasses are never afraid of others. Those who are afraid of others always reject and attack them. The grasses are not like this.

Their living is in the full field of their own life, and so they do not need language or thoughts. Reverence their tranquility. Long for their silence.

Young grasses, I've gotten tired of my own falsehood and my own cleverness. I deeply adore you from the bottom of my heart. Because I truly love myself, I throw away all the external shells that covered me and – I can't help it – I want to kiss you.

Haya Akegarasu

(From "Shout of Buddha"
Trans. by G. Saito, J. Sweany)

R. A. 4/11/2015

When I look around these days I see that everything is bursting with life: the lilacs, the bushes, the tulips, the daffodils – everything is bursting through the ground and through the branches of trees and so forth. But it is Rev. Akegarasu who puts it into poetry, not only poetry but the teaching as well. Flowers to him are not just flowers. Grass to him is not just grass. To him they have a spiritual essence beyond what we normally think of. There is something in him that is urging him to seek an organic soul that he can find only in nature and as in his own nature, too. Then when he sees it through his mind's eye, that is, through the intuition of his mind – the most pure and honest mind appears, and he comes upon what he describes as dirt, the dirt that lies within the surface mind of conceit which has covered-up this naked mind – and can't help it, he confesses to the grasses his falsehood and cleverness. Unbelievable!

This is not a mere confession about this or that fault. Within this confession he sees something about himself that is covering up his essential wish. When he sees that which is nakedly shining and then compares that with himself, the light clearly allows him to discover the truth as to what he is. It is not that kind of confession that people make in order to improve themselves. It is that kind of confession that goes to the very roots of the problem with our contaminated mind: attachment to self, the one most difficult to transcend as we are so blinded by our own self-love. It is self-love that creates this notion of a conceited position, and from that conceited position we create all kinds of falsehoods in being the clever person we think of ourselves as being. The flowers are not like this. Certainly the grasses do not broadcast themselves as being clever. What is wrong with us? Why can't we be as naked as all this life I see growing and pushing up its way so single-mindedly, so strongly, powerfully, as if they just can't wait to bloom! The very early ones are already blooming! I see them everywhere – the daffodils braving the snow – now shining so briliantly, the little dwarf tulips, the crocuses. I bend over – the tiny wild iris, the "sweeties" – I want to caress them as they are so cute.

Without a spiritual life we have no real life – just nothing. It's not just about flowery decorations, or the feeling of compassion-ism towards others. For if so we haven't really touched upon the miraculous truth that comes upon one who has an empty mind that goes beyond language, rules, and set religious formalities, and into that solitude of mind and quiet where one can erase and throw out all that which otherwise can't be done by our own power alone.

One's confession does not come to me by reasoning. It comes to me by some power that is beyond my power to control. The mind that sees into the power of nature sees into the power of life itself, the ever-moving, ever-changing nature of life to which we humans must pay close attention to; for this is our teacher without words, and we are its student. This is the main thing that Akegarasu is thinking of, and why he bows down in reverence. I feel his nembutsu here, worshipping these plants and with feelings of adoration towards the grasses. This is what opens his mind, and opens my mind too. We are totally at one; his words and spirit awaken the world, just like his young grasses that cover the world.

"Onceness"   November 22, 1991

    Just touching Akegarasu.... The world cleans up.

  On my kitchen table are some of old Temple Bulletins (in this case, February 1975). I pick up a Bulletin off the top and read from Rev. Akegarasu and my mind becomes clarified. How amazing! It's like having Buddha visit you as you're having a cup of coffee late at night meditating. Because he's so human there is an immediate opening and acceptance in one's mind. Indeed, it is really the Buddha who can do that. I mean, reading him spontaneously as I am, is just like having him here beside me.

    The translation of Reverend Akegarasu is so natural (by J. Sweeny/G. Saito) that his words are living words given by a living man. I have not enough praise to give, really. So these Bulletins remain on the table along with so many other paraphernalia that it takes time to clear away. My kitchen table becomes a meditation bench as I examine what I've written.

    While reading him, all the things that I have been thinking become clarified. The function of the teaching is to have the mind clarified and wakened up to a settled and open mind. This experience touches one's whole being. You cannot just sit meditating by yourself – you have to write! By doing this practice I've deepened my understanding and use of words.

    When someone touches your mind itself, you have to respond even if it is to some unknown person. I sit wondering about my life sometime; how to resolve this, how to resolve that. Reverend Akegarasu is so natural that just listening to him one also becomes at ease, becomes natural. Oh, the natural man! Solutions always appear in a natural atmosphere. These solutions are themselves enlightened solutions, enlightened because they take the difficult burden off. Then when the burden is lifted we become lightened; the burden of our confused state of mind cleared.

    So it is that Reverend Akegarasu as the Buddha transcends the world.

    On top of my table sits the Buddha. His shout more powerful than all the Buddha statues combined. It is like my life meeting with his life for the first time, because every moment is "onceness" when you meet Akegarasu. It is like a fresh spark, a fresh taste. And in this tasting you get into the shallow pond, or flowing like a river, or gushing like a stream. In the sense of no solution the solutions appear miraculously. The solution appears in the emptied mind. Such expressions as "no-mind" or "suchness" appear in the Zen tradition. But my teacher came up with the expression of "onceness" or "isness" to describe the instant, never repeated life. This nothingness is life itself, the very essence of where creation occurs by some unknowable power that inspires me to create with the will of the spirit. And here the words *onceness* and *isness* come to life. So in this world of creation the feeling of warmth and independence of all things is welcomed into our total freedom.

As humans we create pictures of the world based upon our understanding. From childhood to adulthood these various pictures change according to our individual perception of the world. So often they are prejudicial notions based upon our limited understanding. Our mind becomes clogged with so many of these preconceived notions about religion and/or life in general. It all has to be emptied; otherwise we live in a cave of our own misunderstanding. So often we suffer from this because we remain in a fixed position of stasis with life. Even our bodies can suffer from this lack of movement. We become lethargic, lazy, and sick, and may get diseases that could be prevented. So to clean up the body and mind will contribute to our well being and health.

Thus we come to the Dharma to seek to clean-up this world of ours, but first we have to clean up ourselves. How can we hope to clean up the world if we ourselves are not clean? Where the dirt has accumulated our mind has become dirty and with many rough edges – like a human cactus! Even no one likes to come near us. The disharmony within us creates disharmony and difficulty for others. Do we want to live this way, creating disharmony?

But then, by good fortune, we may meet the teacher who is coming from the same direction of the Dharma. He burns up our one-dimensional or two dimensional-pictures. Actually, he crushes and burns up the self that creates these ugly and distorted pictures. As we listen carefully, we are made humble. As we are made humble by listening to the living Dharma we confess. Self-confession is so important. Without this self-realization we cannot receive the Dharma. So a whole new process emerges in our life. We have a living teacher who directs us properly. He's been there; he knows what the true essence of our life is and what we are capable of attaining. He wants to share with us this beauty born out of simplicity. It is indeed, his love that we call "compassion" and in that he "kills" us, i.e., he crushes our ego-shell. As he removes our ego he creates new life. Actually, we ourselves are the ones that create the new life and fresh pictures based upon fresh insights into our own ignorance. In the end we realize the final attachment to the self that has been creating all these so-called pictures of our fictional, artificial, and unreal world. The self that has created all these pictures has to be burned-up in the hellish flames of our own demise. Confessions don't come as pretty pictures. It comes out of our solemn wish to reach the truth. We all start with this wish. It is our awakening to the true essence of life that pushes us and beckons us forward. Sparks of life generate a new picture, so many in fact, that it is endless.

Thus life itself emerges as the true Dharma. There is no such thing as a clean mind without an emptied mind. Here, we meet with the unknowable life which is the eternal life as manifested in the will of the spirit. It is the universal truth that I discover as the One Soul of the universe. Here joyous, I dance with it. I delight in it. It shines through everything, through the sticky secular world, through the ugly or glamorous picture of the world. And, through the contentious picking up of a stick and fighting with others. Next to this One Mind they are all like transient clouds with no real substance.

Hence, the true value of our life is immeasurable and timeless. People will dance up and down when they think that they hit the jackpot and get the gold. Just like the birds after I feed them. They too, experience the joy of being together after they are fed. But this is not the easy joy that I'm speaking of. Nor is it an "Oceanic Feeling" that is as a coined phrase. For when we come back to who we are, the Dharma is not merely for one's self-therapy for the things we do for the improvement of ourselves, either through mediation practices or to the popular yoga practices. Rather, it is for the 180 degrees transformation (or turn around) that changes our whole perception of life. The inconceivable change requires that the self itself, the one who has been conceited has to give way to a sincere self-examination that brings us to who and what we are.

The fact is that we can be in ignorance. The problem here is that we are blind to see it. This refers to our eyes that can't see. Offhand we are ignorant about many things that occur in our daily lives, everything from plumbing to what is wrong with our car. Experience often brings an end to these kinds of problems. But as concerns the self we have a much more difficult problem; I would say, impossible, for our blindness to see it. Simply stated, we are blind. Yet we leave a trail. As we examine this "trail" we begin to see where it leads, and where it ultimately leads is to self. Buddhism and the Dharma are very intellectual here for we are required to carefully scrutinize our actions and our attitude.

Morals and ethics belong to civil order to the extent that there are rules and laws governing our behavior as individuals. But in the spiritual life of the individual it is the very self that is focused on. Indeed, Shakyamuni's whole emphasis is on the self alone. All other problems that we have followed. He determined that it was the limited self, or the relative self that caused us to suffer and to address this issue he came up with many dialogues that later became sutras after he passed away that specifically targets the self as the culprit to attend to in our individual lives.

To live to our true potential as human beings we first have to be truly human. Buddhism as such then, intends for its followers to be naked (free from artifice and falsity) human beings. Surrounding the false self and attributable to it are the three poisons: greed, anger, and ignorance.

Encapsulating this is the shell-of self, or ego, which is fortified by self-love. So the whole set-up is one tough nut to crack. But we must break out of this shell, so to speak, if we are to be set free.

My teacher once commented that we should all write our own book. Along with that he also added that we should form our own sect. Then he, with a smile on his face said that what we were learning was "Saitoism". I also remember that while gathered in the Hondo area observing the statue of Amida Buddha clad in bright gold leaf (symbol of brightness), that we should become this Amida Buddha. At the time, and knowing nothing about Amida Buddha, his statement really surprised me. But now I know he was so correct.

Here he was respecting our independence. All the teachers I have been reading wrote their own book, discovered their own life, and formed their own sect, each while going their own way courageously and independently. Work at the Dharma, listen to it – come up with your own life! Then you will capture the essence of Amida Buddha as to shine your essence.

* * *

The belief and faith in an external entity outside of us has done nothing but produce a confinement that saves the evil self, as to those who believe that they can be saved through the worship of a supreme being along with religious practices through the will of self-power. These are the burdens we carry until we awaken to our emancipation which frees us from these shackles and burdens. It is dependence and attachment to an external entity that has done nothing but brought about great grief and war among peoples; individually and collectively as nations. Whereas religion should bring us together, it has split us apart in so many ways as a result of these static entities under the entitlement of "belief". What a burden we carry here.

In Buddhism we have the expression, "Come as you are." Infinite light, the most pure light within us will give us eternal life, the life giving source which will shine through all our so-called weaknesses, capricious desires, and the three poisons of greed, anger, and ignorance – plus our fixed attachment to the secular world. These things are thrown aside, burned up and buried as our newly born freedom transcends the world where these things play and trick us as believers. To believe and have faith in a static entity outside of us that promises salvation is to cling to the belief that we can be saved similar to that of a gambler who believes he's going to win the lottery. Here it is like a mosquito trying to penetrate an iron ball.

Salvation can only come through one's deepest confession: "I alone, am the most evil person." I never thought of or cared to be saved, so for me the desire for salvation never existed for me to put my beliefs into. I'm fine just as I am with no desire to improve myself, so I see no need to be saved.

Since all of us are unique due to our own karma's, histories, ethnicities, and so many other things that make up our individualities, we have to come up with our own shout and understanding. Knowledge pertaining to Buddhism may be useful up to a point in which objective material can function to enrich and facilitate our understanding; but in the end, it depends on our subjectivity to disclose how we really feel by incorporating such knowledge into our lives and then living it in an organic sense. For instance, I may be taught how to dance, but until I actually get out on the dance floor in real time the various steps I've learned will not be my very own expression of that organic reality wherein all the steps are in rhythm with the music and within my own life that no one else has done before. It is very true that this is my style, to the delight of everyone! No two steps are the same; seeking, finding, all within the same instant. Even I do not know what my next step will be until I do it – breaking, breaking, always creating new steps as I go along. If I care to relate it to Buddhism then I'll say that it is "Buddhism in action". A lion is among the dancers, killing the separation! He can be gentle also, to listen and blend in with everyone else and the music. And this is our life actually – the shout is not to outshout others, but simply to come up with your very own life and to the best of your ability at all times. That's true humility. Humility creates love – love thy neighbor and you will in turn be loved by them. That goes into the dance and is one of the most fundamental steps we take whether it is on the dance floor or anywhere else! The whole harmony between me and others exists on this point – I can love them. Within this harmony there is movement within the dancers themselves as they are experiencing one is many and many are one in actuality and in real time. And, the steps we take are natural as we can then experience the moment-to-moment rhythm of life. I make so many friends here; well so, because we all become as friends. It is really a kind of non-denominational church, so alive with life right here on the dance floor. The old self breaks down into an infinite number of points as each step follows another in endless progression until the music ends and a lively conversation takes place.

Buddhism is about life. Who needs religion if it doesn't produce life?

That's why I came to Buddhism – by instinct, not by some intellectual reasoning, or some warmed-up-cozy-humanist feeling. Only when I met the teacher did I fulfill my essential wish, the aspiration to follow and attain the wisdom that the teacher manifested. I wanted to be just like him. It is so rare to have had this opportunity. This is the fulfillment of my deepest wish.

This mutual reverberation then, between myself and all the predecessors that have expressed the Buddha-Dharma through their own life and in their own way is imbedded in my consciousness, whereas I can now go my own way, I as I. And I keep learning because of these moment-to-moment changes. And through listening I learn so much from other people who freshly expose their being, enabling me to be at one: this essential Buddha-nature of the world – in the world where I live, work, and play. And in this world of changing life I find my life. This is the transforming world I worship.

So I joyously think: don't be as a mere scholar filled with judgments towards your life or the life of others. And don't stop thinking that you've reached a dead-end not knowing where to go. Don't become like a half-dead retiree from life, but take up the Dharma, follow the way, create your own steps as you learn and progress into the unknowable life itself. Then you shall experience the treasures after digging to the bottom of the ocean, cup by cup, until you find such a life that Shakyamuni found and all those who listened and independently came up with their own life. "Oh Creation!" says Akegarasu. Creation, as I jump in and feel the splash! It's very simple, just exchanging one's ignorance for the instant of truth. Marvelous, the victory! The frog jumps in – *oneness* – instantaneous combustion!

"Splash!" — R. A.

THOUGHTS ABOUT DESTRUCTION
Haya Akegarasu (1919)

Life develops continuously. It never stops in one place. Every month, every day, every minute it changes. This is true of everyone: The 'I' of yesterday is not the 'I' of today, nor is today's self the self of tomorrow. This continuous change is a difficulty in life. The instinctive wish of the spirit never stops in one place: it is always moving from creation to creation. The concrete manifestation of this creative instinct is our life itself. But by the next moment it has begun to harden; another instinctive wish is unfolding, while the first, already old, has hardened into a shell. This shell is the tendency to become conventional or fatalistic or bound by fixed ideas and circumstances, all of which tie up the real wish and make for confusion. Therefore, in order to make our life develop and grow we must continuously split open this hard shell.... *For the past ten years, people have been voicing thoughts of destruction, revolutionary thoughts of all kinds. As a result, other people have been trembling with fear. But I don't see why they're so afraid. I would rather accept these thoughts of destruction gratefully, as a healthy indication of human growth. *The life of the creative wish is a continuous burning up of self. It destroys the self and goes on. As it destroys the self, it destroys circumstances, and goes on; without this destruction, no progress, ever. *Something new is born; something old is destroyed. Human life is characterized by the dissolution of old cells and the generation of new ones. The life of all beings means that all burn up and cease to be.... Conventional concepts are the most negative thing in this world and the most dangerous. Concepts are only concepts; they are not life. Sudden advance or gradual; great destruction or small: We cannot say which the better is. But the stronger the life force, the stronger the destructive power: Then sudden advance! I want to live all the time. Because I am able to live, I always break. *Why does destruction scare you? My friends let's go forward. Break the self. Break circumstances. Annihilate all of it. With such courage as this, let us be born into the world of creation. What are you afraid of? At the moment I am saying this, you and I are in truth progressing: We are being broken, we are breaking. Already new born, we are participating in a process of cosmic change. Celebrate this life! *No child is born without throwing away its mother's body. No chicken is hatched that cannot crack and break out of its shell. *Strong burning destruction, burning of all being: O creation!

An Article from <u>Suchness</u>. 10/1/1970
Joan Sweany /Gyoko Saito, Translator

The Eternal Life Sutra - The Larger Sutra
An Abridged Edition
Commentary by Roger Adams

    What is a sutra? A sutra is a text in which Shakyamuni discloses the essence of the Teaching to the world of his listeners who were called the sangha, as fellow students of the Buddha-Dharma. To show the brightness of his life monasteries were established by members of the sangha to teach, memorize, formulate, and record his words so that they and others could reach emancipation.
    Listening to the words of the Buddha his biographers came up with various sutras to explain and record it in specific ways addressed to a specific audience. Therefore many sutras came about reflecting the life and teaching of the Buddha. This is particularly true in Mahayana Pure Land Buddhism, as it is in the Theravada tradition.
    But the text we are studying here is different than the other sutras in that Shakyamuni is praising the audience first rather than the audience praising him. All other sutras praise the Buddha alone. The Buddha, looking upon the audience sees in them a reflected light that shines upon him and in this light he is able to come up with the Dharma. It is the life of Shakyamuni that is presented in the form of a story with all of its metaphors and doctrinal aspects. Is it true to our life? Yes it is.

The Eternal Life Sutra – The Larger Sutra

The Eternal Life Sutra or Larger Sutra begins its introduction with the words: "Thus have I heard". (This "Thus I have heard." places an emphasis on hearing: understanding the full meaning of this sutra.

Here the Buddha Shakyamuni was staying in a place called Vulture Peak along with a large company of 12 thousand followers, along with sixteen Mahayana bodhisatvas; Samantabhadra, Manjusri, Maitreya, by name are also accounted for, this entire meeting taking place in northeastern India in a region of Rajagrha twenty six hundred years ago.

Following Mahasattva Samantabhadra's virtues the Sutra describes the various powers he has in throwing off the evils of wrong views, curing afflictions, flushing out the evils of desire and passions, opening the Dharma-gate, and revealing the pure white Dharma. He realizes the impermanence of the world. He has transcended the world. He sees himself in all sentient beings. So many qualities are being described here. It is informing us of the true nature of Buddhahood. Now we can begin the doctrinal aspect.

It begins with Ananda (Buddha's cousin) bowing before Buddha baring his right shoulder (sign of respect) joining his palms in reverence and saying to the Buddha, "World-Honored One, today, how radiant are your senses with joy, how majestic your countenance is, and how you reflect the tathagatha's virtue.", and on and on, repeating the word "today" a total of seven times, each time followed by more praising of the Buddha's wonderful attributes. In that sense we can understand that he, Ananda, has attained the level of awakening in order to recognize the qualities that the Buddha has, and, the fact that Ananda has used the word, today, seven times replicates the Buddha's taking seven steps to his enlightenment which indicates that he too, is awakened.

In response, the Buddha is delighted by Ananda's recognition and in questioning the reason why he, the Buddha, looks so majestic and brilliant. He then tells Ananda the reason why he appears as such: He says that as the Tathagatha, he regards beings in the three worlds of greed, anger, and ignorance with boundless great compassion. The reason for his appearance in the world is that he wants to reveal the teachings of the Way and liberate multitudes of beings by endowing them with true benefits. He then goes on to say that the Tathagatha's perfectly enlightened wisdom is unfathomable and is capable of leading the multitudes to emancipation, and further, that its light cannot be obstructed as nothing can stand in its way including all evils.

The Buddha continues his dialogue with Ananda going into a multitude of attributes that he has out of his compassion for human beings. That even in countless millions of *kalpas* it is difficult to come across and meet a true Tathagata (Buddha). Indeed, the Tathagata's spirit itself has no age, will not deteriorate, is boundless, and has unrestricted power over all the worldly dharmas (the limited knowledge and wisdom of human beings). It is like a very rare and beautiful species of flower, so too is this Buddha.

(Indeed, because of its rarity, how fortunate it is to find such a one, the more to appreciate it by bowing within one's whole being. This is the true nembutsu of appreciation. We may have the form but not necessarily the content, the words but not necessarily the feeling.) –R.A.

The Buddha continues by telling Ananda that in the distant past many, many *kalpas* ago, fifty three Buddhas came into being before him, and lists them according to various names chosen to describe their attributes. (Collectively, they include all the various attributes that Gautama Buddha himself possesses.) He then goes on to list the last of these Buddhas which is Lokesvararaja, the fifty fourth. He too has another appellation which is: *King of the Free Life*. Ananda by this time is respectfully listening to what the Buddha is relating to him by way of a story.

(We can represent the life of Shakyamuni that turns into a story with all its metaphors. It gives us a comprehensive understanding of how a monk called Dharmakara became known as Amida Buddha. Thus the truth of the Buddha-Dharma through him can be conveyed universally. This meaning in Sanskrit is called: Amitaba: Limitless light, and Amitayus: Limitless life. The Name or chant for it is: Namu Amida Butsu.)

At that time there appeared a Buddha named Lokesvararaja the Tathagatha, the Buddha, and World Honored One.

Then there was a king, who upon hearing of the Buddha's discourses on the Dharma was awakened, and decided to follow his aspiration for Enlightenment. He gave up his throne and his kingdom and became a monk called Dharmakara (*Storehouse of Knowledge*). In time, he distinguished himself in the world for his intelligence, courage, and wisdom. His aspiration was to be exactly like his teacher, Lokesvararaja. He listened carefully, paying close attention to what the teacher said and did, and held him in high respect. As time went on his appreciation for his teacher deepened, so much so, that when the occasion arose that provided the opportunity for him to meet with the teacher, he could not help himself: he walked around him three times keeping him always on his right (sign of respect), knelt on the ground, and, putting his palms together in adoration, praising him with glowing phrases (Tan Butsu Ge).

TAN BUTSU GE or <u>SONG IN PRAISE OF THE BUDDHA</u>

1. What a radiant face he has, shining like the peaks of the Himalaya Mountains! His face shows such brightness that even the sun, moon, and *mani-jewel* cannot compare with it. Though they shine with such brightness, they appear dim by way of comparison, as if they are nothing but black sticks of ink. (His face is reflecting the brightness of the Dharma.)

2. The appearance of the Buddha-Tathagata is beyond compare in the world. The great sound of the Enlightened One's voice reverberates throughout the ten quarters. His virtue in giving, morality, listening, perseverance, depth of meditation, and wisdom, are unequaled. (The Six Paramitas.)

3. In his deep meditation he is focused on the Buddha's boundless Dharmas; knowing their deepest and widest extent to the fullest. The World Honored One transcends the three poisons of greed, anger, and ignorance. How brave and courageous he is – like a lion amongst men!

4. His unusual achievements are unparalleled, his wisdom goes deep and noble. How he shines forth with the light of the Dharma that shakes up a universe of an uncountable, numberless worlds. > Now I aspire to become a Buddha just like you, Oh king of the free life, and the Dharma; to liberate all people from birth-and-death, and lead them into ultimate freedom.

5. I will fulfill the virtues of right moral values, single-mindedness and effort, along with meditation into the depths of true wisdom will be beyond compare. I vow that when I become a Buddha, I promise to fulfill all these <u>five practices</u> wherever I go. And to those whose minds are unquiet, unsettled and in fear, I shall give them peace.

6. As there are many Buddhas and Great Sages in countless numbers like the sands of the Ganges River, I shall make offerings (pay homage) to all those Buddhas (Krio, or spiritual traveling).

7. In the Buddha-lands that are as numerous as the sands of the Ganges River including all other regions that are as numberless, may my light of limitless wisdom reach everywhere. The result of this effort will be beyond measure.

8. When I become a Buddha, I will make my country and its land the first, with all the people within it excellent, so enlightened is this place. Nirvana (selflessness) will be this country which will be beyond compare. I will take compassion on all living beings, and help them to live in the kingdom of the first.

9. For all those who wish to come from the ten directions seeking to enter my land will find joy and tranquility, happiness and peace. I beseech you Buddha, to bear witness to the sincerity and truth of my aspiration. I want to prove to you the desire of my aspiration by fulfilling all the vows I have made to you.

10. The World Honored Ones in the ten directions that are filled with wisdom, please be witness to my aspiration. Even though I face difficulty and hardship that is like poison, I will continue to be resolute in my endeavor of going forward with utmost diligence while having no regret.

Then the Buddha said to Ananda: "The monk Dharmakara, having stated his intentions to the Buddha Lokesvaharaja, announces to him that he has been awakened to his desire for the highest, most perfect Enlightenment. The Buddha responds by telling him that he should (first) know himself..."

So that we can visualize this *nembutsu,* the gassho of praise with hands clasped; the Sutra gives us these words to describe the mind of Dharmakara as he meets his teacher Lokusvararaja.

The Sutra tells us that there is something beyond the sun and the moon as relates to us human beings. There is brightness to our lives that encompass the sun and the moon as we are being embraced by infinite life, or eternal life, and once we are awakened to it, it shows in our faces that shine with such brightness. We can then feel the "Face of the Dharma's Light" is far brighter, for it is that which reverberates within our being – the very reason why the Buddha has such a shining face that is beyond compare. Not only can the Buddha, but our friends in everyday experiences with people we meet can be of such too. The only thing is to be aware of it, that there are multitudes of buddha's, even billions of them; beautiful flowers, trees, birds, dogs, cats – whatever we come across – this very Earth with all its creatures including insects – all can come alive and be included in this "Great Sound" within the Great Mind. The great sound of the Buddha's voice is that which reverberates within our life. When our life is awakened to feel the power of life it shines. This is the meaning of the 1st and 2cnd verses. Then when we are prepared to listen we can hear the voices, the sounds, and feel this shining essence.

These virtues, as in transcending the <u>three poisons</u> that are mentioned in the 3rd verse. Yet we cannot claim to have even one virtue by ourselves that is not given to us. We are essentially *inchantika*, as those who have no abilities by our own to attain an awakening. Because we by ourselves are blind to see ourselves as victims of our own greed, anger, and ignorance. We are strapped to the world with our worldly attachments and involvements, and etc. Merely being a "good person" is a delusion, as it covers up our crucial confession as to who we really are. Considering ourselves as good persons can cause us to be blind as to our bad self, our more evil self. Being self-assured with our goodness we fail to look deeply into our static ego-self which is the basis for our evil. So the virtues that I cannot claim to be mine were given to me by the teacher.

He held up a "mirror", so to speak that allowed me to see who I really was. Even my little "surface evils" were exposed by him – he never let me go on anything! Thus it was it was that the teacher gave me my virtues; that is, of ultimately becoming a true human being. But it was mostly through his example that I felt the real need to self-examine my life, still being repremanded by him.

In **Verse 4** Dharmakara aspires to be exactly like his teacher. Long before I came to Buddhism I had a bright and healthy disposition, despite, or because of the tragedy and various difficulties and/or unstable circumstances. To start with my mother was killed in an auto accident at the age of five, which put me in an orphanage along with so many other kids. Things were unstable, or in constant flux. Though the orphanage was a good one, still I felt lonely.

During the year I entered, WW2 broke out. My father was away, working 10 or 12 hours a day as a machinist in a war plant, so I didn't get to see him very much. But if I look back at all those years of my early youth, I see a certain vein running through it all because of the rather unique circumstances of my life. Later on I couldn't warm up or respond to the conventional religions that were preached to me without my seeking them. Instead, intuitively as the years went by, I had to find something that would answer the inner core of me as to what it was as to who I really am. In other words, I wanted to find out "Who am I?" as an inner question latent in me. A kind of void existed otherwise.

I wanted to attain an absolute self in the spiritual sense. Being young and having a blank sheet as far as religion was concerned, I naïvely sought some kind of religion that would answer to a spiritual quest that was lurking in the back of my mind. Then I heard about enlightenment. To get the power I imagined, I wanted to become enlightened. But what really drove me was a sincere wish, the beginning of an aspiration that was the truth behind my real spiritual yearning. So on my quest my imagination pushed me onward. I prepared my stuff, left home and went to the West Coast for an adventure to find the source, a "Zen Master", or teacher who could answer my questions and act as a guide. The lengthy trip was adventure filled alright, but I failed to find the teacher until I came back to Chicago; again, here and there, until I finally met him, Rev. Gyoko Saito of Chicago Buddhist Temple in 1963.

After meeting with him and listening to him and watching his demeanor, I aspired to be just like him. I'm bringing this out because there must be a spiritual quest taking place in one's own life that one can call an innermost aspiration and though rather vague in the beginning it grows deeper as time goes on, and at the same time rises to the deepest wish for fulfillment. How fortunate I was at this time in trying to be just like him.

The Tathagatha is unstoppable as in **verse 2**. It shakes and penetrates the universe of a thousand million worlds! Such unimaginable power of life itself is beyond our estimation; indeed, it is beyond our knowledge and/or thinking. But by putting our total trust in it, relying on it alone, we can move and flow with it, and moreover, manifest it directly. This is what Reverend Saito expressed. When on Sunday he rang the gong sharply at the opening of the service with the pestle, you really felt it penetrating and vibrating within your being. That's how he woke us up to sit up straight and be prepared to listen. He shook the audience up, and I for one, listened. He didn't waste words on a half-asleep audience. Even without a gong he'd crack his voice in such a way as if clearing his throat – that you really had to listen hard, set up for people who came to spend a nice relaxing time in church, or anywhere else for that matter. And then when he spoke of his teacher, Rev. Akegarasu, he would pause for a while which I felt was his nembutsu for the teacher, for he would bow his head and you could feel tears, not showing, but there. You have here, the essence of this sutra in a living being, a manifestation of Shakyamuni's Great Sound and the reverberations that were felt by all his listeners.

Rev. Saito introduced us to many great teachers over the period of years. To name just a few: Shinran Shonin, Rev. Kiozowa, Shuichi Maida, Rev. Akegarasu, and even from the West, such as Goethe, Epictetus, Kierkegaard; and also the poet Santoka, and so on, all spiritual teachers and philosophers whom he studied from along with Gautama Buddha. Of course, his teacher was Rev. Akegarasu who himself studied from many teachers including his own teacher, Rev. Kiozowa; so when I think of it I was so fortunate in being exposed to so many great teachers and spiritual philosophers – the best in the world! Think of it! I never would have come up with these people if it weren't for him. These kinds of Buddhas and teachers are very rare, as is the teacher. But first and foremost, they are all students, this is the point that we can easily overlook. They are not "finished products", for their endeavor is to study from their teachers and predecessors throughout their lives from this depth of historical teachers.

Dharmakara is involved with spiritual traveling, called: *Krio* or making offerings to all the Buddhas, which essentially means that he is listening to them and studying from them. As we are engaged in these practices we can come up with the phrase: *Buddhas contemplating Buddhas mutually*; which is in the teaching of this sutra as stated in **verse 6**.

This is a sutra written for those who aspire to go to the fullest extent of their life. So we have the 6 Parametas and the 5 Practices found in **verse 2** and **verse 5**, respectively. First, they are: Giving (Dana), Morality, Learning (listening), Endeavor (perseverance), Meditation, Wisdom (Prajna). The Five Practices are: giving, mind control, moral virtues, forbearance, and effort. These can be understood only by being immersed in the Dharma, not before.

The underlying theme is virtuous practices. It is encompassed by the word "right"; such as, right meditation, which means self-introspection as much as focusing on the Dharma and its related associations. Or, if we take the word morality, which can be very misunderstood with its ensuing complications and implications of purity, verses impurity; bad karma, verses good karma, and so forth. Therefore to simplify, we have to think of morality in the absolute sense of the term, which simply means, "right morality". Then about being virtuous, meaning an honest person not engaged in tricking others. Again, we have to think of life itself as the only virtue given to us since we are incapable as deluded human beings filled with anything but good virtue. Here we have to be desperate seekers and listeners for the *right virtue,* which has nothing to do with right verses wrong in the relative sense. The same can be said for any one of the Six Paramitas or in the Five Practices. Then think of these practices within the context of selflessness. These virtues are given to us only when our mind is pure and naked. All other practices that follow have the same pattern.

Indeed, this is one of the difficulties that the aspirant Dharmakara will be facing before his self-realization. Inevitably he must have found himself, as all humans are, of being incapable of living a perfectly moral and virtuous life. Just as let's say, Shinran Shonin, who studied this sutra to its farthest end in his KyoGyoShinSho. Shinran confessed as to his incapability of practicing any worthiness or purity in his relative self. But in meeting Honen his teacher, he simply trusted his whole being to Amida's infinite Light. This is the result of 20 years of striving to perfect himself as a religious person: "How true it is, how sad it is." he once confessed, but he experienced the transforming truth through his confession. This is why in the sutra Dharmakara opened the way, through Buddha's compassion for all humans, to put their trust in the power beyond the self existing as Amida Buddha, and in which Dharmakara manifested.

The teacher was virtuous, but I observed some of the things that a few people conveniently called his "faults". But others, such as me and his dear friends and members, considered him as his greatest virtue, that of being such a human being. I love him for this. Yes, there were a few who he did not cater to who caused difficulty. Such things as this occurred at the temple, and this just adds to my feeling and respect for his being.

We all want our freedom. No matter whom you are, no matter where you live in the world, the desire for freedom is universal, so we have the universal truth in freedom. Yet so often we do everything to prevent it. Why is it so true that because of blockage we never really taste true freedom? As we are tied to the surface self and suffer from vexations and fears, where in the world can we find ourselves in real freedom? But if we are not afraid of death then how can all these other minor problems bother us? Facing death forthrightly we can transcend the darkness and be illumed by the light, the brightness of the mind that sees the light.

I do not find the word, freedom, in the <u>Tan Butsu Ge</u> (Song of the Buddha) which here is the English translation of the ten verses listed as above that is chanted during Sunday morning as part of the service. But as I scan the lines I come across the word, emancipation. Emancipation is freedom. But emancipation is freedom from one's attachment to the self.

As we busy ourselves with all kinds of plans for the future on how we can be free, freedom escapes us. As we cling to the relative way of thinking about freedom, it is based upon hopes in the future for something better in our lives from the way we are living now. We want to be free from the binding ties to the circumstances we find ourselves in. How we sometimes yearn for it! Yet once we finally get to the place where we can settle down and become free, we soon forget freedom and start worrying again – or even worse, we get bored! This is due to the fact that our freedom is relative. It is not true freedom. Freedom is not permanent, nothing is. It travels in waves, and like the sea, it moves. If freedom were permanent, we'd all jump in! In Shinshu Buddhism for instance, many people think of the Pure Land as a nice beautiful and happy place to enjoy their freedom after they die. So when I say deluded, I mean that we have all kinds of deluded ideas about freedom: superficial ideas; or freedom from stress and physical pain, freedom from financial problems, all these are included. But none of these places are permanent, as they come and go in our lives. So yes, freedom connected to our imagination is like clouds passing overhead. We must fortify our desires for freedom when we retire, so then we can fix it. Such expectations! What we thought of as our freedom again turns into bondage, because we still carry around the same ole' un-free self. Death of the fixed and relative self is the only freedom given to us. Selflessness itself is freedom. And the honest mind is the way towards the freedom of selflessness.

Our confession is our only freedom. Otherwise our freedom is partial, transitory, even rootless, as it is aside from life itself.

So many people are chasing around, going after every conceivable thing that ties them to the world and thus deprives them of their essential wish to be free. Indeed, true freedom can come only through our deepest confession as to what I really am.

The self has no substance, yet we place our reliance on the self. On the other hand, and, in a 180 degree difference we have selflessness, or no-self, emptiness, or Nirvana, a term which means extinction of self or absence of attachment to the relative self. So it seems that there is an opposition between the two. According to our intellect this seems to be so. But in real life we cannot function as one while maintaining a separation between the two. And that is where real life struggle begins. Well, let's clarify it by saying that the surface self is the relative self, but that the very core of our being itself is unknowable by our relative self and to that extent we are caught with an unsolvable problem. It is as the *One Soul* since it is at one with the organic soul which means our organically felt feeling of continuous change involving the core of our human essence. This movement is the rhythm within our bodies and minds which comes alive. It is not the same as how scientists examine the world and the universe as they already know that it is continuously changing. But they are examining it externally, not internally, as it applies to them. As they are observers to life, they themselves are left unchanged by the changes occurring outside of them. We too can function in the same way.

Our endeavor then, not mentioned in the sutra, is to attain emancipation from the concepts of opposite selves and the transcendence from both a self and no-self dichotomy that form the difficulty of our life. For the problem is that two selves in opposition to each other cause grief, pain, and friction. Our liberation begins with relinquishing the cause of our suffering and lack of freedom, not by combining the two things, such as ½ + ½ =1, but a complete collapse and dead end of such dualistic logic; for we cannot move into the world of One Mind until this takes place. As such, merely thinking about it in terms of logic will do us no good. Spiritual life is not decided by logic aside from life itself. "If the truth has no flesh to it, it is not the truth."

Philosophical speculation provides us with no clue as to the actual self that lives and breathes and therefore cannot be dismissed into positive and negative formula in the form of concepts. Life is not a theory. And concepts are only concepts. The organic fact that is within ourselves in terms of flesh and blood human beings defines our spirituality, not scholarly or philosophical discussions. For in reality there is no definite line between self and non-self, only a subtle self which cannot be defined.

So often, even in daily life, we become like scholars and philosophers, trying to join parts and pieces together like a word puzzle dealing with good and bad. But life goes on unmindful of our scholarship, like the Mississippi River, flowing onward into the ocean and blending in with all the life there.

So the solution is of no solution. Only the indefinable, unusual, unpredictable and subtle self exists, found at the bottom of an unknowable ocean. You cannot put concepts to this; it gushes out as the shout you can feel that resounds within one's total being.

Dharmakara's endeavor is to establish his own land. He describes it as follows: "It will be Nirvana itself, a place most exquisite, its people wonderful and excellent beyond comparison." as it appears in the **8th** and **9th verses** of his aspirations in the Tan Butsu Ge.

Listening to this we can assume that Dharmakara wants to establish a land that we all want to belong to in order to hear what he has to say about the Dharma. But what is the object of our wanting to be there, other than the fact that it has such wonderful people? And further, what is it that makes them wonderful? I'd like to see a discussion group fully participating in asking questions about various words and aspects of the Dharma - getting their feet wet – being exposed to the brightness and virtue of the Dharma through study of the sutras. This most marvelous interaction produces such results. Mostly, this is the world that Dharmakara wants to see and establish throughout all the Buddha-lands. The sangha of students become such a lively group here. This is the land of practitioners that he wants to establish. A community of sangha takes place wherever the Buddha is, into his land of freshness and wisdom.

It is humility that creates life for it creates us as listeners, or, in listening to the Dharma, we become humble listeners, either way. Our sincere desire or aspiration is born here. We desire to participate in this land composed of fellow friends of the sangha; as in the <u>Three Treasures</u>: The Buddha, The Dharma, and The Sangha. We are not concerned with our attached way of thinking, as we are feeling free to express ourselves in a most unusual way, hitherto unknown to us because it is so unexpected. And we can actively participate in its universality across all lines and in every direction. Enlivened ones are created here, with an organic feeling for life. Are we not fulfilling Dharmakara's wish that each of us establish our own land, realizing our full potential here? Each of us can establish our own land of independent seekers of truth. And further, do we actually need a life other than this? Here we are being transformed as into a Dharma that creates transformations, the Dharma in truth. And what we are being transformed into is a flame of creation in which I am consumed and reborn into fresh life. This transforming process is itself creation. Destruction of all that we have assembled of the past self and re-birth of the fresh self is itself creation to the fullest extent. The bright flame of the spirit creates the person of virtue as a "lion amongst men."

So nothingness or nirvana creates this infinite dimension that we call unlimited light and life, which is the essence of Amida Buddha's land and that which we cannot attain within our own effort as here we can face the impossible. But, if we realize Amida's vow transcending difficulty by being brave and courageous we can persevere without regret: the **10th verse**.

The person of nothingness, the humble listener, the person of virtue, while claiming no virtues by himself, experiences the virtue of the Buddha-Dharma and with such joy wants to share it with others. The land that he wants to share with others is the land of peace and bliss or the Pure Land. It is a land that is open for us, but few go there, according to the sutra. It is a place, a land where you, yourself, must establish as a reality. The Buddha attained this place, but now his deepest wish is for us to attain it as well. Having gone there he returns to the world of samsara, to guide us in going forward with our own aspirations to cross over to the other shore of emancipation. While his actions are that of coming back, our actions are that of the guidance we need to go forward.

Referring to the Three Vow Stages (or Three Vow Gates):
The three births as Shinran Shonin refers to them appear among the 48 vows of the Larger Sutra, in the order as follows: the **17th,** the **20th**, and the **18th** vows. The three of them are important insofar as Shinran Shonin is concerned, because, as he outlined in his KyoGyoShinSho, they direct us to what he calls the Three Vow Gates that each student of the Dharma must go through in order to proceed to the final self-realization. Until we go through (be born into) all three gates we cannot expect to realize the full extent of our emancipation into total freedom.

The first gate or stage has to do with placing one's trust and reliance in the recitation of the Name (Namu Amida Butsu), and in Amida Buddha's inconceivable power known as Other Power, or power beyond self. When chanted it is known as the Nembutsu which is bowing before the truth.

The 20th vow starts out by thinking that we can perfect ourselves by our own abilities. In a way it's very true. By the same token, however, it is untrue. In what way is it false? It is false in the sense that it is our relative and ignorant self attempting to clean up our relative and ignorant self. We don't seem to be getting any closer to our real self here, our religious self. We try and try, but nothing we do by our own self-effort, either by prayer to a Divinity or being a good moral person observing the Precepts give us any real feeling of being blessed into thinking that we are saved.

Being in the 20th vow of the second birth or gate is the religious stage in which a person seeks to improve himself by religious practices in order to purify him by getting rid of all the bad things within him and to encourage only the good things. But, here we can become hypocrites. Those who seek to be saintly seek an identity with a Supreme Being, and being so inclined tend to live in an enclosed environment that is isolated from the world such as a monastery or live in a confining cocoon where they can control their purity more easily. Such a person could harbor a sense of superiority and conceit, and so they tend to stink of religion.

Monks and priests and such, can be living in a secular mind-set of a scholarly interpretation of religious practices and texts. A misgiving among the falsely settled, thus it is also provisional as in the 20th vow.

Rev. Akegarasu once commented that priests, ministers, monks, and the like, are the guiltiest ones when it comes to fixing religious practices which they then preach to others. They have no idea of what is bad, for if they did they would stop preaching. Reverend Kiozawa said that it is better to put a stone in your mouth before you start to preach to others.

We strive to perfect ourselves and put ourselves into the mold of self-righteousness, and that of good moral and ethical conduct. Here we are very much attached to the notion that we can by our own power, control our virtuous self, thereby eliminating our evil self. But our evil self pops up unexpectedly anyway; and so the harder we try, the more the evil self asserts itself. So in the end we realize that we are doing nothing but pouring gasoline on the fire. For the more we try to control ourselves as well behaved, moral, and decent good people, the more we add to our blindness. So on Sunday we go to church in order to be cleaned-up. It's like taking a mental shower. The secret evil here though, is that we want to be perfectly good. They believe that cleanliness is next to Godliness. Worst of all, Buddhists may think of Amida Buddha as a kind of God who bestows on them special benefits. Such people think, either by worshipping Amida Buddha as a kind of demi-god, or, that Amida exists outside of them in the sense of a dichotomized relationship. In innocence or naivety how can this be thought of as evil? But it is the results that can turn into evil as we can get attached to the notion we can relax in one's own faith-based religion and need go no further in the critical examination of one's laid back attitude. Conventional thinking as regards religion and its purposes can lead to blindness to see the truth about ourselves. If religion is for our convenience wherein if we prey to a Supreme Being we will get something in return then it is nothing more than a superstition. So in all our religious ideas we must clarify the real purpose of religion in our lives and not just settle for a lukewarm two-dimensional interpretation based on our own smallish views. Meager and insufficient efforts will produce no results as we can live in a cocoon of our own making. Here we can wear an artificial religious gloss covering up our real problem. Shinran saw all this as not being true religion.

Amida's infinite light does not discriminate between the good and the bad. All people are accepted, seekers and non-seekers alike. That is the compassion of the Buddha of Infinite Life. For as Shinran stated: "Even if good people are born into the Pure Land upon death, then how much more, I, Shinran." All that is required is the total recognition that I am the most evil person, an inchantika, one who is incapable of being enlightened and living in hell. We who think we've attained something good in ourselves and are proud of ourselves for having attained such a level of goodness lack the humility to see ourselves as being the most evil person by way of a conceited person. Being conceited is the worst of all.

Truth reveals itself upon our self-reflection of, "What am I?" The reality of seeing ourselves coldly and objectively outside of ourselves is our awakening. Contrast that to those who believe that they are already saved simply by chanting nembutsu's – all the while seeking to be saved? Do I think that this useless self has any value that is worth saving?

I have to ask myself if I am capable of doing meritorious good deeds. Am I capable of being a good religious person? Am I courageously honest and forthright, even if the outcome may in some sense hurt me? Am I presumptuous enough to think of myself as a good person already enlightened? Do I have the necessary virtue to judge between good and bad? Do I go around just looking for good things or bad things in people based on my thinking alone? What criteria do I use to decide for sure? Can we see that some people are wise on one hand and foolish on the other? Can we really see and appreciate all people without merely judging them, seeing them as good or no good but thinking of ourselves as good? What kind of moralistic scholars have we become here? Can't we just hug others as brothers and sisters? Why hesitate, for we all breathe the same life. Gautama Buddha accepted everyone. We have to go beyond our relative bias in order to touch anothers' life is seeing ourselves in others.

As dishonesty brings about its own punishment, we must be watchful.

With our limited capabilities for goodness, which includes our selfish desires, then how come our anger in not getting what our greed desires? It is our ignorance in not being able to see it clearly. Aren't we anything but a chunk of ignorance led by our often blind desires? I think so. I think that we are all guilty of being caught in the net of our desires. To which when we fully confess appear small and insignificant; awakens us to the fact that we are such smallish individuals, incompetent to assume the role of the good person. Yet we stubbornly refuse to accept this recognition, and go on trying to improve ourselves. Like a blind person trying to climb the top of a mountain reaching for the impossible. Here in this blind position, are we not the most ignorant? We indeed are the most ignorant, and within this total confession, I can live as a free person. I can live in the freedom from ignorance. But being as I am a foolish person, I can fully and freely accept the good and the evil of what I have been; for as such, impermanence, or nothingness, will cause this karma to disappear. So we needn't try to fit ourselves into the religious mold of the good person feeling guilty over the fact that we cannot comply. As such I can live the life as a free person, being free of past karma's and restrictions by the sincerity of a confession, as ignorance finds no roots in the Buddha.

The Buddha exists as an ordinary person living in the world of samsara, this very world where all other sentient beings live. He blends in with the natural surroundings, but because he is as he is, people may call him an unusual person. He transcends the world, yet his life's spirit embraces the world. Thus it is the very place of his creative life – it is in the very movement of the world that forms his creative life!

*   *   *

Think of the fixed and finite circle, and we are in the center of that circle called ego-shell. Yes, we may try to expand that circle by increasing our wealth, power, prestige, education, family, accomplishments, good merits, and hope for the future with all its expectations, and so forth. But with all this, are we made any freer, have we touched upon being truly settled here? Or, are we just expanding on to and shuffling around in our fixed circle. If we are so fortunate we will meet with the teaching that will remove all of our fixed positions, and by doing so will expose us to the infinite circle that has no fixed point. An infinite circle has no center since its outer perimeter cannot be defined. An infinite number of points exist in this unbounded circle and all the points are moving! This is what is meant by an infinite number of buddha's that exist for Dharmakara as he visits them all. He calls this the universe of Buddha-Lands; and spiritually visits them where unbounded numbers of buddha's exist, paying respect, making offerings, and receiving teachings. This is called *krio,* or spiritual traveling. He is awakened into a fully emancipated person with no fixed place, so he is able to travel freely wherever his spirit leads him.

This spirit has the power to transform everything, from a set understanding to a living understanding. From death to life, this is what Dharmakara sees within himself. The main protagonist, Dharmakara, is no longer a fixed figure in a story but comes alive, as we ourselves live his life. This is birth into the final stage of the **18th** vow of the Larger Sutra.

We get caught in a net of our own devices, and as a result we suffer. So, with sincerity of heart we turn to the Buddha to try to save us, and we turn to the Precepts in the hope that these practices will save us. But alas, it is our delusion (dualistic interpretation) that prevents us from really being saved, for we are in the end left alone, deprived of the very thing we want the most. It is unfortunate, yet ironically most fortunate, for faith based on a dichotomized understanding has collapsed into nothingness; and in this abandoned condition we are left alone facing the truth. Here, absolute nothingness (or emptiness) only exists. A spring-like freshness enters our spiritual life that is just beginning. This earth is filled with such wonders. No matter how dark things get we are free, for the noble light within will come as the Tathagata to transform one's darkness into light. Now as the "Gateless Gate", by creating sparks of life that we wouldn't have conceived of as the inconceivable life and light. And in this freedom a birth shout, which is transformed into words that are alive with the brightness that Amida represents. Here the light of the Dharma shines in all directions, including all sentient and non-sentient beings are illumed by its light. This sutra, focusing on Amida Buddha as it does, has such power of life, such an enlightening feeling, simply by placing one's whole trust in the power beyond self. This, I feel, is Shinran's meaning of: "There is indeed, a reason beyond reasoning." linked to the transforming power of Tathagata.

Such joy here, at the very tip of the discovery of life itself! This is the fruit of our resources, the treasures brought about by listening to the True Dharma. The ordinary mind that dwells in peace is such a beautiful thing right here in this place, right here near a shallow pond where the bottom can be seen exists the flatness of ordinary life – which before was taken for granted – now has so many interesting things to reveal and teach me.

All these things as Dharmakara will realize and recognize within him. How could he not bow to the light that has taken him so far beyond his control? The light of Amida reflects back on Amida. This oneness is complete. Such things compose his spacious spiritual life. As he gives life, life is given to him. He willingly shares his life with others helping others to cross over to the other shore of emancipation. He walks and works as a free person, the man who has found himself. With single-mindedness his deepest wish is realized when he is liberated into the final stage and blooms like that of a flower that opens up into life itself. (the **18**th Vow)

◆❖◆

The Five Vow Selection (out of the 48 vows Dharmakara makes)

In this particular selection of five vows, Shinran expands his list of vows to include the **11**th vow, the **12**th vow, the **13**th vow, the **17**th vow, and the **18**th vow. It is important for us to listen to what these vows have to say regarding enlightenment. But once the Buddha attains enlightenment he does not stay there, he returns to the world of samsara. This is expressed in the **22**cnd vow, so therefore there are six important vows altogether, if we add the **22**cnd vow to his list. (Note that all forty eight vows that Dharmakara makes are not listed here.) We can start with the **17**th vow (aspiration within the Name):

> The **17**th vow refers to praising and glorifying the name of Amida Buddha throughout the ten quarters.
>
> The **12**th and **13**th vows refer to with one's attaining infinite light (Wisdom), and infinite life (compassion), which describes the Name, Amida, as limitless. (Sans.: A-mita-bha, and, A-mita-yus.)
>
> The **11**th vow refers to Nirvana. Here I will connect Nirvana with selflessness. Extinction of self is the formal definition. It is the pure fresh self stripped of all defilements, suffering, and delusion, as within the atmosphere of emptiness, or the naked self. It is within the assured, settled state of Nirvana where we live in an enlightened state of tranquility and ultimate peace.
>
> **18**th Vow: (The final "blooming flower" stage or shinjin):
> The contents of this vow contain all those listed above. As such it is as to the "onceness" of shinjin, or being at one with life itself.

Then, in finishing what is being said above, we have the **22**cnd vow:
> Upon attaining enlightenment, the Buddha enters the land of *shaba* as an ordinary person; a Bodhisattva, to join with others in the world of suffering and ignorance. Using expedient means he allows them to realize their fullest potential and, in encouraging their deepest aspiration to become truly awakened persons.

Going further into the aspects of this Sutra which has to do with Amida's limitless wisdom and compassion is this unlimited light and life that Dharmakara becomes. He now is a symbolic figure, as he finishes his 48 Vows, no doubt to the delight of his teacher Lokesvararja.

From that of a Bodhisattva he becomes the "Bowing Buddha" known as Amida Buddha. Amida Buddha within his deepest aspiration now becomes reality within the true aspect of Nirvana. Total negation is total affirmation. The negation of self – cremation of self – brings birth to the total self or naked self in selflessness, not confined by any evils. This includes the five greatest offences and the abuse of the Dharma which Amida's light penetrates, embraces, and absolves: as no human evil can prevent it's shining through the dark clouds as such in the evils of one's darkness. This infinite light comes to us as continuous change, the Tathagata, which in Sanskrit means: "Coming and going, thus comes" (continuous change). Life itself is this continuous change which is the whole basis of Buddhism as it is based on impermanence. It is totally different than the static ego-self along with religious beliefs based on a static and external entity concept, or as a concept of Amida as existing outside of oneself.

So in Shinran Shonin's work and in his seeking through the Larger Sutra, he was able to determine which of the vows led to eventually being able to free oneself of the conceptualized or self-based religious practices and into the "Wide Vow Gate" (**18**th) of freedom. But this came within his deepest confession that he too could very well be an abuser of the Dharma, and as a result, a good for nothing hell-dweller. "Hell is my only home." he once stated, in full recognition of the fact that he was like an inchantika, one who is incapable of being enlightened. From this confession hell was to him a way to freedom, indeed, the freedom of being a hell-dweller as a devil. He just left it alone, and in just leaving it alone he was free. He felt no need for any action on his part whatsoever. A "Foolish bald-headed Shinran" as he called himself, an ordinary person, he arose from hell with no fixed self left for him to improve.

The tathagata is formless. To give it form, i.e., life, we have the Name of Amida Buddha that we can manifest, indeed, be at one. This is the practice reflecting the **17**th vow, and concluding with the **18**th vow in shinjin.

♦❖♦

In establishing his most perfect land, Dharmakara wants to make sure that it is a place of universal truth, for if it is not then it will not apply to all human beings (here as Buddhas) in the ten directions, meaning the world itself. We hear of many truths, but these truths are so often on the purely relative scale, and, along with that, many teachings given by wise people and sages; but they are also relative in their wisdom, thus they are called, "dharmas" with small letters; as well with their "wisdoms", also with a small letters. They are referred to as sundry practices and knowledge's – they apply in some cases, but not in others, to some people but not to others, and etc. Thus, if the truth is not universal, it is not the truth we can apply to our daily lives no matter where we are coming from, across oceans and continents; irrespective of race, religion, and culture. Universal means all human beings have within them the potential and capacity to attain Buddhahood. But for those who have limited capacity, limited learning, limited understanding, and limited ability; for them, once they have heard of the brightness of Amida's all embracing compassion, and upon saying the name even ten times with the desire to be born in his land – shall crosswise – attain an emancipation into his land of peace and bliss. In other words, all we need is the sincere trust and desire to be born in His Land.

All three stages have this as their content as we are born into their respective gates, being pushed and beckoned by the Buddha into the final stage of fulfillment within the truly awakened person of shinjin.

The necessary stages or "Gates" of the focal point, **17th**, and vanishing point the **20th** vow reflecting practice, now become the deepest aspiration for the fulfillment stage of the "Gateless Gate", the **18th** vow, which contains the contents of them all. Being reborn into a 180 degree transformation that this vow reflects is the one thought moment of shinjin.

◆❖◆

Such an enlightened person Dharmakara is. He achieved the blooming flower stage, fulfilling his deepest aspiration. He had to dig for it as it was buried within him. With total effort into the depth of himself he found it.

When I think of how deeply buried the very essence of our life is within us, I think of something that corresponds to this in the sutra that says:

> "One who determines to clean up the ocean is able, after
> a billion years (cup by cup), to clean up the ocean and is
> able to take Treasures from the bottom of the ocean. If a
> person seeks the way honestly, diligently,
> without giving up, he is able to reach the goal,
> any kind of wish can be realized."

How difficult it is to get to the very bottom of ourselves, the core of our being with so many things in the way. Yet with perseverance and dedicated effort it can be done, for it is our life, and we must seek it.

"Know yourself" the sutra says: "You should know yourself by what practice you should establish the wondrous Buddha-Lands." Knowing yourself means knowing yourself as a true human being and as the quiet person who is well settled and who doesn't create noise.

In mentioning practices such as the five practices found in the **5th** verse of the Tan Butsu Ge are to be after we've been awakened to the light of wisdom. Chief among them is *Dana,* or giving life. How can I give life?

Somehow out of our depths is our true nembutsu, which is bowing before Eternal Life. It can also come about through praising of those that we are bowing to. Therefore the phrase: *Buddhas thinking of Buddhas mutually.* In this expression of humility, in the act of bowing we are sincere persons willing to listen to our teachers, who themselves, are the embodiment of the nembutsu. If we really feel this nembutsu then we shall enter the deepest part of the Tan Butsu Ge within the Larger Sutra, and in realizing this go straight through to the true essence of our life crosswise. "Crosswise" means "straight into" without the lengthy and difficult practices taken by monastics and ascetics. The solemn truth alone is the Nembustu.

For in the end, this is why this sutra was created several centuries after Shakyamuni's passing, to give us his true intent. Though many sutras were written after his death, this is the one that gives me the deepest feeling; not only for this sutra, but for the Pure Land Mahayana Buddhism itself. It is the Buddha-Dharma for the people, people like you and me, and untold numbers of potential seekers of the truth that this sutra speaks to. This is the sutra that speaks of Amida Buddha, and how it affects our lives. For the deepest part of our feeling is the membutsu, and is the light that reflects and directs our attention on Amida's inconceivable truth.

The words that carry the truth are the truth. Being as I am, I have continued that which I sought after as a young man instinctively seeking the power of life that was within me, and the guidance to be able to realize it and put it into words. O teacher and teachers, I bow to you who gave your life, allowing me to find my life. You beckoned me, taught me, and gave me all that I needed to find myself, with nothing but a feeling of bowing in front of you for all that has been given to me.

◆ ❖ ◆

R. Adams 12/15/14

Sun lights up the window –
hidden behind the drape –
an amaryllis in full bloom!

This Christmas (2013) a cousin of mine gave me an amaryllis bulb in a box as a gift. But since I was so busy I never had a chance to get the proper potting mix, take it out of the box and transplant it out from a container that came with the bulb. So I stored it in the cool darkness of the basement near the door.

Every day I passed by it, hoping that someday I could get around to planting it, but never did. Then one day I opened the door to put something out – and there it was, a single shoot over twelve inches high, poking through the box with two one-and-a-half inch flower buds needing the sun's light so they could burst out of their sheaths and bloom! Right away I took compassion. I so pitied the poor flower that was shut in a closed box for two months with no water and food in such a cold place and in such darkness. And so the first chance I got I went to the hardware store and got a bag of potting mix (the soil outside was frozen solid) to put the flower in and gave it some water and stored it upstairs on the window sill behind the drape since the rather tall stem was too weak to hold itself up. Within a week it began to bloom and two buds opened up – red flowers – bright and shining! I'm so happy this morning seeing this surprise!

This is our life in a box, living in an enclosed mind. The essence or spirit of our life trying to get out, but it is so difficult. We may think that because we enjoy such lukewarm conditions that there is no real need to get out. After all, we are too busy, so why bother. So we lie half-dead, we will never bloom. Here, we are even more unfortunate then the poor flower, for its only wish is to get out. Its only aspiration is to be born as a flower and fulfill the brightness of blooming. Its total life is put into reaching its full potential as a blooming flower. How it can be other than being bright? Here I think of Dharmakara and his deepest aspiration to fulfill his life.

In the Sutra the word 'Virtue' is used so many times. It appears everywhere. Buddha's Virtue, The Tathagatha's Virtue, The bodhisattva's Virtue, Amida's Virtue, The Virtue of Amida's Wisdom, and so on. Then what about this flower as it is so bright and shining, so filled with the organic virtue of an unfolding life. Can we see this connection, or, are we so unaware that not even a flower can melt our cold mind? Somehow we have to melt this ice, this frozen flame, but we may go back into our little box and close the lid. This is the problem for so many who get stuck in a box they seem not to be able to get out of. We are born as human beings with all the freshness of our birth and now we merely exist within a box of enclosed darkness? Where is the light, the flame within our life which brings us out of the box and into life itself? To fulfill our life is to bloom! This is the miraculous power of life so exemplified by the gift I received. Now I am reminded of the **18th** vow.

I love flowers. I love to watch them grow and bloom, so like a loving parent I watch over them and take care of them. I've painted flowers many times using different techniques and mediums through the years and what has attracted me the most is their simplicity and beauty. They are so naked. They simply shine in such freshness. The lilies especially attract me. And I can't help it; I'm instantly captivated by them. There is something clear that they're leading me into, a purity that they show without any struggle on my part. The instant of truth given to me by the flowers entered my life without any struggle in seeking it. The virtue of simplicity and beauty that so inspired me to create them into paintings.

As I think deeper into this, I think of how embracing my mother was who was suddenly taken away from me in a car accident. I was 5 yrs. old at the time. Is it deeply buried in my mind that her embrace comes to me by way of flowers, or is it ithrough a religious teaching? As Dharmakara has this embracing spirit, it is quite possible. Something in the deepest, earliest part of our life somehow comes to the forefront.... wherein I sought a religious teaching that could embrace me.

That which was taken away has miraculously been given back to me. For flowers act as a teacher to bring us back into the reality of ourselves in thesimplicity and beauty life. When we think of the essence of virtuein nature is it not to be found here? We don't need to struggle to be virtuous. We don't need to prey to a divine authority to get all the virtues that we think we need. We can relax within this natural environment within the peace of the happy mind that is receptive to the words: "Wel come" or "Come to me" in the unfolding of a flower that captures us instantly with its beauty as we can't help but be captivated. Yes, this "Come to me" is the warmth of o ne's mother or father, or as eternal motherly that she represents, beckoning us into her bosom oflife that shines in the face of a flower. So flowers represent the feeling of nature's life that we should be at one with as they have the power to move us.

"The Sutra of Eternal Life" along with what we can gather from its teaching, which has to do with the nembutsu as its ultimate expression. Thus the solemn wish that exemplifies this sutra is fulfilled as we hear the beckoning voice of, "Come to Me." and "Welcome!"

We too, can be like flowers. We are like flowers when we burst through our buds and open our lives to the life that is given to us. Why must we remain in the "bud palace stage" (Shinran Shonin's expression) of religious duties, and not open to bloom in the life giving stage where we come up with a shout. Isn't this what all flowers are saying when they unfold their life, their essential and original wish? Isn't this where I find my true self? Isn't this the fulfilling essence of my being? Do I need anything else other than this? I'm alive – that's it! I feel natural here – totally at one with all things. So I don't need to force myself into a small box, feeling cramped and bounded by such study and practices that lead to nowhere, but instead feel the energy cursing through my body just as life curses through the whole of nature. Oh natural man! It is here that I can hug myself as I feel the essence behind all things. Even in difficulty nothing can stop this pervasive light that cuts through and shines through everything! Brighter than the sun – even as the sun causes all things to grow and bloom. The light that is brighter than the sun is the spirit within the human being that shows in one's face!

All along we were seeking virtue for ourselves, because we wanted to be pure and decent people. But we can make a mistake by identifying virtue with morals and ethics, thinking that we could become good Buddhists and persons by doing so. We were being directed this way by our relative mind, the one who is discriminating between the good from the bad, and etc., with our so-called surface virtues tied to fit into our judgmental values. No way could we establish our wish to be virtuous this way. Here we are going in the opposite direction of our true wish, which is our deepest aspiration for birth. No wonder we experienced guilt feelings, saw ourselves as hypocrites, and told lies about ourselves in order to cover-up the life of pretense.

This pure spirit itself – to be born into the Pure Land is the reason for its inclusion in Mahayana Buddhism as it inspires us to move in this direction, beckoning us to "Come to the Buddha-Dharma". In so doing we acquire its virtue.

A great silence appears, like the atmosphere of Nirvana. The opposite of this is the secular world of birth-and-death. What is it that so many happy here? In the surface world, is it the Emmy Awards? It is as if this is what so many people in this country are transfixed on at this time. They can't wait for this Sunday evening to come and bring into their living rooms all those Hollywood actors and actresses with all the glitz and glamour that the people of show biz have to offer. This is exactly what people want to see, glitz and glamour – an extravaganza of it. They will be happy here for a little while, watching all this stuff in such beautiful displays of egos, or little devils in full costume! All their diamonds, jewels and gowns borrowed for the evening to really <u>Wow</u> us! But nothing here really moves us. It just feeds into our greed for lust and passions – all the things we cannot have, but desire for. And then when the show is over and all the laughing and joking is over? Life is but a stage, as Shakespeare noted, where we have our time and then have to depart, signifying nothing; whereupon, we then go back to our lonely lives. This is the meaning of birth-and-death. There is nothing here of significance to our very lives, and in that which we've wasted our time.

"Buddha is the one who has compassion for all the lonely people in the world", Reverend Akegarasu once said. It is such a profound statement that applies to all of us. He used the word lonely rather than the rich or poor because all of us have the universal feeling of longing and aloneness. Yet for him, loneliness or longing for others is an essential part of our being. Therefore it is not something to get rid of; it is that which makes us want to be with others. If we were not lonely we would be perfectly okay living an isolated existence.

He wanted to help all the lonely people, but he never used the word:"save", as in "save them". He never would use the word "save", for as he stated: "It's better not to be saved than to be saved". Or, "What value do I place upon myself thinking that I'm worth saving? Better to discard this worthless self than to try to save it". To that extent, he lived most of his life being totally free, being saved from the useless stuck-in–the-mud he otherwise would have been had he been saved! So ironically true, giving up wanting to be saved actually led him into being saved into enlightenment!

It never even occurred to me of being saved. For it connotes that the Buddha acts as an external savior, to whom he is not. Many people have taken Amida Buddha as a kind of external demi-god or savior, and by saying the nembutsu hope that their wishes will be granted. Many traditionalists have been influenced into thinking that they can avoid evil by chanting the nembutsu over and over. These are trusted but provisional understandings, as they express doubts when their wishes are not granted. The reason for this problem is that Amida Buddha is not a God to be worshiped, such as in the West. This can lead to laziness, indolence, and self-indulgence in that this belief is all that is required of them. Then they can just sit under a fruit tree, so to speak, and let the fruit fall into their mouth! This is just a religion of self-convenience, not at all Shakyamuni's intent, nor Shinran's intent, nor anything to do with Buddhism itself. Amida Buddha exists as a symbol, a name, and stands for eternal light and life, not a God. God exists as One (as in the jealousy God), whereas Buddhism is directed towards "One is many and many are one." a completely different understanding with completely different results. That's why Buddhism does not fight with other religions. Whereas a God who exists as "One only" will inevitably fight with other Gods, who themselves are trying to control the world. No two Gods can peacefully coexist with each other, except if they decide that it is in their best interests to make "peace agreements". But again and again fighting and war will be inevitable. This is what happens within the static God concept, actually based upon the super-ego and self-love. The hardened ego creates static entities, that when projected outwardly in terms of the absolute, inevitably turn into a Supreme Being that is also permanent, static, and immovable. There is no need to worship an external entity that exists in the other-world. Nor is there any need to speculate on who or what created the world. "When I was born the world was born, and when I die the world will die with me." – H. A. This absolute certainty answers the question of who created the world. If we don't see the world subjectively through our own life then how can we see the world? Yes, we can fall into concepts that so–called religious theologians have preached to us, or that scientists speculate about. But in fact, there is no such world to begin with until we ourselves were born into it.

On the other hand, Amida Buddha is as the Tathagata, i.e., life of continuous change or impermanence. We can identify the Tathagata as the absolute movement of the universe itself including who we are within the universe itself. We can call this the One Soul of the universe as it is the organic self-realization of the soul. Here the term, soul, means an organic and subjective understanding, not an entity as separate from the body just as is our spirit that cannot be separated from our body. Without our conscious awareness there can be no spirit or soul. Otherwise we are dealing with superstitious beliefs. There are all kinds of these idealistic superstitious beliefs under the name of religion, and many people believe in them.

The Tathagatha is a person of freedom. He enters into all the dharmas of the world (small relative wisdoms). All that we see or do not see is a manifestation of the universe. Thus this world we live in is itself a manifestation of the eternal life of the universe, and that includes everything seen and not seen, sentient as well as non-sentient existence. As such, we can worship the world itself, just as it is!

We have flesh and blood therefore we exist. We are declared human the moment we come into being, i.e., our actual birth. Upon our birth we let out a shout of our entrance into the world of life itself. We marvel at the new world we are just born into, and it is here that the world is created. As a bundle of flesh our faces have such a wide-eyed expression. Our parents love us and are so attached to our every move. The very first experience with God in the flesh is with our very own mother to whom we are totally dependent on. Soon enough, however, we will naturally be seeking our own identity. This will gather momentum especially in the teen years, when so many physical and mental changes are taking place. So dramatic are these changes, that we could even describe them as our second birth. Then through high school and college we will be preparing for our future. All along we will be developing friendships, and our limited world will be expanding greatly as we will be meeting and working with other people, and in so doing, we will be trying to understand other peoples' lives. Yet, we will still be seeing everything through our own eyes, or subjective self. We already have certain desires and passions installed in our being. We will try to fulfill them. If we cannot, we get upset, just like a child is when we are denied something that we want from our parents. We are naturally selfish. We selfishly desire for things we want.

But the world does not cater to our wishes always, and as we are denied as such, we face difficulty. Because of our difficulty we seek release, and so we engage in so many practices in order to be happy. Here, we are seeking happiness externally. We also want to be independent and free, so that we can express ourselves freely and be ourselves as we want. In other words, in back of all our wishes, desires and so forth; the desire to break out is now looming stronger. Along with our desire for independence looms the question of who we really are. Something we are seeking in terms of the absolute self is subconsciously driving us towards in an as yet an unknowable goal. This desire for self-power becomes fixed and is our ego, the all important "I". The "I" is fortified by self-love, which becomes fixed also. So altogether, is the so-called relative self or surface self that dictates both the rational and irrational aspects of the mind, affecting our judgmental values as well as our emotional and intellectual values. This is again greatly affected by our pedantically set educational system, with its tendency of teaching in terms of conceptualized methodology, which leaves us with sixteen to twenty years of sophisticated education set in a dualistic understanding of life – words set apart from life with no organic soul. These set principles will be useful in being able to get a job or being able to communicate with each other with the standardized rules of language, or being exposed to different worlds for us to explore including the arts and sciences.

But yet, because all these items are basically secular in content, where in all of this is there any life compared to the sense of words as squiggling fresh truth? Simply we are bounded by the words we use that are coming from our limited reasoning, the same kind of reasoning that we were taught in school, or by the religious who are coming from the same direction. Once Rev Akegarasu observed in himself, "I've become like a huge head walking around on spindly little legs!"

As youth our bodies and minds are filled with passions and desires and since they constitute our organic flesh and blood they are our organic body that proves to be much more powerful that our mind is to control them. The power of nature cannot be denied. Here we look for a lover. Finding such a one we fall into one of the most transforming occurrences in our life. It overwhelms us to such an extent that we lose our smallish self-identity to become at one with our partner in love who also loses their identity as we mingle together as one. The term love, then, is not just a pleasant word, it kills us. This is the pure force of nature that sees to it that we reproduce. But it is this organic fact that breaks down our objective mind, the one we learned in school and used so often, into a life experience that touches the very soul of our subjectivity and shows us the importance that nature has within our bodies and emotions. Since the main of our thinking is based on subjectivity, these uncontrollable elements enter as organic flesh and blood which is instinctual to the very nature of our life. Rev. Akegarasu said, "If you don't like women you will not attain enllightenment."

The "unknowable something" is the infinite life. But in the early first stages we don't know that as yet. We turn to religion to provide an answer, but alas, all we meet with here is more of the same morals and ethics and restrictions placed on our self that we were taught to as a child, the "should and shouldn't" aspects of our behavior. But at this stage, these appear as restrictions on our desire for freedom to do as we wish, even though society and social control demands that they be taught to us. So we become rebellious against authority as we identify it as an external control. All these difficulties enter our lives as we are still groping and exploring ourselves and testing our powers. As we grow into adulthood we may begin to question the traditional religious teachings that were inculcated and preached to us by the ministers and priests of our respective religions. If we are so fortunate, and in our search for who we really are, we may find out or come across an entirely different dimension that challenges us in every direction: Buddhism. But this may become confusing for there is so much information out there at this time that can be false, misleading or confusing. And so we ask the question of which way to go in our search for the truth. Here we are taking the very first steps, important as they are, in seeking the truth. Thus we become a "truth-seeker". The way is clear when for the first time I meet the teacher, who knows me better than I know myself and through his compassion guides me carefully and in the process empties my self-set, my ego. From then on, my life begins to change.

One is many, many are one. The "I" which was as independent as before the meeting with the Teacher took place is now composed of multitudinous beings. I begin to see a way beyond the smallish self-contained domain and begin to circulate among those of the sangha, fellow students studying from the Dharma. As this process goes forward my universe enlarges to the point that I begin to understand the world of seeing myself in others, deepening my self-introspection.

"The Buddha sees himself in all sentient beings." From a statement made at the beginning of the Larger Sutra, the Buddha establishes his doctrine of "One is many, many are one." It is said that when alive and traveling among the people he accepted all persons, regardless of who or what they were as friends. This shows how magnanimous and embracing he was, not letting any ideology and differences get in the way of his yearning and needing to be with people. In that sense we can say that he simply loved others, human to human, unconditionally. I would be perfectly relaxed and comfortable with him. We see now how this "One in the many..." has a value to our lives. This kind of oneness he demonstrated warms me up to the fact that he was a true human being.

There is always a feeling of friendship, togetherness, and vibrancy among a group of people who get together, if for no other reason than enjoying each other's company, irrespective of the occasion – even after a funeral! Yes, even before, during and after the funeral, where one has gone through much grief, crying, and sorrow, it empties into nothingness – where from there a fresh world opens wherein together we taste a sense of relief and peace together at dinner with the cracking of jokes and laughter. This is the transcendence of birth–and-death while living in birth-and-death, and wherein we are at one in human-to-human contact. This is the world of Buddhas mentioned in the Larger Sutra, and the Buddha's Dharmakara is thinking of and those he pays homage to.

The lands of the ten quarters is the world itself, all created out of the feeling of "One is many, many are one." Here we can love each other as brothers and sisters. I'm sure that everyone has had this experience. Then, if that is the case, we've all tasted the very opening round of Buddhism! Indeed, we are already in it, into the flow of life. It is as playfulness as our savior, for it allows us to get in touch with our human essence in a well-rounded whimsical way. Taste it, for it is an aspect of our true religion, stripped of all the various decorations and encumbrances. It opens the Dharma-gates for us to enter as our mind is ready to receive it openly. So often it is the simple things we overlook that have significance, a sense of playfullness enters, and wherein it bring a sense of joy to our life.

As I think of this, I think of the world of birth-and-death, and see that I too, am part of it, for I live in this world that consists of birth-and-death, otherwise I am not truly alive – this moment-to-moment, birth-and-death; the final gate being my own death which my life comes as a complete stop. Pari-Nirvana: complete combustion, positive and final; that now I think of as a solemn ending of this fulfillment of life itself and the infinite creation of life, which includes death and its destruction, all within a meaningful life that has had real substance.

The open air and spacious world is where I live and gain my sustenance in the freedom of being in this wondrous world where all things come and go, and is where I work and live as such. As the world of birth-and-death transforms into birth-and-life, in a sense that it embraces the world as a positive element in a *continuous discontinuous continuity* as it transcends the shaky, relative, birth-and-death life-style of the secular world, the world of samsara.

Samsara is Nirvana, and Nirvana is samsara, as they say in Zen. At the core of samsara is our life of birth-and-death, according to the secular mentality of the world we live in. But nirvana means extinction of self, such as in no-self, or selflessness; opposed to the relative mind as it is based on a dualistic, distorted interpretation of life. Superficially we can carry around so many deluded ideas, concepts, judgments, errors and misunderstandings all based on self. To straighten this all out a removal of all these artificial layers is necessary. This is the function of the Dharma and especially in the hands of the teacher or teachers who put a mirror in front of our face, so to speak, to let us see who we really are objectively. But it is we ourselves who must complete the process through our own self-introspection. This then is the subjectivity that turns around the secular world of samsara into the flowing, free, spacious, and well-settled Nirvana.

Then how can samsara be nirvana? It is precisely because of samsara that we are seeking nirvana. The process of seeking into the truth begins with oneself. Though I live in the world of birth-and-death I am not caught by it. Thus the birth-and-death world of samsara transfers into the birth-and-life world of Nirvana, one's newly born self. Instantaneous transformation by the power beyond self through actional intuition defines death and re-birth in our lives and in all places in the world of samsara where we live and work. The reason that goes beyond reasoning is the transforming power that transforms the relative birth-and-death into a living birth-and-death originating in one's organic and subjective self. This is the inconceivable Gateless Gate, wherein the bud miraculously opens into a beautiful flower and from which this freshness transcends the difficult birth-and-death that everyone experiences within secularisim, which is a two-dimentional subject and object framwork attached to self-love. As we stay here we can never experience Nirvana. Only our deepest confession will release the bondage we face within secularisim.

* * *

Last night I went dancing. Since my friend was unable to attend, I went by myself. I needed the exercise and wanted to get out of the house and meet with people. It was really a necessity. I have a special place I go to, a pretty nice place with a good atmosphere. I recommend that all middle age people on up go to a place like this and take in the rhythm of a lively band along with such lively dancers! Do your dance! Loosen your stiffened bones, and get in real tune with the "Bhodhi" spirit. Or, put in another way, "Buddhism in action". Anyway, this is the action of dance that I do. When the band is really in tune, my feet start tapping, my body starts swaying up and down and sideways – I can no longer sit still, I have to get up and participate with the crowd on the dance floor, who are swinging and swaying in such rhythm. It is sometimes unbelievable what happens. Sometimes several people get together in a circle, and, moving in and out amongst each other, with each person doing a dance in the center of the group, the floor becomes one group of humanity as one. Now this one has significance, because it is composed of many as one. And these many is not standing still. We see many, but they are altogether as one. Therefore in terms of oneness, the one cannot exist without the other. Simply it is impossible. Speaking of losing oneself and finding oneself in the other, this is what meant. It happens spontaneously. It doesn't come about from a prefixed idea. If you are self-conscious about yourself, looking askance at all of this and say, "Wait, am I doing the right thing?" and so on with cold feet, it won't work. It is a spontaneous decision done by a collective group that leads everyone to be in harmony with each other and the group as a whole. In this playfulness, the joy of which innumerable buddha's appear dancing their way into the Pure Land, creating the way together instantly. In other words, only by throwing your whole self into it without thinking will the spirit of the dance in the one thought moment come alive, and, is selfless.

But the question is, can I be at one with those who disagree with me or who are disagreeable? We need a well-rounded understanding of the term "oneness". If one's notion of "oneness" only applies to those who agree with me then my understanding is limited. Shakyamuni, for instance, accepted everyone, regardless of who they were or where they came from, or even what they believed in. He chereshed everyone, and that is true oneness. Because of this he was well-loved.

On the dance floor, for instance, there is not always a sense of oneness. Not everyone dances the way that I do. In fact I'm the only one who dances the way that I do. I see many different styles of dance. In fact, it's incredible the various styles that I've seen throughout the years – all of them different and unique expressions of the person(s) doing their dance. But since I'm so intent on doing my own dance I don't pay too much attention to what the others are doing, being just focused on what it is that I'm doing. Then others may join me, as it happens every so often. Or, I may join others with whatever it is they are doing. Then what a happy crowd of lively dancers we are. It is amazing or even miraculous over what happens on the dance floor when the rhythm of life enters our bodies and manifests itself through actional intuition, a phrase that means: I act as I see, and see as I act. This describes the intuitional one thought moment as in the quick steps the dancers are doing their dance. You see by doing and you do by seeing, the feeling from this is oneness, and joy.

Because I lead, and hardly ever follow – except when catching the spirit of the group. I am an independent person respecting the independence of others as they are alive and expressing their own life. I dance with others wholeheartedly with sparks of energy that I do not study, contrive, plan, nor think about – for exactly and irrevocably at the very instant it happens. Therefore I say or do whatever I want without any attachment. It is here where I love others as myself because I'm in harmony with others in the "isness" of life. From an unbounded and unknowable power comes the truth. This is oneness. As the person mingling with others without hesitation and in the manner of a person bravely and courageously seeking into his own life. Here I feel at one with all others as I love the spirit of the group itself. If I say so, this is the essence of Buddhism; or rather, this is true religion. The worship is in the spirit and the spirit is one are many and many are in the one. Can we understand this principle? For otherwise there is no spirit, no rhythm, or no religion.

The spirit is within the body, inseparable from it. The will to live is what gives the spirit life, so the spirit has a will. If we extrapolate from this, then all of life has this will and spirit. As long as I am alive this spirit can manifest itself in so many ways. But it is not an entity outside of our selves. For without our consciousness, our sense organs, and along with our body as a whole – without life itself which exists within the body/mind, there is no spirit. We must see ourselves as a whole, as indivisible, not a bunch of parts that can be pulled apart and put together someplace else, and consider ourselves as a living human being. Therefore it is a delusion, a terrible misconception to think that there is an afterlife in which after the body dies, and the individual's soul and spirit departs to the other-world leaving the body behind. Without the body, the living manifestation of the soul and the spirit; along with the conscious mind that resides in the body, how can anyone preach about a life after death as nothing more than a wishful fiction? It doesn't matter wherever it goes, to heaven or hell, the whole process is a result of our not living our life to the fullest right here on this earth, and so we must go on to another life to fulfill it because we didn't really discover our true life while we were still alive. But if we live our life courageously and to the fullest, fulfilling our deepest aspiration for birth in the land of recompense as non-returning and well-settled, then I can be well rewarded and feel satisfied to be able to pass on right now with no regrets and to a full stop. But not yet! I have much work to do feeling the spirit of life within me and sharing it with others. I'm alive because I'm inspired to live!

It is a huge mistake to divide or separate the body from the spirit, for then we have a dual existence from which all subsequent dualities will take place. The totality of life then will not be understood properly. We will be living a disconnected existence from the spirit in the world of living beings. In fact, religions which divide the body from its living spirit have no real spirit; they and their set doctrines do not have the slightest understanding of the organic life of the spirit. A faith-based religion that is conceptualized on the basis of mysticism and sentimentality and dogmatized by religious priests and scholars who are observers to life and not actual participants in the true sense; i.e., they did not die to be reborn into the flame of life itself. Thus they remained cold to any organic understanding even within their own bodies, and thus were cut–off from any spiritual life which must include the flesh and blood of the body itself. It is only natural that from here that they focused on morals and ethics, considering the body with its fleshy existence as a temporal and as a preparatory relationship with God while on earth hoping to be rewarded in heavenly bliss after death. Organic life is dirty and filthy; they must seek holiness in the pure realm of an eternal life concept, in the other-world as secluded from this world of birth, desires, passions, suffering, sickness, and death. We will be rewarded they say, if we live a pure and moral life while having faith and belief in a supreme being. We will pass on to the ultimate bliss which is heaven and be with His glory after we die, everlastingly!

Actually, it is their fear of death itself that push people into thinking that they will be saved from death and go to a better place away from this world of suffering, struggle and disappointment. Rather than be comforted I'd rather seek deeply into my life to express the living spirit. The way to death is to fulfill our lives right here and be happy with the knowledge that we have lived our lives fully, courageously, bravely, and creatively. Then the conscience is clear and I can pass into eternal sleep with no problem; for there is a solemnity that doesn't compromise with our ultimate death, but faces it directly. This thought gives me satisfaction, actually. So death can be positive as another term for life that is positive. It's all a matter of what I choose. For when things come to a complete stop, such as in death, all manner of discussions come to a complete stop also.

When my father remarried after my mother passed away, he married a Catholic who then became my stepmother. After a year or so she had me taken to a Catholic Church for Baptism, Holy Communion, and Confirmation, all within the time that I graduated from grammar school. The priests who preached to me took hold of my mind so that I remained Catholic-minded in my thinking even after several years of entering Buddhism. Catholicism is a natural result of Judaism, Rev. Maida said. I, an innocent child who knew nothing about religion got caught. My Teacher once noted this in class, recognizing the problem that I was not even aware of. And since I became Catholic-minded (fixed thinking), it took time to shake it off, even some time after I was exposed to the writings of Buddhist teachers.

What it is that I was doing is how I converted living teachings into sets of conceptualized understandings which then became fixed like so many blocks. But I was not alone as all of us did, and especially another person, a Mr. D., who was the only philosopher in the group, and who got the appellation of "frozen flame".

But come to think of it, so often beginners go through the same process of storing the truth into abstractions and concepts, accumulating these concepts in one's head, referred to as "head knowledge" – which we attach to in terms of being fixed so that they become like so many dead sea-shells.

So too, we can experience a set life in a cocoon-like enclosure. We may try to beautify it by decorating it and ourselves with beautiful objects, but come down to it, we can feel very isolated and lonely here. Ha, we can also spin beautiful silk within our cocoon, which only further strengthens our illusion of ego-satisfaction. It becomes our prison of self-enclosed ideas and life-style. We must strongly seek a way out of this tightly enclosed space and break out of our shell-of-self, out of our cocoon-like enclosure and into the wide spaces of freedom. Indeed, we can pass through a whole lifetime without ever waking up to our essential nature which is both spiritual and alive.

This was my instinct when I sought into a way to progress forward. I wanted to find something that matched my instinct for life. It was the Dharma that caught my attention, and in a sense it pulled me forward into a whole new world that I never imagined or expected. But along the way, I created my own cocoon(s) as well. It took the teachings of the Dharma to see what it is that I was doing, that even I confessed of not being able to go forward with my life. This is what the formation of one's cocoon can do to stop further progress. Release or breaking out from our self-made cocoon is the transforming process of liberation whereas we break through this stationary covering and unfold our wings to fly freely as does the butterfly breaking out of its sheath and arising freshly out of its cocoon. A rebirth!

It is not surprising that the statically held self, or ego, will invariably create a static entity in the form of a static God, externally. This entity can be called any name as long as the name means that of a Supreme Being and enters the language as such. People seek a permanent prime creator, one who holds power over all beings and all life. Giving it a name through our language, we can then communicate it and worship it. They want to become at one with the name of one who is absolute and immutable and who controls all things and who is the origin and death of all things. Such is the entity they look up to and worship. This is the basis for most religions and religious practices regardless of names and forms.

Many people have delusions about what their God will do for them, and so they cling to the notion that they will be blessed, and so they feel comforted and do not go further. In Buddhism it is the same thing, for if belief in an Amida Buddha as a fixed notion of a savior is all that is required, why seek beyond that? If religious practices settle for rituals, what good are they? Who and what are we worshipping here? This is in the world of abstractions; therefore it is for the falsely settled as in the **20th** vow.

Shakyamuni himself began his seeking for the absolute in terms of Atman, the Hindu equivalent for God, so in that sense he began as a religious person, essentially no different than any one of us. The way it turned out however, is that for all his efforts, and they were extreme, became more and more doubtful as to his power to eliminate all that stood in the way of attaining the absolute Soul (seen as God. Ironically, the closer he got to his dedicated goal, the more his mind would conjure up dark thoughts and delusional dreams, so much so, that he came to an iron wall of the impossible. "Oh Avidia!", "Oh Darkness!" was his confession.

This was the last of his seven steps into awakening from his provisional religious self to his true religious self. We must conclude from this that Shinran Shonin was quite correct in stating that all such religious practices are from the falsely settled mind.

Actually, Shinran went through the same process before he met his teacher, Honen, who taught eternal life through the Nembutsu alone (the Vow. So again, without his bowing through the nembutsu as embodied through his teacher he never would have succeeded in finding the essential question concerning his deepest aspiration. Otherwise, self-power efforts intended to grasp the infinite essence of life ended in futility. Trust in the power beyond self moved him beyond the impossible.

Buddhism starts with the Four Noble Truths. The first one begins with the statement: Our life is suffering. The second Noble Truth is: Find the cause of our suffering. What is the cause of the suffering? The answer is the self. This self is deluded into thinking that it is strong, all powerful, self–righteous, smart, intelligent, and superior. But on the opposite side, the self wants to be seen as pure, and so it wants to be morally correct, honest, giving, unselfish, and caring. But in back of all of our self-affirming deeds and thoughts is still the attachment to self through self-love – the hidden one that we cannot see that lurks behind all our efforts to show to others how good I am. It is truly amazing as to what it is that we are willing to say and do to impress others as to our powers of attainment or meritorious good deeds. Here is where self-love exposes itself nakedly as attachment to self, an unbreakable attachment and the final one. While it is called self-pride we tend to overlook it since it is so commonplace in our life. Here we are like blind sinners unwilling to confess anything wrong about ourselves because we take it all for granted, or hide it from others as it makes us look weak and vulnerable.

Our "sin" as it were, can be defined as a static, dichotomized and academic understanding of life in which we go about categorizing things into good and bad, a scholarly procedure that we do all the time. But the moralistic religious priests, ministers, and scholars, thought it was our immorality and unethical conduct that created our sinful behavior as the cause of our being impure and defiled – but not so. It is the attachment to the relative self, our scholar nature – which they themselves are guilty of which is the cause of our problem. Being scholars and religious philosophers they study life and religion from their standpoint of *being*, i.e., a static being attached to one's self-identity. But they had no idea about emptiness or non-being as the core of life itself. Thus, all their discourses on spirituality have no real substance, since they are all based on a self that they themselves are attached to. This invariably led them in the direction of logic (*logos*) to solve the problem of humanity and its spiritual difficulties. But this cannot be resolved by fixing on a being that is set apart from life like that of a stone. Spiritual life has an essence to it that cannot be figured out by way of logic. Being mystical they then turn to faith and belief as a result, sounding even more mysterious. People merely accept all these things under the name of religion, but unfortunately it is not true religion, but the appearance of religion that satisfies the general public. We get fooled by the appearances until we really get to the bottom of what it is that we are asked to believe in.

The very bottom has to be experienced by one's death to the self, that is, the ego-self. The deluded self cannot figure out the enlightened self. Only the Buddha can know what the Buddha is. Nor can it see itself as being deluded either. Only a power beyond the self can reveal our ignorance. It is the Buddha-Dharma and its teachers that enable us to see it by opening-up our critical mind's eye, enabling us to see into ourselves. It's like our eyes can only see outward, not inward. It is the teachers who give us the "wisdom eyes" to see ourselves outside of ourselves. So we must have the wisdom eye of a true student, and know what to look for. This means that along with ourselves, we must look into the face of others, along with the voice of others, we can determine where and what they are thinking, so the face and the voice express what we are. My teacher always had a crisp voice, along with a clear expressive face.

For us beginners, Rev. Saito chose a course that was open to all, that is, he brought out the feeling of his teacher, and through this he would focus on the teachings. Feeling came first, and then once we had a physical feeling we would be ready to listen. I believe that this is the most sincere way to approach Buddhism.

In one his articles entitled, "The Seventeen Article Constitution", Rev. Akegarasu discusses Prince Shotoku (6th cent.), and the way he handled his anger: "I am not always right and the other person is not always wrong". Reverend Akegarasu deeply felt this in looking into his own anger. This is how we must listen carefully to others.

It was such a well-rounded understanding that he had, and what Rev. Saito wanted us to understand, rather than begin with the doctrinal studies which would have been way above our heads in any case. But mostly, he really wanted us to taste the truth coming from his teacher's understanding, and, since he was intent in translating Akegarasu's writings anyway, he used us "guinea pigs" to test out his translations by way of our feedback. This was especially good for us as students, for we got many live teachings from this. These live teachings are very important for they really sink in.

Always we had lively discussions that took place as a result of our exposure to Akegarasu. Indeed, in examining each other's understanding, the discussion group became quite active, to wit, we got into some heated discussions on various disagreements about matters of opinion regarding these teachings. Some arguments would erupt because we were coming from different directions. So as a group you have ten of us representing various aspects of humanity discussing various aspects of the Buddha! That was okay with him, because if you are really learning, you are at the same time changing, which creates sparks because in the process we become alive, not just like sacks to be filled with knowledge passively sitting back waiting to be fed! Indeed, we had to write down our various understandings, and not sign our papers, so that each person could then criticize or comment on another person's work. You could not get lazy in his class; you had to be an active participant. All of us as individuals at various times would be given the "hot seat" treatment in which we had to come up with our very own life in response to questions put before us. These red carpet sessions, along with the teacher's comments, made such a difference in allowing all of us to get to know each other and the teaching. Then afterward we'd continue the discussion and get more into each other's understanding, even more on personal issues, along with some joking and laughing at the restaurant, forgetting how late it was getting! It was through these sessions that I got a real taste of Buddhism.

So often, as we were listening to the points he was bringing forth, it was quiet and introspective, as the dialogue between him and we became deeper. I believe that this atmosphere gave us the feeling of nembutsu without words.

What is remarkable is that he never showed to us or explained the nembutsu, but rather manifested it with his whole life. This is the difference of a true student that he was. We could call him a "bowing student" as an honorary title, for he continued for the rest of his life to be as a student. Because of his humble attitude he never looked down on us, except when he thought we were acting like "roshi's", i.e., thinking that we were "know-it-all Zen masters"; in which case he could look at that student rather coldly. But there was no dualistic idea that we were his students and he was acting as a "Teacher" in that he would be explaining things as he would then be talking *about*

Buddhism and then giving it to us dualistically. We would then be functioning as receivers of that which he was giving to us. Because of this dualistic function of him as teacher and we as students there would be a divide on both sides in which he would have been "preaching" to us. In this kind of dualistic procedure, the nembutsu would be relegated to a religious practice. Often this is the difficulty that teachers make in that they preach a scholarly form of religion as referenced in the second stage of our religious practices as in the **20th** vow of the Larger Sutra. But there is something in listening to the truth itself that produces sparks; listening to a person who awakens the truth in us that creates life, which is the **18th** vow.

Out of this comes the nembutsu. As Rev. Saito noted, so often we get into one-way conversations with each other, sounding like we are trying to control each other's thoughts, maintaining our own position, and etc., and as a result we don't express our feeling towards each other, but try to control the other. And so it is that the essence of the nembutsu is in our real life association with others in the form of respect for the others' life that we experience our oneness with each other. We are by listening to the other, bowing to the others' life, not just asserting our thoughts over the other person. It makes for a dramatic difference in our communication.

* * *

One morning while having a cup of coffee, a thought came up in my mind out of nowhere: "Foolish is okay". Since I had no direct reason to think such a thought, I then began to think that being foolish is okay and I'm perfectly comfortable with that, so long as this is not the same kind of foolishness that is relative with that of priding myself, thinking of myself as wise or smart. In other words, I am comfortable being myself just as I am, with no improvements necessary to make me a better person. This is the first thought of morning meditation. But when I think about it, can I feel the same way about ignorance? I cannot be comfortable being ignorant as ignorance is blindness of not knowing oneself. But selflessness is the result of working in the atmosphere of nothingness or no-mind that removes the dichotomy between subject and object. Here I am the subject and object as one. Thus when I say I am foolish I am saying that once I understand myself as such, I can be playful. Being playful was one of the features that Shakyamuni had in his teaching.

Foolishness accounts for much of what humans are capable of doing. For instance, we may be proud of the fact that we are wise in doing so and so, wisely. But as things are in a constant state of flux we may be wise one moment and foolish the next. But on the other hand, if we begin with knowing ourselves as foolish, we can more readably understand the foolishness of others and this allows us the wisdom of being wise. So I recognize myself as a foolish person having discourse with another foolish person, for instance. This is what gives me the freedom of foolishness. In other words, to recognize it one has to acknowledge it within oneself. Thus wisdom is when I confess that I am foolish. So what begins with foolishness ends up as wisdom, then to return to foolishness, then again wisdom, and etc. Thus it is like a horizontal forward movement with no ending. If I stop somewhere and get caught by one or the other it will appear as already hardening. As a result I will either think that I am a foolish person or a wise person. Since this is a relative position I may either look down on others, or look up to others, depending on which side of the fence I'm on at the time. Here, there is no freedom because there is no movement that tags one thing into another. Thus we have foolish Shakyamuni examining foolish Shakyamuni. In being foolish, self-awareness that I am a foolish person is as the middle way, and as a natural confession as to one's being foolish. This is what leads to playfulness.

While we try to do away with our ignorance, yet we remain ignorant. We cannot be satisfied with that; we continue to pursue an enlightened state of mind. It is like the proverbial bull that is pulled by the nose, thinking that ignorance can be done away with one's own self-power through enlightenment. This is completely dualistic and cannot survive the test of reality. We are ignorant before the inconceivable life of which we have no idea. This confession of our humility before the truth shows us that we are ignorant as we go about seeking our own self-enlightenment.

Within the freshness of life there is the freedom from ignorance. Easiest to understand! Here I return to my original self, who didn't know any better but just being himself; after all the education and seeking, being just an ordinary person is okay. I can be comfortable with that; going to where being wise or foolish are but two sides of the same coin, rolling along, presenting no problem.

We must have a well-rounded view of the world, not just a limited-to-self-view. This is the context in which the Pure Land was conceived. But we cannot be born into the Pure Land without our deepest confession. The honest mind is the Pure Land. By confessing, "I myself am a devil"; and as such, incompetent, and good for nothing, the Pure Land opens up as the world of freedom. The world of freedom is the world-wide view, whereas the limited-to-self view is bounded by self. Now something must go. You can't have no-self co-existing with a relative self for that brings about friction and unhappiness. Two selves will oppose each other; therefore the one that is causing the friction must go. But if one tries to get rid of the other it is impossible because one turns into the other as one. Same way, if one realizes that, "Alone, I am a devil." then the self that is a devil must disappear into the freedom of being a devil. "The freedom of being a devil is our only freedom, the only freedom that is granted to us." – (Shuichi Maida)

"Extreme bliss": extreme means the unlimited, both horizontally and vertically, while bliss refers to happiness. So the land of "peace and bliss" refers to the Pure Land where Dharmakara wants to establish his land (Verses **8**, **9**) of the Larger Sutra. He states that his land will be Nirvana itself, and that it will be beyond comparison, i.e., absolute. Since Nirvana means extinction of self, we must assume that his land will be selfless, i.e., without self or no-self. But in that case, where does the self go?

Logically it has to go somewhere; it can't just float into thin air. Actually it goes into Hell where he the devil exists. That is where self-extinction occurs. Because the self is a devil; and as a hell-dweller realizes that this is his only home. Indeed, his self being as a devil, enters the flames of hell, and is consumed by these hellish flames, to be reborn like a Phoenix (as in the ancient Greek mythological creature) to arise again out of its ashes letting out a birth shout as when he was first born: "Alone, I am noble!" Alone, the birth shout is most noble – then self and no-self are as One Self.

Thus having no other place to go, the worthless good–for-nothing self finds itself in no other place other than hell. "Hell is my only home", states Shinran Shonin. He, most serious, was not afraid to call it as it is. In facing the truth about himself, he made an open confession as to his incapability to perform any good religious practices. The harder he tried, the worse it became. All his efforts came down to this statement.

Frustrated, and after 20 years of struggle within the Tendai sect of traditionalist Buddhism on Mt. Hiei, he fortunately met his teacher, Honen Shonin, who was in the midst of forming a new sect based on the Nembutsu (Shinshu Buddhism) as in the essence of Amida Buddha as contained in the Larger Sutra. Self-power attempts at being a good religious person were transcended which now became *other-power* through the nembutsu, which is what Shinran focused on for the remainder of his life. Thus when once criticized for deviating from Honen's teaching, he answered by saying that between him and his teacher they shared the same nembutsu.

As he threw away his self into the farthest reaches of Hell and himself along with it, and then was reborn as a true human being, nakedly standing alone. Trust in the nembutsu completely changed his life, for now he began to realize the bright and embracing light of the power beyond self which led him to create the Kyo-Gyo-Shin-Sho, a six volume work: The Teaching, Practice, Faith, and Enlightenment, in which he examines the basis for his teacher's nembutsu along with the six other Patriarchs who he studied from within the context of his own life.

What does that tell us, those who are still reaching for perfectibility of self in our desire to be such good religious people? Do we wish to find ourselves in Hell? No way, as far away from hell as possible! We want to be in heaven on earth as well as heaven after we die. In trying to perfect ourselves, we reach out for so many practices that will give us a good, healthy life. Life is difficult. We therefore reach out and embrace that which gives us a sense of happiness. And we do find happiness for awhile. But the flux of life changes our happiness into unhappiness. In some ways it's like a rat race leading to nowhere. There's no real focal point, and so we try to grab after and attach to whatever comes along – friends, family, house, car, sports, T.V., entertainment, hobbies, and of course, social media on our I Pads. But behind it all we live in fear, fear of death, death of all that we cherish and hold dear. Strange isn't it; we were born to live our life to the fullest, only to get bogged down and entangled with so many things that confuse and trouble us, some to the extreme. What are we to do? "If we are not afraid of death, how can small things disturb us?" – (Manshi Kiozawa)

Where is the truth? The truth is within us, the very core of our being that we didn't even know existed. This is what we must seek with our total being. Indeed, this is our life to discover. And the relative self, our surface self, and our conscious intellect, so useful in picking out good apples from bad ones at the grocery store and etc., will not help us here. We have to dig far deeper into our very life to come up with the squiggling truth. Otherwise we can relapse into fear. Do not pin your hopes on a transitory life of worldly gain, for the truth enters when our expectancies fail.
Life is unpredictable, surprising, unusual, and unique; as well as quiet, resourceful, courageous, and brave, as in this rhythm of the infinite life that supports us.

Expansion, expansion, we want to expand ourselves in so many ways. All of our efforts lead us in this direction. No matter, for our greed here inevitably self-destructs into pain and suffering. For in the process of obtaining whatever it is that our greed desires, we will do whatever it takes to fortify and protect it out of fear of loss for that which we've worked so hard to obtain. We must be worldly here, even if we didn't intend it in the beginning. Meanwhile with all these distractions, anxieties, vexations, and attachments, have we found any peace to it all? Aren't we seriously cheating ourselves? Where among all this stuff that we have to put up with – is it doing us any real good? Isn't all we are doing is just expanding the limited circle we are bounded by? We've done nothing to rid ourselves of that small fixed center of the enlarged circle of expansion we are bounded by; whereas infinite life which has no fixed circle has left us behind. In all our efforts of expanding our limited circle we are still left facing ourselves bounded by our greed. We have deceived ourselves. Unlimited expansion occurs when we touch upon infinite life, not when it is confined by one's limited circle, and which leaves behind the limited circle of the worldly life, thus freeing us from this self-imposed bondage.

The ego-self is evil. It is not maybe or if; it is a lying, cheating, licentious, artificial, pretentious, erroneous, sophisticated, superior, immoral, ugly, usurious, impervious, blind, smelly, static, arrogant, hypocritical, vindictive, and calculating chunk of ignorance – and whatever else one cares to add to this heap of trash that ultimately has to be put to fire. We have got to throw this whole baggage of the useless self into the fire-pit of Hell! At this point I am open, I did nothing to control it; nothing to protect it, improve it, perfect it, or save it. I just let it go – and in letting go, discover who I am, a naked human being standing alone with a clean empty slate.

The nature of man is filled with desires and delusions. Up to the time we face our own death this can be our way. Close to our death these will fade away into nothingness. Still we will be clinging to our life. We want to live, yet we must die. A solemn quiet will enter our mind. The flow of life entering death will move us into the ultimate truth that we are mortal finite beings entering the infinite life. The infinite life was always present, but unfortunately we did not see it and fully appreciate it, otherwise we would have worshipped it, and put our whole trust and faith in it as the sustaining power behind our life. It sustained us, yet we knew it not. It supported and guided us properly, but we knew it not. It was the truth itself, but we knew it not. We were so taken up by so many external and fruitless things. It could not be seen, so we could not see it until the end. Then we, knowing the absolute truth that will be coming, become so quiet. When we face death itself we wake up to our birth in the Pure Land of unknowable life, whereupon our eyes are opened by an absolute truth facing us directly. In the throes of one's darkness and pain the truth appears as this shining light.

Here we come across the true nembutsu, bowing to infinite Light and Life. It is not of our making. We don't need to show it to others. It is not a product of self-love. It simply exists within our very being. It addresses itself to me alone, to you alone, and to all those who with the passage of time have devoted themselves to the recitation of the Name.

*   *   *

At the time of my teacher's memorial service (some nine years have passed since I last saw him), I met with Bob Kikuchi, who was in a wheel chair guided by his son. I was really surprised that he was still alive. I went up to him and told him rather loudly: "Gee, I haven't seen you in such a long time, I wondered if you were still around! Good to see you!" He simply smiled, and his eyes were sparkling bright. He nodded and continued to smile, and then told me that he continues to see Reverend Saito's grave along with his wife's grave that are placed right next to each other in Montrose Cemetery. He too, wants to be buried next to him. I've known him for a long time, and knew that he loved the teacher as so many did here at this temple. Then he stuck out his hand and gave me a "thumbs-up" sign. I responded with a "thumbs up" of my own, both of us in such a positive way, with me bowing to him in the wheel chair.

Knowing him, I know that he lived his life to the fullest extent, to the fullest potential that he was capable of, and how instrumental he was in building the new temple, and how happy and satisfied he was to see it completed after such a long struggle. So now he is satisfied to pass on with such a positive attitude, giving me the "thumbs-up" sign. Pari-nirvana, or complete combustion, is given to our life that is fully lived. One's total being is burning with such a cool flame and in such a way that he can face death fully satisfied, with no regrets along with a smile. One doesn't need or desire for a replacement of this life for another life after death, because he didn't fully live his life here on earth. This is our appreciation, and yes, our ultimate reward for listening to the Buddha-Dharma. I too will go into the unknown and unknowable life, get buried next to him, along with the Saito's and the rest of the temple members who are buried in Montrose Cemetery facing the far outskirts of a frontier of Buddhism that Reverend Kubose and Reverend Saito gave us. Then too, the Issei's, Nisei's, and Sansei's who were so devoted to the temple and who shoveled the coal, so to speak, that kept the fires burning and the temple alive.

All share in the same and undying spirit that the temple represents. For they have no real death in a deep sense, as their spirit is alive in all of us. They never really died as I can remember their life and their spirit. This is what is meant by the timelessness of infinite life, as it never perishes. In death the body dies and along with that our consciousness of the world that will die with it. Yet our spirit by the way we lived will carry on right here on earth.

Now it is up to me to see what I can do in the frontier of the "Cemetery facing the woods", by going forward with my own life. This is the spirit that they had, and in which as a whole they shared with one another. For they were among the frontier people; those of them who helped establish Shinshu Buddhism in this country; those ordinary ones who did unusual things with single-minded effort, the kind that they were capable doing. We too, can clean-up the world to keep their spirit alive and welcoming. For to clean-up the world along with our selves is our main practice.

For if Buddhism challenges us in every area of our life, it opens our mind to transcendence into the Wide Vow Gate, the Gateless Gate, which for us means living the life of Dharmakara who exemplifies Amida Buddha of The Eternal Life Sutra, wherein seeing into an inconceivable life comes up unexpectedly without seeking it.

If all our self-power attempts to remove the devil from our lives are futile, what hope then is there for us to ever be born into the Pure Land? I cannot expect or think that the Pure Land is a place that is separate from me. That it belongs to some other shore that is beyond this worldly shore until I die, and/or unless we die to the self that contrives evil and greedy thoughts and desires. In fact, this is the whole point: Do we reach the Pure Land upon one's physical death, or to the death of the contriving self? Which is it? This is a real question here. We reach the Pure Land by being thoroughly honest. Thus the Pure Land is not a geographical or physical place, but the naked self.

The land of Nirvana is the beauty of mind that answers this question. This is the land that Dharmakara wants to establish, and to do it he has sworn to make his 48 Vows as proof of his deepest aspiration to attain it. In so doing he has to work hard and go through many difficulties to attain his aspiration.

In thinking of this I am reminded of Gautama Buddha's six steps prior and the seventh of his enlightenment. He examined himself as to whether or not his near physical death had anything to do with his spiritual life. To test this out he became a monk who practiced extreme asceticism which left him as nothing but skin and bones. In his thorough self-examination during this process he discovered that the real cause of his suffering in trying to reach the absolute Soul was none other than a power that he thought he possessed. Near death, anguished by evil thoughts and delusional dreams of dancing girls and marching armies; or being besieged by Mara, the Devil-King who tempted him with all sorts of greedy and pleasurable evils. He reached a point in which he realized the absolute and immutable Soul was nothing but a delusion, since he could not seek an absolute self without the living body of his organic self.

He was doing nothing more than providing fuel for tormenting himself that was raging as a fire within him. Alone and tortured by his own thoughts, he discovered that the problem was coming from his own self, his own self-inflicted mind, the very one that was the cause; and, creating evil as it divided his body apart from the concept he clung to as Atman, the impervious Supreme Being. His ego-sophistication most certainly had led him in this direction. This is the natural course for all persons entering a religious life, for they mistakenly assume that their self-power ego can overcome all they see bad in themselves and to better themselves they attempt to live the life of two separate attributes: the mind that he clung to as absolute; and the other, that of his relative mind or self that he thought was the one that he had to extinguish. But it was his relative self or mind that created his concept of the absolute self to begin with. So it was all a matter of a conceptualized understanding based on an objectified understanding. One's spiritual life cannot flourish or be fulfilled on this basis.

He had thought that by practicing extreme dietary controls along with difficult yoga practices he could rid himself of his relative mind by relinquishing the needs and desires of the flesh to the barest minimum so that he could get total control over his mind and body and thus experience Enlightenment. But in actuality he was preventing his enlightenment by way of creating a fixed position for himself. Atman was seen as Holy, that is, free from all defilements. He must first get control of the body, as the body is filled with defilements, thus his ascetic practices. In conjunction with this he must gain control of the mind, thus his complicated and severe yoga practices. All mendicants were engaged in these yoga practices. The teaching he got corresponded with Hindu texts. So altogether he was on the right path towards assuming the absolute goal of Atman, the Godhead and the apex of the Brahman ideal.

But what happened? Was it his self-efforts which failed him? Were his practices imperfect? How extreme and pure need he be? No doubt these were the things that occupied his mind during the first six steps that led up to the final seventh step of his religious experience. In the final stage he simply got up from his seat of meditation and introspection, and outside of himself saw how impossible it was as he was totally incapable any of his ascetic and religious practices as they had left him with nothing more than delusions of mind that corrupted his mind and left his body totally deficient as skin and bones. He examined himself very carefully on that seventh step, and came to the conclusion that the path that he was following was completely wrong. Realizing it finally that he had become the very evil one, left him with nothing but the sense of futility. An iron wall existed that with his self-power efforts he could not break through.

Beset by his self-torture, both body and mind unable to go any further – he let out a shout, "Oh Avidia", "Oh Darkness" (absolute negation. In this very darkness he realized the devil himself, arose within his noble self as the very flame of his life. He emerged from the very bottom of the abyss with his birth-shout of total independence and freedom (absolute affirmation). His birth-shout appears as his enlightenment.

In the solemnest of this moment he attained infinite light and life. This is the cool flame within his mind that came after the flames of struggles within the abyss, the flames that burned up his useless self. He transcended Brahmanism along with all its Gods, to become this independent person as an <u>Anatman</u>; opposite that of Atman, as the Ordinary person. He returned as a Bodhisattva, which is a uniquely unusual return.

The God and/or gods that he transcended are located in the first two lines of his shout as recorded by his biographers, as there are many such Gods or demigods in Hindu mythology. In throwing off such Gods he realized his total independence from such Gods and all such religious practices attaining to them.

He arose from his place as a totally free person, indeed, not as a special person, but as a person who is free to go his own way. As he climbed down the mountain where all the other mendicant monks were engaged in ascetic practices, he was shouted down by them as being a "back slider" who had failed to attain the Brahman ideal of Hinduism. That was okay by him, for he knew what the living truth was within him.

He bathed himself in the river and went down into the village as he thirsted for a drink. He came by a water well where he met a milk maid who gave him a cup of milk yogurt. Now refreshed, his face became as bright as his body and his mind responded with such joy. Now he discovers the pure white soul, the flame within him which he called noble – this coolly burning flame of his awakening.

How noble is the Buddha, how virtuous is his being, the sutra opens with. To remove our afflictions, quench our thirst for the truth by burning up our greedy desires and evils and by opening the final gate to our ultimate freedom.

I am inspired by this story of how this person left his domestic life and ascendance to the throne of the Shakya clan to become such an ordinary person who taught the infinite life to all his listeners as the Buddha-Dharma; as it is today and as it was in the past for untold numbers of people. The <u>Larger Sutra</u> comes from here, where we come across Dharmakara, as well as bowing before the infinite light (the Tathagata), and life (organic subjectivity), and the true meaning of compassion.

So the real question here is how the Pure Land is viewed in the eyes of one's practice as to how it will be interpreted. The simplistic way of viewing it will be that of a convenience for the one who has no real interest in the Pure Land other than what he or she can get out of it in terms landing in the heaven called: "The Pure Land", or upon uttering the nembutsu so many times in order to practice worthiness. This was not Shinran's way. Shinran never thought of the second gate, the religious gate, as a semblance of true religion in any case, but a provisional stage for the final gate of self-realization and emancipation. If the Pure Land is a place we physically go to after death, our understanding is primative. Shinran stated: "If good people go to the Pure Land after they die, how much more, I, Shinran." Pure Land Buddhism was not established on the basis for the worship of external entities. Seeking another life after death and calling it the Pure Land is one of those entities leading to practices which have nothing to do with true religion.

It is the awakening to the fact that "I alone am a devil", which immediately opens the Gateless Gate of awareness. The devil cannot stay as a devil, he must move on. On the other hand, the person who considers himself as a good person must inevitably become a bad person. The bad person is a devil, indeed, that's how the devil came into being in the first place! The devil came to start out as a good person, but the good person discovered that he was not as good as he originally thought he was. Trying to maintain his "goodness" he attempts to get rid of his "badness", i.e., his bad qualities that every so often keep cropping up. It is here where he became bad, insofar as his trying to control the badness in himself. Only by awakening to the truth of his trying to control his self that in itself is evil did he realize that his whole self was a nothing but a chunk of evil.

Awakening to the fact that his whole self is bad, he settled down to the self-recognition of living in the freedom of ignorance of the bad and the good. So often it is a matter of karmic circumstances and conditions that makes do what we do. We get caught by external circumstances and based on this we can make bad decisions. So it is not so much that we make a decision to be bad. Because of all these conditions we really don't know what is good or bad, thus we settle down with a sigh, and say: "I don't know". This "I don't know" is an honest confession of our ignorance, and it is here, within ignorance itself that we experience the freedom of ignorance! But since ignorance is a form of blindness we must have our eyes opened. The one whose eyes are opened does not know what is good or bad as in the form of discrimination.

"I am a devil", is a confession that I acknowledge the wisdom of not knowing what is good about me. In other words I have no way of judging the qualities in which the good and bad play with each other. That is to say, the discriminatory standards upon which judgments take place have been removed, and, because of the most sincere confession I am released from it. Released, means emptiness, and in this emptiness freedom comes in as the tathagata that changes my whole direction from being attached to good and bad, onto virtual non-attachment; that is, freedom away from the relatively fixed – bad, good – impurity, purity – ignorance, enlightenment, and all that are considered as set goals in a subject and object relationship that is fixed.

This must be surprising to those who are stuck on accumulating a store of good merits as above, thinking of themselves as worthy of going to the Pure Land upon one's death. There are many sincere believers who follow such traditional teachings as this, and unfortunately there are others who think they are already there, so they can just sit back idly not needing to introspect themselves carefully. After all, Amida Buudha will protect them and embrace them so why bother, being satisfied with this understanding considering themselves as good Buddhists, or religious people, they can just lie back under the fruit tree and let the fruit fall into their mouth! Merit transference from Amida Buddha to them is a sure thing! Just stick to the well-traveled formula is their thinking. Seeing this, Shinran exclaimed: "Even if good people attain the Pure Land upon death, how much more, I, Shinran." Having transcended religious practices based on self-improvement, he made this unique statement.

How can freedom exist within ignorance? Ignorance itself is darkness. We see it everywhere played out on the world stage. But wait, our time will come when we are presented with our own ignorance. For we ourselves are ignorant of the very thing we accuse others with. We are guilty of our own misdeeds, but so often, blame others. The truth is that we can be guilty of the very thing we criticize others of. Sensei told the story of a woman in Japan, who upon seeing that her neighbor had holes in her shoji screen widow, and was critical of her for having such holes. But she was looking at her neighbor through the holes in her own shoji screen!

Leaving everything up to eternal life is the only thing we can do as human beings; not out of a sense of weakness, or surrender, but out of the awareness that comes with the realization that I am incurably a devil. What good can the devil accomplish, nothing but bad comes out of the relative self that tries to control life. Infinite life is what supports us all, embraces us all, both the good and the bad – and even further, includes our stupidity over what is good or bad, which includes our ignorance of it. We are so inadequate in our secularized way of judgment that it is incredible, especially when we get into the question of ignorance of which we are indelibly guilty. So there is no solution. But there is a reason beyond reason that if we touch upon it, wipes away all these discussions, leaving me bare with an empty mind. It is the relative self that divides things into good and bad and all other set entities that form the criteria for our judgments.

We ourselves are the product of an incredible numbers of karma (cause and effect circumstances) starting from our very birth itself, our entry into the world itself – which is continuously changing – and we are to judge what the ultimate truth is? It is therefore laughable for someone to say that he has grasp on the truth that allows him the power to judge between good and bad. All such terms are merely relative to one another, and there is nothing that is immutably solid and unchanging here. Therefore, from here we are forced to rely on a power beyond the self – the infinite life which cannot be divided into parts and pieces. It is our thinking that discriminates, not the unknowable life itself.

God, as in an absolute entity, exists as the One, and we humans exist as the many. But we humans are not able to be the absolute One (aside from the many), therefore we are not able to become God, and so we are not included in the One. But Amida Buddha does not fit this picture because Amida Buddha is not a God. Therefore, there is no need to prey to an external entity. As such, it is a representative of what we must become. Also, there is no need to chant or verbalize its name in the hopes of obtaining special merits or favors thereby, or thinking that we will be saved, for we are already saved even before we embark on this negative fear of survival of not being saved.

Incomprehensible life created this universe and all things in it; indeed untold billions upon billions of beings are being created and are perishing at this very moment, all within the flux and movement of the universe itself as one.

There is no "I" as independent from all others who are also independent. From here, the "I" consists of many as infinite as the "Sands of the Ganges River", a number which cannot be counted. As such, it is transforming itself into the life of others and at the same time is within itself, independent. Absolute negation of self is birth of a fresh self. That means that "I" is giving back to it; transforming in a movement from negation to affirmation and affirmation to negation, as a process of continuous change foreword. This subtle self within the organic body is in the soul of the world and is within the light of the One Soul of the world.

Let's say that we were created like little devils. Then leaving us as cute little devils, what is next, our freedom of "devil-ship"? But being free, then why should I create evil? In freedom it is not necessary to involve with evil since I have no need as it complicates and disturbs my life. I don't want to become a saintly person either, for if I am a saintly person thinking of myself as something special then I will quickly turn into a devil as a way to relieve the boredom of saintliness! That's the dialectic between good and evil. However, it is we ourselves who unknowingly create good or bad according to our karmic actions, not like when we were first born as perfectly naked and free from "sin". What is "sinful"? In Buddhism there is no such a word, except in the case wherein we don't live in *mujo* , Japanese for continuous change, or when we don't fulfill our life which has to do with self-realization, i. e., an awakened person.

We are at times like a dog that clings to its bone, as we humans cling to our attachments. Sometimes we get all excited about our attachments and accomplishments and can't wait to show them off to others. Sometimes we like to show off our accomplishments because we are so attached to ourselves, and happy with ourselves. However, we don't like to show off our weaknesses; rather, we try to cover them up and hide them. For that will show to others that we are vulnerable. Aren't we like cute little devils? Thus we live as relative beings, bounded as to our relative thoughts as to our successes but hiding our failures. This is the cute evil devil that we are. We get jealous and envious when someone appears better than we are except when we are perceptive. When we begin to recognize that, after all, we are just ordinary foolish people and we no longer care to fight with others for supremacy, so we just leave it alone. This is the freedom of the foolish ordinary person. This freedom leaves us open to the world-wide view of humanity. The world is upset with so many problems. These are caused by all sorts of little devils that are fighting with each other despite a landscape of peace. Unmindful of their beautiful and peaceful surroundings, they continue to fight and argue over who is the best and most beautiful of devils – it's called the beauty contest! But all it breads is ugliness. That's okay too, because we get tired of all this "beauty" and want to see some ugliness and violence from those who fight over who are the most beautiful. What a stage that is set showing humanity playing the role of "I am the most beautiful". From our politics,sports, and the culture we live in, from the entertainment on T. V., to the violence for the sake of violence in the secular culture of downright ugly violence; it is for the sake of some action in one's lethargic state of boredom and stasis.

So God is this huge Devil that created this landscape composed of little devils in the survival of the fittest contest of life here on earth! A one way only, or a one sided lifestyle, would be too boring! It would never work for another reason, as it would never lead us to an understanding of what we are as a devil disguised as a nice person, only to discover he himself as a devil.

This is Dharmakara's experience as well, as Lokesvararaja explains in detail of the good and evil natures of those heavenly and human beings living in the two hundred and ten *kotis* of Buddha lands. His glorious land will reflect this, whereby through the accomplishment in all of his 48 Vows, he will include all the good and evil natures of man to establish his Land of Bliss, or Nirvana.

As the Pure Land is born with the awakening of: "I alone, am the most evil one", so too, is the mind emptied of all defilements by listening to the true Dharma. Here, just by listening with all sincerity, I can feel the Land of Peace and Bliss. As such I can transcend the dharmas of the world which is composed of the relative good and bad, and realize the non-arising of these dharmas, or worldly wisdoms. Even if these dharmas should arise, they can be swept away by the power of the light within us as cloudy mists without any real substance or reality; belonging to the realms of illusion and delusion, or appearing as secular knowledge's. The power of the Dharma is Amida's light and life that penetrates the cloudy mists of the attached mind and reveals the self just as specks of dirt are revealed, thereby showing us the dirt that somehow we could feel but not clearly see if it were not but for Amida's light within us. These specks of dirt represent the various aspects of our ignorance, which are multitudinous in their karmic relationships. The more we listen, the more dirt we see. Finally we self-recognize our foolishness and stupidity. I can no longer self-affirm that I am a good person, as represented by these particles of dirt that need to be washed away. It's like taking a shower to wash away all the dirt that has accumulated on the body in order to feel clean again. So here any idea of feeling the purity of the body can be applied to the mind. Throw away the dirt stuck in the mind.

I may have thought that I was a good person, and in these ways was self-affirmative. The self needs to be satisfied with it, otherwise it can be uncomfortable. The self needs to accomplish certain victories in order to be self-assured, and thus happy with it. I think that this is a normal process by which we accomplish what it is that we wish to do with our lives. If we are successful we will be happy and to that extent self-affirmative. We have no reason not to be. But there comes a problem even if we are successful, and especially if we fail, of not looking deep enough to find out who we really are in all these excursions into the self. We seem to be dealing with the surface side of our life, i.e., the surface and relative side of our nature. Even in religion the same can be said. If we are so fortunate, we will come across the true Dharma that will awaken our aspiration for something deeper that heretofore existed as a seed that never sprouted and thus lay dormant, or the bud that never opened.

But listening to the Dharma is no easy thing. It challenges our perception of who we think we are. It challenges our understanding of how we think of religious ideas. It challenges one's understanding of Amida Buddha as a kind of demi-god to bestow on us his blessing. Who we are is not as important as to what we are once we listen to the Teaching. For the Dharma will not pat us on the back and tell us how good we are, or confirm our ego, or promise us heaven if we become believers. Rather, it will crush our sense of worthiness, a conceited notion of my being important and good.

The Teaching then, is like a sword that enlightens us. Indeed, my teacher, with a smile on his face, once commented that we were little devils but he was this huge devil! I remember how at least this one time I thought of him as this huge devil as every once and a while he had to reprimand me that felt like a pound on the head. Now that I look back, how fortunate I was to meet such a person, who was such a good friend. Ha, we even joked about it much later – all those bumps on the head that I received long ago. When I showed him a picture of Bodhidharma with that enlarged bump on the head, he said, "That looks like all the bumps I gave you!", and we both laughed!

While the Dharma gives us the doctrinal texts in the form of sutras taken from verbal transmissions given by Shakyamuni to his disciples, it is the historical teachers who interpret these Teachings for us that enable us to understand them subjectively, that is, how they apply to our lives. To do that a teacher is necessary to explain their meanings. But in order to do that the teacher himself has to be a student, not only of the sutra that is under discussion, but someone who examines it within his own life. This requires a great deal of self-examination in a lifetime of study and experience to be able to interpret and translate its meaning. In the process, the teacher becomes a true student, a member of the sangha who listens carefully to what the Buddha says regarding our life as humans, in terms that for us is difficult for us by ourselves to understand and properly interpret. In Buddhism especially, these words have to be translated into our common language specifically so that we can understand their meanings. In this case, so much depends on the teacher that the teacher himself becomes the Dharma. We then get a living person who manifests the texts for us and gives us by way of his own being that which allows us to feel for that which appears basically objective in nature. For instance, sutras focus on the doctrinal teachings, and let us provide the feeling by transferring objectivity into subjectivity.

The Dharma functions to challenge our understanding and the conceited notion of who we are as individuals. To really show us how evil we are, including his care for us, he in the end had to become like the Devil. Or, as Sensei once stated: "I cannot be frank with you people." Meaning we may not come back! His concern in this statement demonstrates his real compassion for us. That's why, as Shinran stated: "We have to grind our bones into powder and flesh into pieces to hear the Dharma". "How difficult it is to be a true human being", my teacher repeated on various occasions. He showed us very well how to be human being. Despite or because of it, he had to be the person whose job it was to awaken us. He had no intention to control us, but rather, to awaken in us our deepest aspiration towards being the best students.

We can call it the Buddha's compassion. But one mustn't take this expression lightly, for compassion can be a double-edged sword. Real compassion will kill us; it will crush our hardened shell, and our isolation from others, and give us a new life. True compassion is when I die to the self. So real compassion will bring us new life with joyous rebirth.

In Buddhism the truth has already been established long, long ago. Once we touch upon this truth through the total understanding of Amida Buddha's deepest wish for all human beings, then from this comes the truth as it freshly pops-up. Actional intuition works by direct intuition. It comes into being as the spirit pushes me forward, and this spirit manifests itself intuitively.

I am beckoned by this intuition as with the spirit like that of a lion. The lion is most happy when he comes up with fresh insights. The Dharma is a living, moving force, not stale or dead. Going his own way he finds the infinite variety of life and the wondrousness of the natural landscape to inspire him. The work is difficult, but herein he tastes the world of creation, and through dedication to it is well-rewarded.

* * *

Among the 6 Vows that Shinran also selected out of the 48 Vows is the **12th** and **13th**, that are important since they describe the attributes and meaning of Amida Buddha. I've abbreviated them so that they can be more readily understood.
  12. If my light should be finite, may I not attain Buddhahood.
  13. If my life should be finite, may I not attain Buddhahood.
Amida Buddha has been described as having two main attributes; that is, infinite light, and infinite life, as above. Along with the fact that he has been described as the "Bowing Buddha", Dharmakara (Jap: Hozo) acquires the name of Immeasurable Light and Life, or, "Amida". Herein, the "Bowing Buddha" now becomes Amida Buddha.

We cannot think of Amida's light as a special entity outside of ourselves. It comes from our deepest aspiration to live the life of Dharmakara and to realize his life and effort within one's own total effort. Here then, is where we share the light of Dharmakara and Amida Buddha as one and the same within our own life.

Transcendental wisdom is the light. The subjective realization of the light is the life within that comes up as a shout. The birth shout of Shakyamuni the Buddha is where his emancipation and release from the depths of darkness was to come with a shout:
  "Above the heavens, and below the heavens, alone, I am most noble."
Stripped of all gods and religion and left alone, only his pure clean spirit was noble.

Self-recognition in the land of Nirvana now turns into abiding in the land of samsara. He leaves the Pure Land and selflessly enters the world of suffering with the compassion of being a Bodhisattva, as an Ordinary person to give life to all those who are as dead. He playfully travels while enlightening all others using expedient means, following the virtues of The Way. This is the essence of the **22cnd** vow.

We can feel Dharmakara's realization of The Larger Sutra, as the most cherished of all the sutras, a real treasure of spiritual literature that goes directly to our heart/mind as it holds within its phrases the most important teaching that we can come across. The focal point of Amida Buddha and Buddhism itself is contained within its chapters. For in its essence it has taught untold numbers of people how to be true human beings. How grateful I am to have been exposed to it for this reason, among so many others that have been brought to life because of it. Therefore I shall go further to answer the call of, "Come to me.", as beckoned by the shining light of this sutra.

"The Cosmos" Oil painting 36" x 40" R. Adams

MIND OF THE PURE, CLEAN TRUTH　　　　　　　　Reverend Haya Akegarasu

    To clean and purify the body is to wash away the dirt from it. When we wash away material that has accumulated from the outside and has been produced from the inside, then we feel that the body has become beautiful and clean. Saliva or feces or urine or sweat or body oils, after being excreted or secreted from the body, become dirty. When something adheres to the body which does not circulate like blood in our own life, then we feel that it is dirt. Therefore, to have a beautifully pure, clean body we have to wash away all dirt, whether it has come from the outside or inside, and be a naked body as such, without having anything attached.

    With regard to the mind, what is dirt? All thoughts and feelings produced by the mind become dirt after they have been produced. The mind that remains attached to these external things is dirty. Wash out, wash away all this dirt. The naked mind, mind as such, is the most clean, pure, beautiful mind. It doesn't cover itself with ornaments or patches. This mind as such is the truth and is clean and pure. This is what we call the true mind or pure mind or the single mind or the real mind. This mind, not covered with ornaments and patches, is the strongest thing in the world. This true mind, naked as such, is the most beautiful thing in the world.

    "The honest mind is the Pure Land." This is it.

"PURE LAND"　　　　　　　　　　　　　　　　Oil Painting 58"x 38" R. Adams

Living the Life of Shakyamuni

1/5/2013
R. Adams

    The Buddha is never a finished product. If he is a finished product then he mine as well be considered as a frozen statue. No, he was as we are a human being, as living flesh and blood. As such, he was always learning and studying, for that was part of his brightness and why his teachings are so transforming for us as humans. I, as well as all others, upon hearing the true Dharma, travel basically the same path he did so long as we devote our whole body and mind in searching for the truth. Indeed, this learning process is going on right now as the doctrines he put forth are being transformed and transforming me, thinking of the buddha's I've met, studied from, and continue to listen to – all enter my life as flesh and blood living beings. Even if I should consider the writings of my predecessors or contemporaries as "droppings" of the past, or even errors and evils of the past, they can be useful as fertilizer for the fresh life that springs forth as living material for the present. That which is living produces life. That which is negative becomes fertilizer for the present as we can see how important they can be in giving us a fresh insight for the present understanding going forward. So altogether, past, present, and future, becomes at One in this very moment-to-moment life that I am living. This tathagata, or continuous change, allows for the movement of all things. Not being attached to names and forms is important because I am not bounded by them.

    Not clinging means non-attachment, and that means not stubbornly attaching oneself to one's own judgments and understandings no matter how good or evil they seem to be. That which comes upon us will in turn disappear by the same tathagata which moves life. For the movement of the tathagata creates suffering or happiness according how we live and/or how we think. This can be directly affected by the secular world, which in and of itself produces the suffering within the attached self that is not in accord with the ever-changing nature of existence. We suffer because we are going against the movement of life, indeed, the very blood that is flowing within our bodies at this time. So, as result of our fixed mind as it is not moving, we get stuck in a pattern whereby we feel the friction, agitation, and fear that comes from our own secularized view of life based on the self. The Buddha taught emancipation through the flow of eternal life. Emancipation means freedom from self.

    Shakyamuni discovered the causes, conditions, and reasons for his own suffering and difficulties. His ascetic religious practices were due to his artificially induced projection of himself to become a perfect version of him – a religious person following the tradition of the Hindu religion. Following this tradition he would have to be that of a mendicant monk which included studying religious texts, esoteric yoga practices, as well as living on the smallest possible diet in order to control his emotions and/or wayward mind to better control the arising of evil thoughts. He would also have to abandon the world, live in isolation from it and seek a place where others also practiced in isolation from the world. These were the earliest monasteries usually placed in mountainous areas far from worldly traffic.

    The intention here was to become an <u>Atman</u> the closest thing to becoming God or Godlike as is humanly possibly in order not to suffer from the passions of the defiled world that he had left when he abandoned family and palace along with the princely thrown where he was heir apparent in a principality of far northern India. So he was already a high class Brahmin. Now he would have to complete the course and validate his ascendency to the highest level of religious perfection in order to attain absolute Selfhood, the essence of which was the pure soul. The other issue was a human one: a question of, "Who am I?" But first he would have to cleanse himself of all impurities in order to accomplish his main goal. Down to mere skin and bones in the attempt to control his mind he only increased the suffering manifold by having delusions, including dreams of dancing girls and marching armies (he came from a warring clan), the result of his self-power attempts to realize for himself the most perfect and ideal state of Atman, the absolute Soul or Godhead. He failed when he realized finally that it was all in vain. Abruptly he shouted: "Oh Avidia!" or "Oh Darkness!" If the first six steps were devoted to rigorous self-examination, the seventh step came in the form of a transformed person of total freedom and independence with his birth shout: "Below the heavens, and above all the earth, alone, I am noble!" He arose from this place never to return.

    The crucial point that Shakyamuni realized upon his enlightenment was that his religious self-power attempts to cleanse himself of all evils were futile and ended up in failure. Indeed, the more of his self-power he put into his endeavor, the more evil attended them, until it became quite impossible. How was he to get out of this dilemma as he reached a total iron wall in his efforts? Isolated, cold and hungry, he must have reached a point wherein even his body revolted. Meanwhile nothing in him had essentially changed as his mind was concerned; it remained the same as when he first began his practices. Yet the more he went on seeking the wisdom within the Hindu ideal of Godlike perfection; the goal which was to reach the absolute self-identity of permanent Selfhood, unchallenged by the relative world that contained its sufferings; the more he must have anguished over his inability to master its presumed goal, and to penetrate into its assumed infinity. Only God is omnipotent, both creator and destroyer of the universe and all its inhabitants. The Gods of this religion are manifold, he must attain them all, worship them all, a huge task, indeed. But here was his mistake: As God (Atman) was beyond his power to achieve he realized that he had unknowingly created a gap between himself and the absolute identity that he wanted to become. Thus the closer that he had become to the absolute the farther he was away from it. If there remained even the smallest separation then it became magnified proportionately in the opposite direction – how impossible! He introspected that the cause of this problem lay hidden in the fact that essentially he was dealing with the duality between subject and object; and further, that all of his religious practices began with the false assumption that God(s) existed as entities outside of himself as conceived objectively to be worshipped as such and attained. This basic ignorance, though religious in purpose, had nothing to do with the moving spirit within his being that was forcibly being covered over by religious practices. This in and of itself was a mistake that he was perpetuating that he could not realize until the very end. In other words, all the various practices that he was doing for the past six years were themselves distortions based on the original delusion that an entity he had to attain consisted of a dualistic relationship that existed outside of him. The question of "Who am I?"

was answered by a power that he never knew existed, and that was the power beyond self. It was true – he now could feel as a human being who could taste the infinite within himself – he could be himself as such without pursuing anything outside of himself. The whole contents of life itself existed within him and he could feel it as his brightness! Now this was his real spirit that he could express. How enlightening! Not trying to be a religious person, nor attempting to be a saint, he felt the reality of truth existing in the world itself as he must live in it, even as he transcended it. This was the very opposite of what he had previously tried to escape from and deny. What a shout must have come up when he made this discovery.

It is beyond that of a human being, being mortal and of flesh and blood. The mind itself could not be controlled absolutely, and as it was beyond his self-power the whole edifice of self-power collapsed. He was left alone. Six years (or six steps) of this produced nothing of a transformation and so, after his desperation in experiencing what amounted to ignorance, the very paradox occurred within his confession of darkness, leading him into the light of emancipation. The seventh step resulted in the deepest introspection as appears in his birth shout (as above) leading to the open or gateless gate that he passed through with the expression of total freedom and independence. The true essence of religion comes from here.

He was no longer a so-called "split person", being on one hand, a man of the world (secular defilement), and on the other, a religious person (moral piety). The self that he clung to existed as an entity in itself; a thing most difficult to perceive as separate from the totality of him. The static self that he thought of as absolute became in itself an entity aside from himself which was in effect, dualistic and separate from his real self. Thus, oneness could only come from discarding the static self. Actually, it was the static self that created this dual or dichotomized himself. As one mind he no longer needed religious practices nor get involved with worldly affairs in trying to improve them, but just letting them stand as they are. Nor was he other-worldly, considering another life after this one. He was coming from the fact that when he was born the world was born, and when he died the world will die with him. Living his life to the fullest he knew that when it came to death it comes as a full stop, not to be followed by another one after death for the lack of fulfillment in the present life. Thus he had the lack of fear, whether or not that he was sufficiently prepared for the next one. One's body is not like a temporal shell that contains a soul, as this is a static concept thought up by those who separate the body from the soul hoping to be with a Supreme Being in everlasting heaven. Buddha focused his life in the present, bravely, not thinking of himself as living in some illusion-based human desire to continue on with our life forever! "We are born, we must work, and we will die." Rev. Akegarasu answers this question flatly and emphatically with no addition. Abruptly put, there are no flowery ideas of what our life should look like.

As for God, it is a name put on the concept of a "Prime Creator". People have need for a name that helps to describe the absolute creator who created the universe that people believe in. Lacking as they are in goodness; seeing ourselves as the fallen one's, filled with the sins and defilements that they themselves have created gives them hope and support. Out of one's weakness and fallibility they seek a God along with a religion that describes our identity and relationship with one who has absolute power over life. By believing in him we can seek his blessing. By doing so, and by obeying his precepts and commands, we can thereby be saved. Thus we have created a channel, a religious one that on one hand exposes our vulnerability, and on the other, clings to a name and permanent entity that gives them a sense of power. But it is all external; belonging to the other-world, but not of the living world in reality.

There is a moral attachment here however, as the weakness and defilement that we fall victim to must fall under the control of a supreme power that can then punish us if we disobey his commandments. This has a controlling effect on human behavior. These moral restrictions furnish some good, for it makes everyone accountable for his or her behavior. It makes us want to be good people, as we are being watched over by a Supreme Being who gives us the support we need if we are good people. But actually, do I need to be watched over by an entity outside of myself? I'm fully responsible of watching into myself.

Shakyamuni never spoke of a God or life after death. But he did speak voluminously on the Dharma that comprises the <u>Sutta Napata</u>, which contains some thirty five sutras regarding questions as to doctrinal matters, now with a commentary by Shuichi Maida (trans: by N. Haneda). In these sutras he describes the person of transcendental wisdom in the midst of the secular people of the world. Transcendental wisdom is the key that opens us to the way.

He was the greatest and most humble student. His humility was shown in the very clothes that he wore, no more than discarded rags taken from cremation sites in which he would then wash clean and sew together to form a cloak. Or in summer he wore a bib as he went his way seeing people and carrying a begging bowl as was the tradition among mendicant monks. This shows us the empty-handed purity of mind that he had. Stripped of all artificial ornamentation, he was such a free naked person. Indeed, that was his teaching to us people who crave worldly goods. Not only of worldly goods, but of the titles we wear as well.

For this he was loved by some and disliked by others who criticized and looked down on him as nothing but a beggar. Why didn't he work for a living just like them? But for those who knew him there was a respect for someone who transcended the world and didn't care about fashion and what cloths he wore, but rather saw him as this shining figure, an ordinary person bravely standing tall with a smiling disposition that welcomed everyone.

Shakyamuni's birth shout begins with: "In the heavens and above the earth"... which refers to all the Gods, that in his birth shout he transcended. This is followed by: "I alone, most noble." The light from within is the one that is most noble, and since he embodies it, "I" is used. The use of, "I, alone".... is his shout of total independence. After a long time his biographers gave much attention to the Buddha's shout as they came up with this expression. Though worded as such, this was his inevitable shout upon awakening to his noble being.

Before, when we were just born, we expressed such shouts as, Ah! and Waa! then later we learned the use of words. If we go back to Helen Keller's experience when she was a young child then we can use it as an example. If you remember, she was born both blind and deaf. Very unruly, her parents had a difficult time with her. Just keeping her quiet was a big job. If she had a means of expressing herself through words then maybe she would quiet down. So they decided to hire a teacher/baby sitter to keep her under control and to accomplish the impossible task of teaching her English. Some time went by but it was no use. Helen threw tantrums and was increasingly difficult to handle. Reaching the breaking point her teacher decided to become nothing less than that of a Devil, a huge Devil, and put up with her wild behavior no more. So every time that Helen got out of hand her teacher would immediately correct her and force her to clean up her mess. It got so bad that even her parents wanted to fire the teacher, thinking that she lacked compassion and was being too severe on their daughter. But finally it came to a point where it was either do or die. She simply could not pronounce a single word in English. All methods of teaching her failed. But then out of her intuition, her teacher came up with an idea. She would take Helen out into the garden where there was a well that had water. She would have Helen lift up a bucket of water in a wooden bucket and stick her hands in it and describe what it was that she felt. Then as she tread the water with her hands she suddenly shouted, "W-a-t-e-r!" A success! How difficult it must have been! Comparing ourselves with her it is even more difficult for us to come up with living words, for we simply take words for granted, and so we can go on with the rest of our life using words that function as abstractions in a two- dimensional context with no real life to them. Like so much roundabout and chit-chat conversations we have with each other. Many of these are typical examples that switch us over into scholars to become as observers to life, who so often use words as explanations that express a surface life that appears two-dimensional, flat, and dry, thus having no power to spark our attention and move us. They are in fact, lifeless words. In that sense it is very easy to see how they (religious scholars) can think that words come before life. This is the mark of the scholar, such a one who thinks he is religious but never is really jumping into the depths of the water of life as helen Keller did – a true nembutsu which manifests the true spirit of religion itself.

    Here we can gather the teaching of an organic and subjective understanding which opens-up as life itself. Furthermore, it is this understanding which makes us human, and which involves our spirituality in its fullest extent. True religion is not based on abstractions that form the basis for words, but on the shout coming from one's subjective self. Religious scholars who do not understand this are more or less confined within the boundaries of secularized education that is primarily focused on all the relative dualities that education teaches, primarily the differences between subject and object. As this is what we are taught it is natural that this secularized methodology will enter our thinking when it comes to religion as well. We are essentially blind to see this. In terms of negative verses positive, we like to seek everything that is positive. In terms of discrimination, we seek the good over the bad, and discriminate according to a set of concepts that give us a fixed format and mental outlook and the criteria upon which to judge things. It all comes with words set in two-dimensional linear combinations. It lacks the time dimension that living words have such as in "W-a-t-e-r" that Helen Keller experienced.

Concepts are only concepts; they explain what humans do in the world of abstractions, ideas, names, and forms. In the purely secular context all these words are adequate for the use we put to them. But it is very different when we approach religion. In religion we are seeking a spiritual basis for our life that goes beyond the secular world. For this to occur we must find a teaching that focuses on the spiritual side of our life that education does not give us. For instance, we leave the school system, even after college, without any real idea of who we are. Here we are experiencing a total shortfall. Is it no wonder that we wander around to and fro not really knowing where we are going? It is like we are in this huge crowded casino betting that we can make it. Here we find dancing girls wildly dancing on platforms, slot machines and card tables where people are seeking their fortunes; all sorts of people jumping up and down to the kind of boom–boom music that is supposed to encourage you to put more money on the table! Profit and loss! Is this where our educational system ends up as? Or, maybe it's a reaction against the system that answers our secular side but leaves the spiritual side completely vacant. Come to think of it, isn't it a kind of wild rebelliousness against that which seeks to stymie our freedom, but gives us an outlet to be greedy with the pleasures of winning false money and sensuous pleasures? We live vacant lives until we get out of the system that puts us in a box of secular imprisonment. Gambling is one way to get out of the "box" and feel some excitement to our lives. So much of human society is distorted this way. Whereas, to be truly happy and content with what we have and who we are is the most important thing to us as humans. Upon enlightenment, Shakyamuni lived in the simplicity of the ordinary person, not considering himself as special. So to that extent he became a Anatman, the opposite of Atman, the holy personna that he was seeking earlier.

From here we can see the importance of coming up with our very own language, the language that expresses my life and your life; not that of the other, but an expression of one's very own life. Here the words are no longer mere abstractions that we learned in school but living words that move us and move others too. Words coming from the heart, from one's own experience; crisp words, words that feel like a shout, words that are solemn, words of joy, and sincere words that change our life. Don't listen to the dogmatists who insist that their religion is the best and only one, thinking that their truth is superior to all the others. Abandon the religion that insists that only they have the truth of the highest authority – for it's not the fresh truth that is alive. This is the very thing that Shakyamuni abandoned when he got up and left the meditation seat under the Bhodhi tree, and came down from the mountains and into the village where he was welcomed back into the world by a milkmaid who gave him a cup of milk yogurt. Refreshed, the world came alive!

Originally, when Prince Siddartha ventured out of the Palace walls where he had a wife and two children, he could easily see for himself what the world was like. What it came down to was old age, sickness, and death. While his world was protected, the outside world was struggling with ignorance and difficulty. But alongside this he met an old man who with shining face and bright eyes who stood out among the others as a wise and free person.

Wanting to become like such a one he took teaching from him and upon listening decided to give up the world, which also meant that he would have to give up his domestic and princely kingdom in the process. He had everything that a young prince could want, a beautiful horse, a wonderful wife and kids, Lord of the estate, and so on. But with all of that he was still dissatisfied. Something was egging him on, beckoning and calling him to seek beyond worldly pleasures, comfort, and security, and into a world that the old man as his teacher embodied. He wanted this power and freedom for himself, a kind of self-power motivation that all young people are seeking to have for themselves when they want to establish their own self-identity kingdom. Therefore, he vacated the palace where he lived and sought into isolation from the world, in order to attain the most perfected identity with the absolute Soul or Atman. All the religious practices that he went through to attain this goal led him ultimately into such darkness as he was led into an iron wall of the impossible.

Jesus Christ too, identified himself with God. His mother, Mary, told Joseph that he was the son of God, sent by God as the Messiah to explain why her virgin birth. In the four years of the Bible on Christ's life it came to a point with Christ's enlightenment on the cross with his pleading: "Eliot, Eliot, Sabatini?", "God, God, where art thou?" In the darkest hours of his agony God was nowhere to be found. Alone and abandoned as he was cast into hell, said: "Forgive them Lord for they know not what they do." And as one of his last shouts: "I thirst!" which has been interpreted as his thirst for humanity. Here he was no longer a savior, but a pitiful human being accused of thinking that he was the king of the Jews, or for thinking that his kingdom was not of this world. It was the priests who killed him. He threatened their authority. He came into this world bearing a sword with which he cleaned-up the world with his teachings. But it is because of his crucifixion that he and his teachings live in our hearts.

That which goes beyond our knowledge or understanding – the great unknowable, inconceivable power beyond the power of man is working here. The power that supports us and gives us life is also the power that transforms us and negates our beliefs. Here we cannot hold on to even one of our most cherished beliefs. Once this power enters our life we needn't discuss, dispute, argue, nor think that such a thing exists outside of our life.

We must discard trying to be religious scholars or philosophers coming from a position thinking that in any way we can interpret the infinite simply by putting a name on it and then worship the name itself as a kind of conceptualization. Infinite means spacious freedom.

Not clinging to name or form, the Buddha went his way courageously. Here he could say as Rev. Kiozawa stated, "If you believe in God, he exists for you." He never argued with those who felt their beliefs subjectively. These are the main reasons he was well-loved. He never opposed those who cherished their own beliefs. He could love them all, regardless of their religious beliefs. His understanding transcended one's limited understandings, as he could see beyond their beliefs to get to the truth as to who they are as human beings.

So it came upon me in my travels that the most important thing for me is the human essence. Once I touch upon it then I am satisfied as it is our most basic truth. So when it is said to come as you are, this is all that is really necessary. When we come as we are we can hug one another as human beings. "All others are expedient means to my enlightenment."

wrote Haya Akegarasu. And it is so true, when I think of all the others I have met and learned from. Even being at the very bottom of the abyss – even as a hell-dweller – all are embraced by Eternal Life. And this noble light in each of us is what Eternal life supports.

Human greed creates the casino. This New Year's Eve I'm supposed to go to this casino. I have to join with the others in this place; see others jumping up and down to the noisy "boom-boom music" that the younger generation likes – replete with girls dancing on platforms! Do I to just stand there so wanting to get out of this place? No, with a smile from my friend (she wanted to come here along with her friend); I will create my own dance as I usually do, and then others came to join us, and pretty soon a whole bunch of us together are in a rhythm that transcends the loud music. As balloons fall – Happy New Year!

This is how we turned a negative into the positive – as all three of us went home happy that night. The profit and loss hell-hole of human desires called the casino thus became a place – believe it or not, where we could dance our way into the Pure Land! The spirit of "oneness" takes place with the power of the spirit. Out of the profit over loss stuff that they sell; which ends up as your loss and their gain – comes a light and life of actional intuition from our lively steps that turns a negative place into a positive center of oneness by the will of the spirit that cleans-up and pushes aside those money changers and greedy practitioners.

So too, Gautama Buddha demonstrated that of sticking his finger into cow dung and quickly washing it off, how the impurity of our defied condition turns into virtues. I, lacking in virtues and not wanting to be pure, find that there is no self to claim them. There are no qualities that I can attach to or be attributable to myself, nor any merits accumulated, for if that were so I would stink of myself as being superior. Since merits and virtues are not what I am seeking, but at times a burning desire focusing on the truth alone, I have no need for these accumulations. Becoming a virtuous person is not of my doing. I do not read the Dharma to improve myself, nor do I listen to others for the same reason, but to experience the power of the Buddha-Dharma. It is here where negatives are turned into positives. This is the Tathagata of impermanence, an ever-changing life that even within one's difficulty is being embraced by the light of its transforming power of compassion, miraculously!

When I meet with my friends, family members and others; or those I haven't seen in a long time, I forget religious differences or cast aside that which acts as a barrier preventing me from thinking of my friends. Our life is being with our friends – not with concepts!

In transcending conventional religious ideas we can focus on the life of the spirit only. In the life of the spirit I forget all that which separates me from others. For in the life of the spirit I expose my human essence. Our humanity comes to us as we touch upon each other's life. This is true happiness and joy. Here the world is at one, and this is our true feeling for each other, and here is where I experience the great movement of life. Just our nakedness of spirit is all that is required, no more needs to be added.

During Mrs. Toshiko Saito's memorial there were some people that attended that I hadn't seen for a long time who were former members of the old temple (now demolished) way back some forty or fifty years ago. We simply lost ourselves in mutual greetings and heartwarming remembrances. I felt love for all those I met, this lively group of people from the past when Rev. Saito was head minister; even their kids who showed up, and so many others. But the point is that of a feeling of respect out of a feeling of bowing in adoration to others no matter where they are coming from. Being exposed to the Dharma completely changes one's life. Being open-minded towards others enables them to be open-minded towards me. This is the meaning of living the life of the Buddha.

The struggle to seek the truth is the truth. The truth in this case is focused on me. Since this is the case the teaching is for me alone. For instance, I find that I am the one that is guilty of the very things that I accuse others of. Buddhism and Shakyamuni's teachings were founded on the basis of rigorous self-examination, for this is how we arrive at the truth about ourselves. To that extent then, the truth is found within oneself and is brought to life and realized by listening to our predecessor's who convey the Buddha's teaching through the sutras. They awaken us to the truth that is asleep within us and that we may not even be aware of. So seeing into oneself is the way that the Buddha lived his life.

When seeking the truth leads to non-other than myself and finding myself as the one most guilty of a number of things that anger brings to the scene then I feel that I have made a terrible mistake.

When going through all the struggles and difficulties that have transpired I am left alone. Through self-reflection I am able to see myself clearly, and seeing this to its full extent I am humbled into regret, and feel so sorry. So fortunate to listen to the Dharma of clarification.

Enduring the high heat of the day and having to perspire and sweat, then towards the evening taking a shower to wash away all the dirt of the day I sit in the garden to enjoy the atmosphere of nirvana. Here I notice that many peonies are blooming gloriously. The afternoon storms far from where I'm at have passed and so there are the cool breezes along with the setting sun which give everything a warm glow. These peonies reflect this glow and they literally shine their essence in their pure white petals. I am in this atmosphere, alone, and in this being alone, cleansed of contamination and attachments to this and that. It's just me and the peony. I look at it very carefully. In feeling at one with it, I enter its essence. The peony does not try to be saintly. The peony does not try to be moralistic or ethical. It does not interfere with others' lives. The peony does not try to force itself into being something that it isn't, something artificial. It straight-forwardly seeks into its own real wish, which is to grow and bloom. I cannot help but admire its beauty.

So with this feeling I watch the phenomena of nature, blooming, growing and shining. And here there is this feeling of hope – for no reason other than this shining hope itself which miraculously removes interferences enabling this spacious emptiness to appear in my mind as nirvana – the absence of self, or, true self as emptied of self-attachment and the defilements linked to the secular world that has its motivations, noises, and corruptions; the secular world that we should abhor.

The pure white peony is clean of all such dirt and human accumulations. It is itself the essence of religion drawing me into its unfolding beauty, shining in its purest and simplest form. It is here where I bow as I focus on its life; the simple nakedness, and the spirit and will that is in the natural organic life of nature. It is here where one is at peace within the serenity of a quietly settled person – how pure and beautiful is the mind that is joined with nature. Free from the defilements that man creates, and has created for the world also.

Shakyamuni himself led such a simple and pure life. But I believe he was active in forming a sangha and giving lectures on the Teaching that later became sutras. So living the life of Shakyamuni is the same as living the life of Dharmakara in the Larger Sutra: discovering his life within our life and in so doing discovering a lively and noble essence within ourselves.

6/3/2015 R. A.

(Note: The formal name for the Buddha is Shakyamuni (sage of the Shakya clan), whereas Gautama Buddha is the informal or given name to the Buddha which the teacher used as it was more amenable to us beginning students, but both are synonymous.)

"Park Scene" Acrylic   R. A.

The Buddha says that each person emits a noble light. No matter who they are, even those who live in the darkness of ignorance, or in the fires of hell as a hell-dweller. Once we hear the true Dharma we come to a light that cleanses all darkness, and enlightens all those who live in hell. Then we can live in the landscape of life that shines within us, and into the playfulness within the unhindered freedom of one's travels, as within the way.

Living the life of Shakyamuni means to discover our own true life in our own free kingdom.

The Seeds of a Revolution

11/12/2013
R. A.

    I think that anyone looking at the history of Japan would marvel at a nation that within the period of roughly fifty years was able to progress from that of a feudal society into a thoroughly modern society able to compete as well as hold her own next to that of the Western Powers is nothing short of a remarkable feat. While she modernized at a tremendous speed she was also experiencing an internal revolution as well. This internal upheaval had far reaching effects, not only secularly, but spiritually as well. Century old traditions were being questioned by those who saw these traditions as being too staid, formalized, and unresponsive as to providing any life for a generation that saw these age old traditions as ineffective and even blocking the way to a growing population that was expanding and progressing into the modern age. These reforms were taking place everywhere. Studying, learning, and borrowing from the West in all levels of scientific inquiry was going on; everything from philosophy to mechanical and electrical engineering to the medical and educational formatting and beyond had dramatic effects on a society just emerging out of a feudal order. A revolution is for the brave and not for those who are fearful of change.

    This all took place at the beginning of the Meiji era (1868 – 1912) through to the Taisho era (1912 – 1926). With the enthronement of Emperor Hirohito, Japan was at its zenith as one of the five "Big Giants" of the world. The militarists strengthened their hold on the country's weak government turning it into a militaristic and nationalistic country. Zennists gave it additional support, and a kind of "Devine Wind" energy took hold, thus adding to an invincible and mystical super-ego. In effect, they were "feeling their oats", and were emboldened after defeating Russia's Baltic fleet in the China Sea, during the World War 1 incident. This also involved Japan's attack on neighboring China's Manchuria. Japan was going through an industrial revolution along with a scientific one and needed oil, coal, and other mineral resources that she began to greatly need as a growing and expanding nation from 10 million to 90 million in population in this period of time. The necessity for outward expansion was the outcome of her ambitions to become a world power and take her place along with the "big five" nations. At this time the only way to accomplish this was with military power and the use of force to overcome the obstacles that were in her way. The idea of super tankers had not as yet been invented nor any of the things do we take for granted such as "International Trade Agreements", and etc. Thus nationalism and the roots of imperialism began to take hold. It is either "to be or not to be" one way or the other; either you stand still, or you move forward. Given the time and place, and the inconceivable karma's of circumstance, the option Japan took was to go to war.

    Early on Japan must seek its national identity along with the other nations and not be isolated. Other colonial powers, themselves imperialists, might very well look to claim her on the basis of her unpreparedness and vulnerability as a still feudal and ill-equipped nation ripe for the taking. Observing what they had done to China; indeed, all of Asia and

Africa itself provides a glimpse into the future for those who remained unprepared. So there were historical reasons here, but as a result of all of this you have World War 2, and its aftermath, the unconditional surrender of Japan, having exhausted all her resources, along with the dream of being a leader in Asia.

A nation on its back becomes humbled, and in this case, very humbled. It seeks a direction. Yes, recovery instituted by the U. S. under General McArthur strengthened a democratic Diet, which now had to listen to what the people were thinking is one way; but still, this applies to the secular world. No, there must have been a direction for seeking the truth, a yearning for a spiritual teaching to fill the vacuum that exists in disillusionment while seeking to rise from the ashes of defeat, and that would by peaceful means, revive itself. The nation of "The Rising Sun" would once again cause us to marvel at her ingenious creativity in all kinds of manufactured products; everything from super tankers to automobiles, computers, televisions, mobile phones, and etc., many that the world uses on a daily basis.

We cannot merely sit in judgment of another nation's actions aside from the actions that we ourselves are capable of committing. Just think of the Vietnam War under presidents Nixon and Johnson as a perfect example of world domination under our own flag of nationalism that we expose even today. We too, hold on to notions of world supremacy based on self-love. Greed, anger, and ignorance are no different collectively in nations than in individuals, and for that reason we must listen to the Buddha's teaching that exists in the quiet person who dwells in peace, and not involving with worldly affairs, but leaving them alone. Irreversible karmas are created on the world scene that leads to barbaric actions and bloodshed. Picking up the stick and fighting with others is a warning given by Shakyamuni. He himself tried three times to quell fights between his principality and others with no success. The Buddha saw no need to fight with others over supremacy, superiority, and greed.

I remember the last time I met with the teacher, while walking together he stated: "Rev. Akegarasu transcended the world." This I feel was directed towards me specifically. He was so sensitive to where I was still attached, as in his reprimand.

Founders of a Reformation

Those days of war are long gone, but they provide a background, so to speak, as to Japan's real resource regarding religion. Indeed, most importantly, the greatest of her resource was and is the Buddha-Dharma, in which Rev. Saito came to give us. But he too was coming from a post-war Japan, and in this case his teacher was Rev. Haya Akegarasu (1877 – 1954). In turn, Rev. Akegarasu's teacher was Rev. Manshi Kiozowa (1863 – 1903). Another important teacher was Shuichi Maida (1906 – 1967), who was also a student of Rev. Akegarasu. Although he came before Rev. Saito they were both closely associated as friends and fellow students of Reverend Akegarasu.

All these teachers, plus others who were from this framework, came out of this tumultuous time in Japanese history and revived, if not transformed the Jodo Shinshu sect of Buddhism, which for some centuries since the passing of its founder, Shinran Shonin, had become marginalized by the over-dependence of traditional nembutsu practices, thus falling victim to misinterpretations of its intent by its original founder. So although it was the largest sect in Japan following the Mahayana Pure Land tradition, by and large it was losing its real effectiveness by becoming too institutionalized. Various religious practices became set in a formula that required no need for real investigation by the parishioner. There were exceptions, but beyond that it was becoming more of a faith-based religion set for retirees. Shinran Shonin questioned the validity of such laid back practices, seeing that they had no real reason other than being respectful formalities.

But a wake up was to come, a revival to take place that would shake-up the Shinshu followers and that would take place beginning with Reverend Manshi Kiozowa. A re-examination would take place going all the way back to its original founder, Shakyamuni himself. But in real terms it began with his Mother, who expressed "paper thin" doubts about the nembutsu (Namu Amida Butsu). Because she questioned the Shinshu faith he began to think more seriously about it (He was the son of a Shin minister himself). At the time he occupied a rather good position as a philosophy professor at Tokyo University, belonging to the highest elite among the intellectuals at that time. During this time Japanese officials were willing to pay high salaries to those who not only had good English but who also had firm knowledge of Western philosophy, so hungry were they of Western knowledge, along with the teaching of the English language. But he was troubled with guilt. Plus his Mother embarrassed him as she no doubt criticized him for wearing such expensive Western style suits (high collar) and traveling around by way of expensive rickshaws.

Facing his Mother, he became very sincere. Perhaps he thought: "I may have diverged, but now I will investigate this issue." Therefore he set about clarifying this problem. Here I will quote from Rev. Saito's description: "He became a high school teacher in Kyoto, and tried to understand Buddhism through the experience of life itself. At the time Akegarasu met him, he was experimenting with the minimum possible way of life, not eating regular human food but a diet of pine needles and resin. As a result, he became little more than a skeleton, and a half year later caught the tuberculosis which was to become terminal in about ten years. All this time he was intensely active in reforming Buddhism."

He was known as a great experimenter, and thus he wanted to experience Shakyamuni's asceticism the same way that he did during the six years prior to his awakening in India. He had to find a way to physically re-live Buddha's life of asceticism and also through the study of the Larger Sutra which Shinran Shonin wrote extensively on with his six volumes: Kyo Gyo Shin Sho, which took many years to complete. Respecting such writings, he became a student of Shinran Shonin. This study opened the way for him to get a closer understanding of the nembutsu which was the reason he undertook the project in the beginning. According to Shinran the nembutsu was not relegated to a mere practice, in which by mere recitation would deliver all what the practitioner could desire; such as that of becoming a good or worthy believer, a store of merit making this person pure and free from evil as a candidate for the Pure Land upon death. This would be the same as when a person preys to God for favors bestowed on the believer – a religion based upon one's own convenience. Amida Buddha on a pedestal surrounded by flowers, so glorified; or Amida coming down from the heavens to save the believer acting as a savior, was how it was being portrayed and this is why Buddhism had turned into a faith-based religion for the convenience of the practitioner. If that is the case, then it is quite obvious that the nembutsu has lost its real spiritual value. If all you have to do is chant the words, then why not? You can very well be self-satisfied here. Chanting the Name continuously as a way of preventing evil from taking place and keeping the mind focused on the Dharma is one way, but even here there may be an element of practice and dependency. Life is not determined by chanting words alone without the feeling behind them, which then can express the depth of feeling.

Being given the Dharma that changed my life and by the teacher(s) who helped me is the nembutsu that goes beyond expressions of gratitude. This is the very reason why Reverend Saito never preached to us the nembutsu, yet living it. He let us discover it ourselves through our very own experience. This is the reason why the other teachers mentioned never preached it either, and why Rev. Kiozowa studying from Shinran, discovered the true meaning behind Shakyamuni's life which came about as his own confession: "I am as useless as a fan in December." He, like Shinran, saw no use in him as performing any good as everything he tried ended in failure.

The closer one gets to the Dharma the more clearly one can face the truth as pertains to oneself as being capable of doing any good. But rather, he left himself totally to the "Mandate of Heaven". His confession was the self-realization of a mandate that was beyond his control and that he fully embraced. This is not a practice for becoming a good person, nor is it attached to a set of religious practices; as this is the very reason Kiozowa broke through the set mentality of what had become of Jodo Shinshu and why it had become flat as a moving force, depending largely on faith. The shout of one's truth was lacking. It had become a place for scholars to discuss and pick up on the smallish details relating to historical truths. We can study history as it deepens and contributes to one's understanding, but we needn't study Buddhism relating to historical examples to reachself-realization. What we need to do is cast off the artificial layers to arrive at the true nembutsu, the most solemn feeling with our bodies fully lowered. Within the context of deepest humility, the true nembutsu gushes out that lacks any conceptualized form.

This is the feeling that brings me to find my true voice, expressed through the language of the first person. Indeed, whenever there is a dead-end, a barrier that exists preventing me from going forward – a blank wall – then suddenly a fresh spark pops up as actional intuition – then again I proceed! Here I can listen to the moment-to-moment inspiration that gives me the forward movement of life.

A fresh truth comes up and clears the mind. *Shinjin* is not just a onetime occurrence. So many think that enlightenment is a onetime experience and that's it. But many of these ideas about Buddhism come from our expectations, thinking as we do, of a goal that we achieve that is self-affirming. We all like to get self-affirmed. But in the process of seeking the truth which I don't understand, that comes up with a confession that is the nembutsu. Shinran Shonin was quite critical of those who misunderstood his teacher Honen Shonin's practice of the nembutsu, taking it for granted as a mere religious practice with marginal validity. His statement, if known by so many of its practitioners would shock those who think that they have a grasp on one of Jodo Shinshu's main features, the nembutsu. Here is his caution or repremand: "It is better to be a cow stealer than to chant the nembutsu needlessly". Nor out of filial piety did he say the nembutsu. Criticized for his views regarding the nembutsu as in relation to his teacher, Honen – who is purported to have chanted the nembutsu 84,000 thousand times a day – he responded by saying that both he and his teacher had the same nembutsu.

What then was the conclusion of what it is they started during this period in the context of a historical movement away from fixed and tired out assumptions? They were not about changing Buddhism, per se, but rather, through their own life they were seeking an awareness of Buddhism to the extent that they could be at one with it. The contents of this Dharma existed in the <u>Larger</u> <u>Sutra</u> through the mind of Bodhisattva Dharmakara. Come down to it, they then would have to study Shinran Shonin's commentary in order to get the true meaning related to the doctrinal elements that formed Shinran's understanding. In other words, Shinran was studying from the Seven Patriarch's and also studying from what he got from his teacher, Honen, comparing and seeking the true meaning behind the words that would have been otherwise difficult to understand. This whole process took a lot of work and total dedication on the part of Shinran. But what came out of it was the realization of total submission of oneself to the power beyond self, as was Honen Shonin's practice. So in mentioning "Mandate of Heaven" Kiozawa is realizing this power, and trusting in it totally.

"Self is nothing more than settling down and observing the myriad phenomena." Was just one of Reverend Kiozowa's many statements. This has the emptiness of one who is living in the ordinary world as an ordinary person and is perfectly relaxed in it.
His life was marked by tragedy – losing three of his young sons and wife early in life – being rejected as a minister in his father's temple – contacting tuberculosis and coughing up blood.... "What more can I lose?" he exclaimed. Indeed, this was his darkest period.

Yet despite all of this, he arose from it to fulfill his life to the utmost and giving us a new movement reflected in all those who listened to his "Mandate of Heaven". This was his way of saying "other power". Converting other power into a conceptualized understanding in which you have faith in it as a truth given to you by an inconceivable power can become a fixed belief that is externalized. But the term, "thus comes" is an apt expression coming from the depths of an unknowable life, the Tathagata. The way to it is not merely through the chanting of the nembutsu, but within one's confession that gushes out as the true nembutsu. The true result of Kiozawa's reformation was that of a whole-hearted subjective understanding. Is there any other way to understand Buddhism other than through our subjective minds? This includes his "Mandate of Heaven" which transcends what we can depend on through our objective intellect. We are as servants to the master as the "Mandate of Heaven", his favorite expression of the unknowable truth.

This year of 2015, the night before Easter, I met with my lady-friend to have dinner at her place. I brought along a bouquet of cut flowers to celebrate our usual get-together every Saturday evening. When I got there I noticed that she had a glass vase in which she had placed some cuttings from the evergreen bushes she had from her garden. Good, now we could place the flowers in her vase and the whole ensemble would be beautiful. After dinner I read Reverend Akegarasu's article, "The Mind of Embracing All Things". Knowing the difficulty she had with certain people she had to deal with being the manager of a 12 unit Co-Op building, I felt that I would have to explain to her how she could feel towards those who caused her so much trouble over a period of years. This difficulty was resolved by Akegarasu so beautifully in his article, yet it is difficult to fully understand. So after reading it I began to explain it this way:

"Suppose you had a bouquet of flowers, all different kinds, and you placed them in a vase with some water at the bottom, but suppose that this water had evaporated. What do you think would happen to all the flowers? They would all dry up and no longer be flowers. Then you would dispose of them in the garbage, wouldn't you. It is the water that has kept them alive."

The only way we can understand Akegarasu's article is to understand where he is coming from. He speaks of embracing all people including the ones who lived the life of lies, those who caused him to suffer; and those who opposed him, threatened him, and wished him as good as dead, casting him aside. How difficult it is to understand how he could embrace these people, as it goes beyond our ordinary reasoning.

Then I looked at the vase that held the water. Suddenly I awakened to the truth of where he was coming from – he was coming from the water that was at the bottom of the vase, so to speak. In other words, the "Mandate of Heaven" is like water that gives life to everything. As it does so it removes our surface judgments and discriminations. Our awareness of it allows us the compassion needed to embrace all beings, and to transcend our limited differences to be the mind of the One Truth.

We should therefore worship the "Mandate of Heaven" as the tathagata of our true compassion and subjectivity. The fact that we all breath the same life gives testament to the fact that – religious differences aside – we are undeniably alive because of it, and if we don't appreciate it we cannot experience the One Mind of truth.

Then when I think of what happened to Shinshu Buddhism and how it depreciated into nit-picking over procedure, management, historical tradition, and to name and form – which ended up by being split into two distinct sects, whereas they don't even want to speak to each other, and so it is rather unfortunate. I began to realize that it took all four of these reformers to restore Buddhism from death, or half-dead traditions which had lost their impact and influence. They however, were coming from the water of life. Through them many flowers were born into the world of spirituality, and my teacher was one of them. He too, reformed the Buddha-Dharma at the temple where I first met him. I lost my smallish personality, but found a life that grew like that of a plant that gives forth a bud among all the others who listened and paid close attention to him, likened to that of water that leads to a flower's fresh opening.

There are those who in living lukewarm lives like to listen to lukewarm teachings. And there are teachers who are like this as well, who also give two-dimensional lukewarm teachings. Without the voltage, they have not as yet tasted the real water that comes with the reality and difficulty of life. They have never really lived their life but just rely on the safest well-tread path that comforts the masses because they themselves want to eat.

In his article Akegarasu sensei examines the issue of destruction in: "Thoughts about Destruction". This destruction that he sees is a positive influence despite the fear that people have, are in part directed to those who are afraid of the destruction of their traditional fixed beliefs which they think is good enough and are satisfied with it. To this he exclaims that we should get rid of it and to pursue our own independent wish for self-realization into the world of creation. This is the way to freedom, joy, and wisdom that the Buddha gave as the true Dharma of our life. How difficult it is to be a true human being, and to have heard the Teachings and to feel the true nembutsu of praise. Praise of the Dharma-predecessors' who with such courage and bravery got rid of the cold scholarly mind to be at one with the ocean of life – how valued, and exemplified are their teachings. We can drink of the water that is provided instead of living in a dried-up desert.

From the Collected works of Shinran comes this poem:
> The ice that melts and becomes the water that flows into the sea
>> becomes indistinguishable from the flavor of the sea.
>
> The more ice the more water, the more water, the deeper the ocean.

AN ARTICLE ON WAR   Shuichi Maida (1952)

    There are signs of an impending political solution to the Korean War, but still the fighting goes on. This is the reality, that we kill each other. We are confronted with this reality.

    What we most dislike in life is the thought of killing someone. If we are forced to do so, there is always some extenuating reason given. But the essential reason for killing people begins with self-love or selfishness.

    As long as we have this self-love, war will continue, we will not be able to eliminate it from human life.

    People hurt and kill each other because of self-love. Where they hurt and kill others is the very place they will be hurt and killed by others. The fate of this relationship cannot be avoided. Thus, because of self-love, people kill themselves. This is not so much interesting as it is strange. As result of loving ourselves, we are trapped into something that has exactly the opposite consequences. This is why human beings are self-contradictory. The true definition of a human being who fights is the person who loves himself and kills himself.

    In its broad meaning war is a variety of suicide. Human beings commit suicide because of selfishness. The true mechanism of suicide is this: A person thinks only of himself and never of others; he tries to fulfill his own desires but he can't: he kills himself then. In back of suicide is the selfish mind. As long as human beings have selfish minds, are selfish, suicide will continue to occur in the world of human life ....

    Self-love is the desire to control one's world. Simply, it is being an egotist. Every individual has the desire to control his own individual world.

    You see, this so-called "love" in our society is not just a sweet word it's a conflict of kill or be killed. You cannot say it so simply, this "Love others." We must be careful to observe that what passes for love of others is a distorted form of self-love. The love between parents and child, man and woman, teacher and student – is a distorted self-love. And so human life, human society is the world that always fights because of the world of human self-love. And for human kind, war is inevitable, from the fight between neighbors to that between races and nations, and between whole blocs of nations, such as the American and Soviet bloc's.

    All human beings love themselves, regardless of whether they are wise or stupid, poor or well-off, women or men. Self-love seems to be a necessary condition of being human. Self-love is an inevitable characteristic of human existence, so fighting and war are inevitable in human history. So in this world there will not be peace.

    Or may we expect peace on earth? Here we bump into an iron wall, the iron wall of self, which is based on self-love. And for the first time we meet ourselves.

                                            From "Suchness" 1970
                                           (Joan Sweany, Gyoko Saito, Translator)

An Article on Love

R. Adams
6/1o/14

    Love depends on feeling, without this embracing feeling how can I express or feel any love? Feeling is all. Connected to this feeling is respect and trust. These essential elements are the backbone of our being human more than anything else that we can think of. Without this how can we claim to be human – how can we think or be alive spiritually? Even dwelling on the various aspects of the Teaching, and listening to others express their life, how can we not respond to what is essential within our own life as well? Love therefore, is most universal within all of us no matter where we come from and who we are and moves us to hug each other as brothers and sisters in the family of friends and lovers. How welcome it is then to be able to participate and be welcome in the world of a universal brotherhood, for this is our life as humans. It is here where we can drop our conventions of discrimination and judgments and really get to appreciate our oneness with each other. Seek into a real dialogue with each other and forget our little self-love position. We can get into a real dialogue with a feeling of reverence in observance to our essential wish in seeing ourselves as, "One within the many, many within the one." Within this understanding we can live a fulfilling life that supports us all. I am reminded of Jesus Christ's words: "Without love what hath you?" That applies to everything we do, for there is something in the inner core of our being that urges us to go beyond the mundane to touch upon this essence, a miraculous power called love which is not based at all on the all-important "I".

    If I look at the Buddha-Dharma as reflected in any of the sutras I don't come across Shakyamuni discussing love in any form specifically. But in all the marvelous credits ascribed to the Buddha I come across words that are like this: "He sees himself in all sentient beings." Though love is not mentioned specifically it is implied holistically, that is, if we can see ourselves in others that we respect as human or all natural life for that matter, an embracing feeling of love emerges. This is what is implied, not self-love that is based on ego self-worship.

    Gautama Buddha did not come about from thin air, he was born of a mother and father, so though love is never mentioned in any of the sutras he, as well as we, came about through love. So love is universal among all of mankind, which also includes the animal world as well. It is pervasive among all living beings. Therefore there must be a manifestation of it in all living forms which we can call an all-embracing compassion or love.

    Should we therefore kill animals and eat them? When Reverend Akegarasu visited Chicago after the war and stopped over at the Stockyards here (when they still existed) and seeing how they were being slaughtered, vowed never to eat beef again. That was his feeling.

Between a man and a woman the emotion of love can be very strong. Through body and mind they want to consume each other so that there is nothing left of the other as separate from them – such an all consuming selfishly burning love!

There is this story about two lovers that Reverend Akegarasu likes to tell about: A young monk residing in a monastery being visited by a young girl who falls in love with him. As the young monk was diligently trying to rid himself of his passions in the attempt to be pure and to follow the monastic precepts, and accordingly tried to escape from her affections. Finally it reached a point where he ran away from the monastery to try to get away from her. But she followed him in hot pursuit. Then he came across a river and seeing her following him he decided to swim across thinking that she could not swim after him. But, lo and behold, she turned into a snake, swam across, and continued her pursuit! Then he spotted a large Buddhist bell sitting above the ground. He decided to crawl under the bell feeling safe. But she wrapped herself around the bell and squeezed so hard that the bell began to melt. Finally he had to get out and surrender to her hot passions and they were united in what became of themselves as one. With a smile on his face Akegarasu tells this story out of his wishes that he could meet such a lover!

There is this story about Gautama Buddha that is told of him giving one of his speeches to an assembly of followers and listeners on the famous Vultures Peak in Northern India whereupon someone gave him a flower just prior to the time when he was about to speak. Many in the audience were no doubt waiting for his speech in anticipation. But when the Buddha with such a shining face stood up to give the speech he simply held up the flower given to him without saying a word. The audience composed of twelve thousand people in such a small space must have been in happiness and joy. He saw that they all had shining faces – they became instantly at one! I'm thinking of myself among those being there. From the Sutta Napata (earliest texts on the Buddha), he could be straight forward on one hand, and filled with compassion on the other. The Buddha saw all those gathered in the audience as already enlightened beings. Thus no words.

How many centuries ago was this – two thousand five hundred and fifty odd years ago? And it is as if I were right there along with others of the sangha, as his presence was enough. Wordless communication – why is it so important? Love is wordless actually – deeply imbedded in our consciousness, and we should be careful how we use it. But if it simply gushes out unexpectedly beyond our control, then it is an expression of, "I love you, why don't you love me?" These are the teacher's words soon after I met him. Hearing this I was amazed.

In his article, "An Article on War" (1952) Shuichi Maida coldly examines self-love. It is a very enlightening article and I learned a lot from it. I wrote this in response to it. He doesn't waste words on sentimentalities. He gets right to the point. But this is the negative side, the egoistic side of our distorted self-love that is merely a reflection of the all-important "I". But without this "I" that distorts and contaminates things; I love the fact that I am alive, and that I respect myself.

But come to the point love has two sides, indeed, many sides, many shades, in fact, it is limitless. In Maida's' case he is discussing the egotistically selfish love that inevitably leads to fighting and war. But when I look into Akegarasu I get an entirely different picture, one that transcends the ego-love that we normally think of as love. For Akegarasu could love and adore everything. You name it: to a newly born snake flicking its tongue out seeming to say: "I love you", to flowers; including everything imaginable from an all-embracing mind, stones and dust included! His yearning and longing are expressions of love, the kind that melts the cold mind. Because of this I love Akegarasu.

And come to that I love the teacher, who was so human. Nothing but an open-minded student who knew so much about the Dharma while studying it and sharing the teachings with us. I simply could not help but love his being, the ordinary person that he was, and that's why I stuck with him throughout all those years and trusted him completely. His spirit is still with me for that reason. It is his spirit for life that I can't get over and still marvel at, and it is this spirit that I love. Shortly after we first met, and in the parking lot of the temple he said: "I love you. Why don't you love me?" Then he added, "Let's study together." But as time went by and he perceived that I was clinging to him, he told me sharply: "My son is more important to me than you are". Thus his love was not of the attached kind but had a special meaning which was to push me forward in the proper direction. He didn't keep me as his student, but saw all of us as independent persons and students that also included him. From here, how could I not love him? And, it was through this love that I know was mutual, that upon his funeral I broke down in such tears that I went bending over. So this is simply love of the teacher. The teacher was not some kind of object, he was a human being. There is just a feeling of warmth through long association. It is very simple as it is clear: it was just the respect for his being.

So in that sense Maida's article sounds fatalistic even though I admire his ability to get to the truth with no nonsense. Presenting us with the cold facts about the relationships within ourselves and others is not very warming. With his sharp scalpel he cuts into the truth about the "iron wall" attachment to the self and the way we love. Yet, how inevitable love is! I cannot write this article without thinking of it. I couldn't have pursued the Dharma without being directed by the desire to get to the truth, working to get to the bottom of self-introspection in regards to this issue of love over self-love. In self-love there is this iron wall; as he says, because it is bounded by self, a sticky situation that curtails and crimps freedom. This is the problem with attached love that we can't seem to get out of and really exposes us to who and what we are as human beings. How can I love others enough to care for them, to be sincere with them? So in some ways it is a matter of fact simplicity which transcends self-love and becomes love itself. I cannot think of others with whom I share my life or experience without this. Yet, on the other side, I want to go clean and free of any attachment that becomes a burden and kills my original feeling that was free and open as an independent person seeking the way as buddha seeking Buddhahood.

Is this a distorted form of self-love? That I'm selfish, yes, it's true, but that comes as a natural result of being a human being. Is that in itself a form of distortion? Selfishness can manifest itself through unselfishness! All living beings are selfish including Maida himself, but is he egotistically selfish? As I go through the difficulties of the thought process love is part of this struggle. Creation itself creates the new and in the process discards the old and this includes love as it is actively engaged which can appear and disappear accordingly. This is what propels me forward into such an unknowable area that we should discover for ourselves. This is how I dance, this is how I play, and despite the struggle or including it, this is how I work. One word follows another in quick succession, crisp, clean-cut and fresh. Love that is conditional according to the way the mind freely goes applies here. This is so different than egotistical self-love that thinks of itself as so important, self-centered, and that is so attached that it is miles away from the simple cherishing that comes from needing people.

With friends I share the feeling of embracing them. And in going back I think that Shakyamuni felt the same way, because it is said that he accepted everyone and didn't fight with anyone. So unless you really love yourself and respect yourself enough to transcend your smallish ego you will never have true peace that goes beyond conflict, argument, fighting, and war; there will never be true love in your heart/mind within the world of embracing all things.

Eternal motherly has as its deepest expression of that which is given to us the moment we were born. Then what does it mean? It means that both you and I are already embraced by a power that is beyond our understanding but has an embracing spirit that defines love of the other, no matter what the other is. It could be anything that the world brings to us. But it could also go in the opposite direction and bring about disgust, and dislike. For our feeling for love is particular.

Among all the mothers of the world, alone, my mother is best.

In this short phrase Reverend Akegarasu sees his mother as the best. Note that he uses the term: alone, to describe his relationship with his mother, so it is his mother alone who is best, not to be compared with someone else's mother. If I use the word absolute, then I will say that this is an absolute expression of what he means by the term: eternal motherly. All of us should say this about our own mothers. What he is saying has far reaching consequences for it describes the unconditional nature of his inspirit into the embracing arms of his mother, plus the absolute nature of his independence to determine the nature of his religious experience which cannot be compared with someone else's. Therefore he is saying that the term "enlightenment" is given to him by a source that embraces him, and in effect says: "Come to me. Don't worry, I will protect you." Then bringing it down to earth he says: "my mother is best". He really felt this way towards his own mother. Eternal motherly draws me upward. This way of expression would be most likely his way of feeling. He is really expressing his life of the kingdom of the first as the best, and his feeling for his mother is his shout as the expression of it.

We are all being embraced by that which is beyond our understanding. There is no "iron wall" here as Shuichi Maida says regarding our inability to transcend our limited capacity to go beyond our self-love position and attain the truth that is beyond our understanding. When you feel this way you don't have to worry about iron walls preventing you from living your life, for you will know the absolute nature of, "alone, my mother is best." is as a oneness with the embracing power of life itself.

"Chrysanthemum Garden"   R. Adams (oil painting)

But what about simply love itself? Is there such a thing as love that allows us to love simply from the essence of our humanity which goes beyond the surface self? In other words, is there a resolution to this problem? There is no resolution other than our wanting to be loved and loving, because first of all, we are human. Then the resolution is to get rid of this selfishly self-centered love and attachment which is the cause of our difficulties in loving others or being loved.

So often when we think of love we are confronted with selfishness which comes in the form of possessiveness resulting in jealousy or anger. These are hidden from our view until they pop up unexpectedly when our love is being challenged and/or threatened. Except for the all-embracing mind, love comes with our attachment to the one that we love or the subject or object that we are attached to. Subject and object attachment is a normal human condition when it comes to love except when it comes to a duality that lacks the one. Dogs, as example, have the same thing but not the same problem. So attachments are not so easy to define. Our emotions invariably have attachment to them. So we cannot merely disregard or get rid of our human condition as a matter of fact.

Akegarasu once said that those who are not interested in women will not attain enlightenment. Now we can take a good look at monasteries and nunneries, as well as celibate priests and others who are engaged in isolating themselves from the world thinking that in so doing they can be "spiritual" or "Godly" or pure like that of a saint. Pure spirituality is simply the life of the spirit and the will to be fully alive, which carries any and all circumstances that we are engaged in at the time, including our interest in the opposite sex which is quite natural, the natural organic feeling of love.

Akegarasu never denied that he was selfish but what he did deny was that he was a person who had a calculating and contrived way of accomplishing his selfish desires; in other words, a self-seeking contriving individual. A contriving individual cannot attain enlightenment.

A critic once challenged him this way: "Suppose there were three people in a desert and they had to split a pot of rice into three portions equally. In that case you would share the top portions of rice with the other two and take the bottom portion for yourself knowing that being packed down you would actually be getting more for yourself". Akegarasu responded: "Perhaps, but I would not calculate such a thing in advance".

Another person queried him: Y: "Who is the first person you love?
A: Myself. Y: Who is the second person you love? A: Myself. Y: who is the third person you love? A: Myself. Y: Besides this who else do you love? A: If you are at one with me I am at one with you".

Transcending the world means transcending that which is being attached to the world. It means going beyond the smallish self with its self-love and leaving the defilements of the secular world alone. Just letting it go as it is while living the life as an awakened person who lives in the world but is not fixed in it. He does not separate himself from others but can sense oneness in everything that is alive as he is receptive to it and leaving the rest alone, and not to get involved with it. That's how he maintains his freedom. Appreciation for all those who through their own efforts provide me with all the goods and services needed in daily life, for otherwise I would not be able to live. So in that sense, use of the term secular, one must be careful not just to label the world into two separate parts like slicing a melon in half, and then calling one secular, the other spiritual.

The mind of embracing all things is the quiet peaceful mind that allows things to go their own way and live their own life; except when it interferes or tries to control my life or the lives of others and at that time I push back. So love then, has many different ways and means of expression and manifestation. So too is compassion, which is another form of love. Compassion for others is a wonderful thing as it is part of our being human. But it too can be distorted by self-love. We should be careful not to be too easily drawn into what some people use to cover-up their feelings of guilt by spreading lots of money around under the name of "good deeds to help humanity", and etc., and make themselves look good so that the greedy side of their reputation is smoothed over.

Someone, a critic, told Reverend Akegarasu that he should transfer his love for flowers to love of the sutras. While recognizing the importance of sutras, they are not alive, whereas flowers are. Indeed, Akegarasu gave life to the sutras by passing through the "bud palace" stage into the "blooming flower" stage in which he transcended fixed ideas and could give lectures on the sutras with authority.

A thought came to me this morning with the words: "Eternal Motherly". Again, it is in regards to the relationship between Reverend Akegarasu and his mother. She always supported him no matter what, no matter the negative occurrences he faced during the course of his life. So he felt her love and embrace as she always supported him regardless how old his age.

So on chilly night while he was in his study, his mother came to the second floor and gave him a freshly cooked warm yam. At this time he thought that this warm yam given to him by his mother at this very moment was more important to him than all the study he had been doing on a sutra. To him everything was fresh and subjective, embeded in a nembutsu the dogmatists have yet to experience.

To him and to me, that which goes beyond study, work, and the difficulties of seeking – is the sudden seeing of a flower blooming that captures my life is something indescribable. The simplicity at the sight of a delightful face of the daylily flower! Words gush up as: "How beautiful!" This is what moves me and you as it kills our separation, and melts our mind into oneness as love.

Transcendental Wisdom R. Adams 4/25/2013

When I stepped outside this morning on this overcast threatening-to-rain kind of day I was surprised to see the daffodils and crocus were blooming so cheerfully. It's been a cold and snowy winter along with rapid temperature swings, yet these early spring flowers courageously bloom as if to say: "I've weathered the winter. Now with the very first signs of spring as the cold has loosened its grip on the frozen soil I can shoot up to greet the fresh spring air and to bloom!" With my little finger I lifted the daffodil flower to see its face – it was so shining, so fresh, and so nakedly shy it brought a smile to my face. And as I looked around I found other spring flowers that were blooming – you know, the little blue curly ones that are about ten inches high – in full abundance showing their whole life so bravely and beautifully.

As I breathed the fresh spring air I took my daily walk as usual when I'm not working, whereupon I came upon the crowds of pre-teens being let out of school. They are so happy to get let out of school so they can be themselves – so playful, so loud, and so gay.

But this one couple were hugging each other and trying to kiss each other on the face. As I came up to them they both smiled at me as I was smiling at them, then he went back to kissing her – so close – rubbing cheek to cheek, nose to nose. I walked another two blocks, turned around, went through the noisy bunches of kids, made a turn and there they were again – still hugging and kissing! I couldn't help it as I joked, "Wow, Wow! Still hugging each other? That's what I should be doing!" The three of us laughed as I continued my walk feeling so natural about everything that I smiled all the way home.

"Walk and the way will open" as Rev. Akegarasu once said.

Then later in the afternoon when I turned on the TV., I heard about the tragedy that struck the Boston Marathon as a deadly explosion ripped through the crowd of bystanders happily cheering their favorite runners on to victory in getting past the finishing line in such a celebratory occasion – when Boom! – ten seconds later another Boom! Suddenly the whole place including the downed runners was in a state of panic as the scene resembled a war zone. The cheerful crowd now turned into a panic stricken crowd desperately trying to get away from this terroristic shock. I too, was feeling the shock as I observed what was going on. So far at least three are dead and one hundred and seventy six were taken to local hospitals, some with their legs blown off, and others with shrapnel all over their bodies and in critical condition.

What a change it has been this day: from flowers and love in the morning to death and tragedy in the afternoon. The thought of this tragedy has burdened my mind all the rest of the day and I can't seem to get rid of these images seen on television. But after all its just television, and aren't these images just images? Am I not just getting attached to this action? Sure there is content, I mean people are getting killed and injured and shouldn't that directly concern me? And yes it does. The feeling one takes away from this is compassion towards the afflicted, as all together so many rushed in to help the wounded and dying, then why not just leave it at that? This after all is not just a movie, it is real life occurring in real time, and just like all the others I am saddened and affected.

Then as I lay down thinking and dwelling on it I asked myself quietly: "What does Buddhism have to say about this." I mean, it's all right to talk about being inspired by flowers, or two kids experiencing the freshness of their first love; but what happens when a horrific event suddenly knocks it out replacing it with a horror scene that I did not seek nor welcome, but instead leaves me shaking my head in disbelief. This is the reason that such an occurrence is called a tragedy. It has to do with man's violence against his fellow man. That's why it is such a tragedy. I struggled with this dilemma for some time looking for some teaching that would allow me to transcend this difficulty. Then a thought came to me that would begin with the words: "Transcendental Wisdom". The Buddha-Dharma has to do with Buddha's Wisdom; or as in Shinshu Buddhism, Amida Buddha's Wisdom, as opposed to the mundane wisdom that pertains to the secular world and its affairs which contain the very world that I was viewing earlier as I was observing this tragedy. It is here that marks a clear distinction between the secular world and the spiritual world; not that the Teaching offers a panacea, but rather in the search for the truth where the truth really matters is the truth that continuously transforms us.

Words like transcendental wisdom have real substance and give us a direction to our life that moves us away from our attached existence as so often we are burdened by it and somehow get lost within a labyrinth of thinking that has no end. Sometimes I think of what a hellish world we live in. Then how can Buddha's compassion free us from this hell? We have to see ourselves in hell just like the Boston Marathon to bring it about even more vividly, emphasized by the fact that the whole nation, if not the world is watching it. A conceptualized and esoterically sophisticated knowledge of Buddhism will not help us. Nor will the knowledge of psychiatry, yoga practices, or philosophizing about concepts do us any good.

Buddhism makes it very simple without extravagant means; the teaching that allows us to cross over the raging river of fire and water representing our greedy, evil passions to the other shore of the Pure Land and thereby experiencing the embracing spirit of life itself instead of the ignorant domain as we witnessed in this marathon that turned out so terribly. It is the evidence of the karma of things coming together as a result of self-love and the warring factions within the world where violence is practiced on a daily basis. This indeed, is the true human tragedy of all those who fight within themselves internally and then strike out externally as they fight with others. The secretly held motivations behind one's self-centered prejudices that end up in hate are being witnessed here. And then there are the runners themselves who desire to win a race against others who are trying to be faster and who are seen as contenders. So it should not surprise us that this is the perfect situation for those who hate this country to practice their violence against us, thus taking out their revenge in this competitive atmosphere of excitement called the Boston Marathon.

Originating from the static self or ego will be the static God concept to bring about the terror of nations fighting with nations, Gods fighting with Gods, religious sects fighting with other religious sects; nationalized ego's vying for supremacy – all as a result of this ignorance and blindness.

That's why then, Amida Buddha's light clarifies our deepest aspiration for peace. The light that penetrates through all the darkness and is unhindered by any blockage put before it in the way of human ignorance. This is the transcendental wisdom that clarifies the mind and breaks through the barrier or iron wall of our difficulty and struggle. This requires our careful and subjective introspection however, the depth of which will reveal the ignorance and evil that we ourselves create, not just somebody else's. We get caught, caught by our own thinking, and without knowing about it so often get into the habit of a set dualistic way of thinking. Life itself is in constant motion and does not stay still for even a second. After all the other things that we are attached to are gone we are left facing this self, a static-shell-of-self we refuse to give up because of self-love that becomes an affliction we place upon ourselves in unfortunate circumstances. If we then hear of the Buddha's wisdom, then we, in spite of our difficulty, will introspect ourselves for the real cause of our friction and the feeling of isolation within ourselves. Is it necessary to go anywhere else to find this wisdom other than it's within in our own being?

"Since I do not hate others, others do not hate me"- (H.A.). This is what I practice. Therefore I do not live in fear. I live in peace and in peace I am at one with Amida Buddha. It is a lively peace as I am continuously going forward into the unknowable dimension. As a result of this freedom the lands that are open are infinite in all directions. It comes out of listening to the mind of embracing all things in the world, and leaving this ugly shore of hate behind.

Our Deepest Wish

4/23/2013
R. Adams

    This article was written from notes that were taken from the Buddhist seminar at the University of California campus sponsored by the Maida Center of Buddhism during the period of July 28th through August 1st 2000, and specifically focused on Rev. Gyoko Saito's presentation and speech regarding our deepest wish into our enlightenment as true human beings. Some thirteen years later I discovered it among my papers and decided that it would be a good time at this point to expose it to the public as reader to show the importance of the Shinshu or Jodo Shinshu tradition within the context of the Buddha-Dharma experience and teachings exemplifying Shakyamuni's true intent.

    These Maida Center sessions were always important to me because I once again had a chance to meet with friends, teachers, and especially with my teacher, Rev. Saito, who I would listen to his words and catch the teaching that he embodied to the fullest extent even at times without much use of words or even with a facial expression in response to some of my thoughts. After many years of knowing him even words were not necessary to convey a teaching that I knew were his feeling as a human being to another human being, life to life. Such a relationship is at the very heart of Buddhism as it is a direct live-wire contact.

    I remember at the time of the his last seminar when he was one of the speakers, while during a break when we got together along with his secretary from Hawaii (as he was now in retirement and stationed as a minister of a small temple there); that I praised him openly and unabashedly stating that his work in translating the work of his teacher, Haya Akegarasu, and with so many of his translations of other teachers were the best, as he just smiled.

    This reminds me of the scene in which the Bodhisattva Dharmakara in the Larger Sutra – upon meeting with his teacher, Lokesvaharaja, went around his teacher three times as a matter respect, and on his knees prostrating himself and putting his palms together in worship in praise of the Buddha. Soon after I thought how true it is that the Sutra came alive in real time, actualized within my own being as a result of my meeting with the teacher some forty years earlier, and how I am still learning from all he did some years later as an inexhaustible source of his teachings. As he passed away the next year on March 10, 2001; it is how I feel now as I had gathered notes on what he said while listening to his last speech.

In these following quotations, he is presenting the   and   Vows out of a total of 48 Vows that Dharmakara intends to make. He is providing us with the human side within the contents of these vows which are not presented in the sutra itself. It's like putting flesh on the bones.

*   *   *

"In the <u>Larger Sutra</u> the 17th vow of Dharmakara means praising the Name. Yes, he was the *Father*. This vow has to do making known the name of Amida. The Name of Amida became a chant: Namu Amida Butsu, the nembutsu that is recited among all Shinshu people, as it is now and has been for centuries since people began to take up the practice. Fulfilling his vows, Dharmakara becomes known as the Bowing Buddha or Amida Buddha. Thus we can assign the attribution of "father" here through the name of Amida Buddha that he wants us to establish.

"In the   vow of the same sutra, Dharmakara makes his wish known to all those who sincerely, joyously, and with a trusting mind aspire to be born in his land, saying his Name. These become the sangha, or *Mother*.

"Accordingly, in this situation – under this embrace – he attained birth in the Pure Land. Under the last of the unenlightened ones – he, the very last of the unenlightened attains the supreme awareness: I, as a hell-dweller.

"These conditions being fulfilled, ignition takes place. The flash, or 180 degree turn – from extinction (of relative self) to true self occurs immediately. The self likened to a Phoenix is reborn as a true human being. Burning his whole self up in total self-cremation, the relative self becomes the ashes and fertilizer for the free newly born self.

"*Shinjin No Go Shiki* (Jap.), a term or phrase that means one's deepest desire to be born as a human (originally from Shan-Tao (Ch.) 613-681 A. D., the fifth Patriarch in Shinran's list, also known as Zendo (Jap.). Or even before that, T'an-Iuan (Ch.), also known as Donran (Jap.) 476-542 A. D., the   Patriarch. This term was picked up by Shinran Shonin in the 12th century – then again in the   century by Manshi Kiozowa, Haya Akegarasu, and Shuichi Maida; thus flowing through the Mahayana Pure Land tradition by way of the <u>Contemplation Sutra</u> as particularly Pure Land Teachings. (Here, the deepest aspiration itself is *Shinjin,* or birth.)"

(This was brought out by Rev. Saito during the recent conference in Berkeley, Ca. during his talk on July 29, 2000. He states that unless we have a crystal clear understanding of this term in the form of a shout, we cannot attain the fulfillment of the Pure Land experience. This is to transcend the world and attain enlightenment.)

"*Ji No Shiki* (non human) refers to the bean, whose deepest desire is to be born as a bean. If the conditions are ripe, the bean will be born as a bean. (This is a story that he told as relates to Egyptian beans some 3,300 hundred years old found in King Tut-Ankh-Amen's tomb in 1922. After being passed about, he finally planted some of them in Hawaii where he now lives. As they grew he examined his life in relation to these beans. They too, had the same wish to be born as did the human being.) How cherishing it is to discover that this wish to be born exists in all of life.

"Rev. Akegarasu picked up on this theme and saw in it the essence of every flower that bloomed, the grasses that covered the earth, and even the baby snake that flicked out its little tongue – such a shout of independence filled his being – such a confession that burst into tears – such freedom in the spacious world. We get from him such brightness in being born as a true human being.

"So *Shinjin No Go Shiki* refers to our innermost desire to be born as a human being – in all of us."

Upon his birth the Buddha returned to the world. He returned as an Ordinary person. As such he saw himself in all sentient beings. In the heat of the summer he wore a simple bib. In the cold of the winter he wore a cloak made up from pieces of discarded clothing from a cremation site, washed and sewn together. There was nothing about him that put himself above others. And because of this so many people came to be his friends and listened to what he had to say about our true life as human beings.

The world that he came back to was no different than the world that he had left before he went from the palace and his family to set out on a journey to discover who he was and the struggle that he undertook. But he came back to the world out of a deep sense of compassion for his fellow human beings who were living in the world of suffering and ignorance no different than the world we live in today as so many tragedies occur in which people "know not what they do". Why come back to the world of samsara and ignorance? Because he too, had lived in the world of hell that were brought about by his thinking – this was his awakening. This darkness suddenly became light as he realized that his self-efforts were of no avail in reaching true spiritual peace and freedom. The light now came from within himself.

At the very end he accepted the fact that he was a hell-dweller. Even though he put his whole power behind it, i.e., that of becoming a Brahman filled with the wisdom of Atman; he, in his final shout: "Oh, Avidia!", "Oh, Darkness!" totally freed himself from his self-delusion brought about by his self-power efforts that collapsed into nothingness, and from here he reached the self-realization of spiritually being born as a true human being.

It may be okay for us to look upon Shakyamuni as a hell-dweller as he sat meditating under the Bhodhi Tree taking those six steps prior to his enlightenment, but what about ourselves? Do we not get involved with hell during certain times in our life, whether it is physical or mental? Therefore don't we get a taste of being on the same path as Shakyamuni insofar as seeking the truth about our suffering experience and how to overcome it?

The plain fact about our existence here on earth is that – at times – the world and/or we are filled with suffering, and because of misery we seek the truth. This is our human capacity for seeking a way to transcend it and find spiritual peace within ourselves. Otherwise we just keep going around and around endlessly without ever recognizing who we really are or where the problem is coming from. Since we are the one's feeling it, it must be coming from ourselves. One's confession turns a negative into a positive.

Our suffering is our hell. Since this is the case why don't we just recognize the case that we've been hell-dwellers, with no way out except for our honest confession for ourselves for being as such? Here we can face the truth. Come down to it – within you there is the life waiting to get out and be born. Given the right circumstances Amida's light will shine through the darkness and clouded over entanglements enabling us to live in the freshness of freedom through one's deepest wish for birth.

But be forewarned, not to be so gullible for spoon-fed truth that merely agrees with what we think. We must be as desperate seekers. Otherwise we will be accepting lukewarm stuff that has no bearing on our real life or our birth. While we've worked hard to bolster and self-enhance our selves, now we must work to coldly self-examine our selves; then we can break open this shell and enjoy. The road to true enjoyment takes work. But at the end – I made it! This comes with the feeling that gives me a deep satisfaction for a life that is well rewarded, interesting, creative – but most of all, feeling the voltage and richness of life itself!

And I will go on listening as long as I live as I go forward where no one else has gone before, from fresh steps into the unknowable life brought about by all those I meet as well as all the things that come alive by just listening to the rhythm of life.

The world is like an ocean. On the surface are the waves of samsara, swirling about in confusion and disturbed by the winds of our cravings. Deep beneath, however, all is quiet and moving slowly where all the treasures brought about by peace lie. Yet both the surface (samsara) and the depths of nirvana are of one ocean, inseparable from each other. We can then worship the totality of life's experience and the liberation into the indescribable one mind, as the infinite spirit of Amida Buddha comes alive.

Studentship of the Ordinary Person

July 6, 2014
R. Adams

    In thinking of Rev. Akegarasu I came across the following statements that I know warrant our attention and that I personally want to explore. These are just a summary of the totality of a large body of work that he was engaged in. But these few came to mind while thinking over the subject of ordinariness and its relationship to flat suchness wherein the Buddha becomes an ordinary person, becoming at one with all humans who are unique but the same in universal brotherhood. Take for example: "All others are expedient means towards my enlightenment." The key words here are "all others". We have in him a listener, not a know–it-all conceited person. As such, he is an ordinary person who doesn't think of himself as a learned person at all but instead is open-minded and sincere, humbled by the truth that has taken away his conceit, enabling him to be a true listener and learner. In emptiness he sees himself as a foolish person. When we are stripped of conceit and self-pride thinking that we know something and therefore why should we listen to ordinary foolish people? All others mean that he has opened his mind to all others, taking what amounts to the lowest position. As such he is a foolish person who is listening to all others who are foolish. More than that, he is thinking of himself as a foolish person. This is what makes him a true student: A foolish person studying himself as a foolish person. Or seen historically in the Buddha, as Shuichi Maida brings out: "A foolish Shakyamuni studying foolish Shakyamuni." If we can fully understand this then we've arrived at the wonderful state of ordinariness, a wonderful state as being playful.

    Shakyamuni returned to the world as a well-settled person, and as such, listened to all others. Is it no wonder that he had so many friends he met with who then, out of reverence, became listeners as well? We then belong to a sangha of listeners to a Dharma of ordinariness.

    This was Rev. Akegarasu's awakening: simply being I as I, this foolish and ordinary person who is open to listen to all others who are expedient means to his own enlightenment. You cannot put someone like this on a pedestal of sainthood and that's why I can trust and respect him feeling that he is speaking to me directly. I feel that this is very rare. This is the essence of what it means to be ordinary, humbled by the truth of passively listening. It is here in the freshness of life where one is an awakened person who realizes "All others are expedient means towards my enlightenment." Such a subtle truth when I think of it, for it is as a quiet listener hearing the truth from those who express it openly and with their own life that enables me to be enlightened by others.

"I listen to the wise man and the fool, and then go my own way." This indicates that he is an independent person and not merely a follower. The wise and the foolish are just relative aspects among all those he listens to. For instance, the wise person may not recognize himself as a fool. He talks above his head; he has a problem with portraying himself as a learned person wearing such a serious face. He gives great credit to his thinking ability. "I think therefore I Am." is the French philosopher Descartes' (1596-1650) remark that leaves no room for doubt about his ability to think. And in fact, he even thinks that his self-power ability to think is absolute, as he states. Since there is no room for doubt, I think of him as a fool for thinking that his brain power is all there is to life. But this is true for all of those who act as scholars and who apply their limited intellect on life, self-enhancing their ego-based understanding in the process, and is at the basis of all those who think of themselves as wise but are actually functioning as fools.

Then there is the foolish person. The foolish person wastes his time with a lot of nonsense that has nothing to do with his very life, but fiddles it away like the proverbial grasshopper, "Floating merrily, merrily, and gently down the stream, life is but a dream." Living in the bog of sloppiness and carelessness he doesn't pay close attention to where he is going in his dream world. He likes to live in the world of indolence, laziness, selfishness, and attachment to greed, excitement, and self-serving pleasure. But attempting to be clever he thinks of himself as wise in his investments – until the market crashes or he fritters it all away.

"The knower who knows", sees into the true value of life and respects himself. He does not play around with things that have nothing to do with his deepest aspiration and so he shuts off all the noises of the world. Here he is deadly serious about the actions he takes regarding the welfare of people. I think of my teacher here in this regard. Throughout his life he burned-up his total being listening to all others: the wise and the foolish. So much of his material came from this source. So much teaching he received being a student and a listener.

He too was an independent person who listened to the wise and the foolish and then went his own way seeking the truth. True independence comes from our being a relaxed but desperate seeker, one who practices true studentship. In no way has it to do with the kind of person thinking he can establish his own religion in isolation aside from others.

This brings to mind Prince Shotoku (6th cent.), who in the article in his 17 article constitution stated: "I am not always right and the other person is not always wrong." This is the world of the ordinary person.

"Among all the mothers of the world, alone, my mother is best."
"Below the heavens and on all the earth, alone, I am noble!"
These two statements, the first by Haya Akegarasu, the second by the Buddha coincide in the sense of using the word, alone. Listening to the Buddha's shout, Rev. Akegarasu comes up with his own shout based on his relationship with his mother. With as few words as possible one gets a sense of him thinking of his mother who embraced him with her love from his birth into the world and throughout her whole life. In a deep sense I equated his shout with that of the Buddha. The difference here is with his own mother and that of being embraced by her in the actual sense of a human-to-human feeling between mother and child; whereas the Buddha speaks from the light within himself as being most noble.

In the case of the Buddha there are the Gods in the heavens and the divine beings on the earth. Of these beings, his being alone is noble. But it comes in the form of birth shout upon his awakening. Alone, here means that he was left alone with no one to depend on, no one to attach to; as he transcended the earthly and heavenly kingdoms of man with his Gods and divine beings, who are said to bow to him reverentially as the Buddha. But I think of Akegarasu's own mother, alone, as her organic feeling is the best. In other words, his organic, subjective self, alone, is the best.

In terms of our human capability it may be our inability to get the true intent of the Buddha's shout. But when I identify it within my own life when I was just born into the world, I too must have let out such a shout coming from my nakedly fresh self. Here I can identify with Akegarasu's shout by thinking of the relationship I had with my own mother; right away in her arms – yes, my mother is best! However, it is not a matter of comparison with other mothers, but simply a matter of the embracing feeling that I received from her. But she in turn, is being embraced by an unknown power that she is organically at one with that hugs this bundle of flesh close to her bosom and thus was able to transfer it directly to me. In other words, in a very concrete way, she manifests the nurturing power of life itself through her own being, and, transferred it to me in the most organic way to understand Eternal Motherly. Therefore, she alone, is best. In such a way I am at one with the Buddha's own shout. "All of us should feel the same way.", as my teacher stated.

This seems far from being ordinary. Nor does it seem to have anything to do with being an ordinary person as the quiet person, for example. Being as such is not the general public. The general public in the case of Akegarasu expected him to "sing and dance", so to speak. He stated that among these people he was most noble. What he means here is the

person that can travel freely and independently in any direction unhindered or unconfined by the artificial coverings people like to cling to.
"Life is like a shallow pond."
Here Reverend Akegarasu tastes the seemingly flat ordinariness of life. He is relaxed finding himself at one with the phenomena of life.

It is the tathagata itself. It has no form or set place. As such it cannot be grasped by the relative intellect. It is realized within the firmly settled mind of an awakened person, the quiet person. In that sense it is the contents of the Pure Land, even a description of the Pure Land itself in human terms and feeling. It is not heaven. Nor is it a conceptualized entity outside of us. Simply stated, it fills the whole universe and is the unknowable working of the universe itself, to which we are an integral part of. Because it is everywhere as the eternal movement of life it is called the tathagata: coming and going, to which we have no control over. This eternal movement, including all the changes occurring in our life, is what we should appreciate, and even worship.

"We are born, we must work, and we will die." is another way that Akegarasu describes the shallow pond of suchness. In other words, life is very simply expressed in short to-the-point sentences which require no explanation, they simply are as they are. Rev. Akegarasu simply is as he is, letting his mind flow in any direction where his spirit moves him, but expressing his life so simply, sharply and crisply. He is at one with the flat suchness or "isness" as it is. We take note of his freedom. We wish for ourselves this freedom and so we listen. As we listen we are awakened by the same unknowable power, a power that is the essence of all life.

It is for all those who are living their lives to their fullest and who are right now living their life as such – always moving forward into an unknown and unknowable dimension. He tastes the simple emptiness through the life of fullness, and so he can easily express himself as a shallow pond, seeing a likeness as being at one with it. He is satisfied with the very simple things that life brings to him. Like the level of simplicity that he enjoys. He has everything he wants in this simplicity. In the spicy apple, in the sweet peach and the juicy grapes; he tastes the natural flavors that are like the fruits of the teaching. He has no hankering for the artificial styles and decorations that others hanker for. Nor does he need to join the crowds or hold up flags for this or that reason. He realizes that worldly things only distract him from living his own life free from confusion, greed, and artifice. But he must work, and the work that he performs is within the world where all such things exist. He is not attached to them, so he can say and do that which makes his work worthwhile.

He is the ordinary person living in the ordinary world without pretense.

The essence of being ordinary is that of being emptied. When I think of it, it is the indescribable power beyond self that it guides me in so many ways that are incalculable to my understanding and the way I live my life.

"Walk and the way will open." he says, when we don't know what to do, get confused, or who are in such difficulty. Our life reaches its deepest point just when it comes down to our lowest point, i.e., expressing the shout of truth coming from the flat self, or *isness*, that we are when we are stripped of all the artificial layers. If it does not do this then it is not true essence of Buddhism; the deepest part of our being human to the extent of having nothing to show of ourselves outside of this naked self.

"Sit in meditation" he says, in self-reflection as to what is the truth. Reverend Akegarasu had such an extensive knowledge of Buddhism, yet he always came down to the most simple and human expressions such as:

> This empty sheet of paper says it best.

Or:

> I have nothing to teach,
>   no students to teach to.
> Just the moon and the twinkling stars
>   in the night sky.
>
> - H. A.

Late tonight I've been watching the clear and bright moon in the night sky. Since I live in the city there are no stars because of the lights. But there is the shining moon – not quite full but nonetheless so bright. My mind is in nothingness. The thought comes to me that from here what is there to teach? Indeed, what is there to say? Everything appears so clear, so beautiful, and so peaceful just as it is.

When I listen to the news I hear of wars or the threat of wars going on in parts of the world that are in a state of war. In a part of the big city almost 70 people were shot during the long Fourth of July holiday. Of that number 15 people were killed. Drugs and young gangs who are in "turf wars" are the cause. Innocent people are so often the victims being in the wrong place at the wrong time. How terrible it is.

Yet there is this moon that has been shining since eternity. I am at one with this moon. The moon represents nothingness. It is in fact as such. I live in the world of suchness – things as they are. So I live in peace even if difficulties present themselves. I take the time to appreciate this peace. This wondrous world, including all what it is, is this one world. I can feel relaxed in it, like this bright shining moon in the night sky.

BIOGRAPHY OF REVEREND HAYA AKEGARASU   by G. Saito

Infinite center of the shining sky-
Sun!
Still and moving...

As the sun moves, the whole world moves. As the author of this poem moves, his whole world moves. The man who sang this poem out of himself was Reverend Akegarasu, teacher of Reverend Kubose and of myself and of all of you. He says to all: Be the sun. Then you will feel that you are the one shining center of your solar system. Don't be afraid. Be it!

Reverend Haya Akegarasu was born toward the end of the last century in northern Japan, birth place also of Dr. Suzuki and of Dr. Nishida, a great contemporary Japanese philosopher.

Reverend Akegarasu lived a long, full life. This life did not end when he died at the age of 78, for he is still living in us.

(B.T.C. Printout 1965)

Biography of Reverend Akegarasu   by G. Saito

> Infinite center of the shining sky
> Sun!
> Still and moving...

As the sun moves, the whole world moves. As the author of this poem moves, his whole world moves. The man who sang this poem out of himself was Reverend Akegarasu, teacher of Reverend Kubose and of me and all of you. He says to all: Be the sun! Then you will feel that you are the one shining center of your solar system. Don't be afraid. Be it!

Reverend Haya Akegarasu was born toward the end of the last century in northern Japan, birthplace also of Dr. Suzuki and Dr. Nishida, a great contemporary Japanese philosopher.

Reverend Akegarasu lived a long full life. This life did not end when he died at the age of 78, for he is still living in us.

"Pacific View"   Three panel shoji screen
R. A.

Dear Mrs. Toshiko Saito, July 16, 2003

    Some time ago if you remember, back in the spring of 1987 while on a visit to the Los Angeles Higashi Hongwanji main temple where both of you and your husband Gyoko Saito were staying, serving as Bishop of that temple. You had your husband give me a printout of a poem by Reverend Akegarasu and requested that I make a painting based on it, who as you know, was the teacher to your husband as well as yourself. I was so struck by this poem which briefly expressed and focused on the essence of Akegarasu's life. Not only for him the author, but indeed, for all persons including myself. For it is the essence of our real life and what we should really aspire to be. It describes the essence of nirvana. It struck me as the shout of the Buddha. It is Akegarasu's original shout coming from his total being. To read into it is an experience of it penetrating into one's mind. Such a wide landscape he has created here. So many times I've meditated and gone over it in so many ways. I even tried to make several paintings devoted to this central theme, but was never truly satisfied. The whole endeavor was to express the very contents of this poem, as well as your wish it be expressed in a painting done by me have led me into many different ways of expressing the meaning of this poem. So I tried and tried to create something that you could appreciate as well as satisfy myself in being successful in capturing this poem on artist's canvas. But finally I made it.

    Actually many of my paintings are inspired by Reverend Akegarasu's writings. I think much of my feeling comes from him. It is to such an extent that I think I'm living his life. If he were alive I think that I would bow to him for opening-up our lives. But then again, my teacher Reverend Saito – I think I'm living his life as well. In this case it's like face-to-face with the Buddha. But among all those I study and learn from, all the various Dharma teachers who have this spirit as reflected in the poem – this oneness comes up – in which case I can live their lives too. The deeper one's understanding goes the number of Buddha's increase that appears in multitudinous forms within the *Buddha–Body* with the sun in the center as our universe. This is what this sun represents as it moves slowly across the limitless sky. This poem encourages us to be the center of our universe. I'm sure that this was your intent when you had sensei give it to me. Thank you so much for exposing me to it.

    All these thoughts did not occur to me until much later after you had given me the poem and sensei's commentary on it. Without his commentary I don't think I could have clearly understood it. For he was actually living this life, and that is why I listened to him for so many years – to reach a point that inspired me to be the sun from a poem that he translated many years ago. Now that the time is ripe, it fulfills itself as I reflect on its meaning.

    So on that sunny day in August when the Dharma lecture in Berkeley was over, the three of us; you, and your friend Sachi and I went across the Bay, whereas I gathered photo's and made this painting that I'm submitting to you fulfilling your request. It is a three panel shoji screen measuring 72 in. x 40 in., and done in acrylic paint. The rose I added was put there to represent your husband, as a compositional element; and as he was this shining sun.

                                                                                   In Gassho, Roger

Memorial Service for the Late Toshiko Saito
January 5, 1930 – October 31, 2012

On November a memorial service was held for Mrs. Saito at the Buddhist Temple at which time many friends who remembered her from the time when her husband Rev. Gyoko Saito was head minister here at the old Temple. Family members, as well as some out-of-towners, the Haneda's from Berkeley, Ca. and Mrs. Ito of the Los Angeles Main Temple, also attended.

She lived a full and active life. She came to this country two years after he arrived in 1956. At that time she brought with her a little boy whose name was Shin. Later they had two more children, Dawn, and Maya. When I first met her she was doing piecework in order to help support the family. Back in Japan she had been a school teacher so education was not the problem. What was the problem was her lack of English. For this she would need to go to school, and she, like her husband before her, would go to Truman College to learn English. Now for a job; because she knew that on her husband's slim income from being an assistant minister at the temple there simply wasn't enough to send three growing kids through college, even if they received scholarships; so she studied to become an accountant, graduated the course, and became one.

I became involved with the family was through my contact with Rev. Saito, who by the way had his own problems learning English. I remember helping him some in this regard. But anyway, as we did various projects together including a tea room so that he could entertain temple guests for New Year's, I spent time with him and his family, in which case he would treat me to dinner. So this time with the family would also allow me to make friends with Toshiko. I always liked her. She was always active in the temple helping out wherever she could. She gained the respect of the temple members so that throughout his tenure there was never a doubt as to her support of her husband's efforts. By this time he had become head minister and the kids were attending grammar and high school so the apartment where they lived became quite busy. With temple members and friends coming in and out, kids coming home from school, and a crowded schedule of temple needs plus family needs that he had taken responsibility for, one can only marvel at it all.

The place was like a Temple within a Temple. I was so fortunate to share those early and formative days with them – even their dog Mariko! This warmth comes now; and experiencing the friendship of being included in an open family, a family that I hadn't experienced before. In that sense it became my family as well, largely due to the fact that she quietly kept it all together.

The Sutra of A Quiet Person   January 20, 2015 – (R. A.)
Commentary by Shuichi Maida
Translated by Gyoko Saito and Joan Sweany (1975)

We use the term "self-introspection" so often in Buddhism that there can be a "slippage" as to our ignorance about the sharp scalpel needed to uncover the most serious attachments we have facing us including self-love, which is our final attachment, the very one that creates all other attachments that prevent our emancipation into the truth of ourselves.

However, since Reverend Saito was a temple minister as well as at the same time responsible for raising a family (a wife and three children) he sought into Shuichi Maida's translation and commentary on a sutra called, "Face To Face With Shakyamuni", or <u>Sutta Nipata</u> for short. This is a collection of some thirty five sutras, of which this particular one is number twelve. This sutra was written from one the oldest memorized verbal transmissions some three centuries B. C., after Buddha had died.

The one that I have before me is a very rare mimeograph copy that is difficult to read because the typed ink is so faded; but just today, finding it buried, I decided to do it to show some of the difficulty when the sword of truth penetrates into our heart over that which we cherish so deeply and cling to so self-centeredly. And so this sutra challenges us to find and locate the difficulty facing our lives and the trouble we face when we don't.

Note that this is a Theravada sutra.

Stanza 1

*It is a dreadful thing to become friendly with people and, moreover, dirt comes out of family life.

*It is the most important thing for a "quiet person" to be away from both friendliness and the family life.

Here in this first stanza the first prerequisite to be a quiet person is being described. The person who is called "quiet" is a dweller in the transcendental world. He is a person who is immersed in play and is a person who has nothing to do with this world. He is tranquility of Nirvana itself. He is a person who has already transcended such desires and sufferings as the three sufferings of life, that is, greed, anger, and ignorance. He is a person whose desires and sufferings were extinguished. He is a person in a free and emancipated state of suchness. He is a person of "nothingness". Therefore he is a person of great compassion.

He is a person who knows peace. This kind of person, first of all, cuts his relationships with the secular world. On the one hand he does not make a clamor with his friends and he does not pass time in gossiping, in idle discussion, in joking and fooling other people. On the other hand he does not put on a serious look and talk a matter over seriously. He does not spend time talking about problems in this world and in short, he has ceased to be in touch with, and, concerned with the human world. What is called compassion is at the core of one becoming friendly with other people. Buddha does not easily approve of this compassion. He is rather compassionless. And compassion further develops into love. This, Buddha says, is also dangerous. He is worried lest our sharp truth-seeking should be worn out by too much friendliness and love. If we become friendly with people we become compromised and affirm each other and forgive each other at a certain point. As we like to live lukewarmly, we allow other people to do the same thing and it is considered as a kind of etiquette not to demand anything more than that from them. "To be friendly with people" means this kind of mutual-recognition and it also means to live life lukewarmly. Here we get away from out sharp, earnest wish to seek freedom and emancipation and we never cut into the hearts of other people hampered by what is called "reserve" and "prudence". Here it is altogether impossible to experience fire-sparkling contact between the truth of one person and the truth of another person... Friendliness is being apprehended here because it becomes a trouble which carries off the feet of those who are seeking freedom in the transcendental world.

    Another thing to be thrown away is the family life. This stanza goes so far as to say that dirt comes out of it. It is because there is selfishness in blood relationships. In this family life where selfishness is allowed the three poisons of life, that is, greed, anger, and ignorance, are being exposed very openly. This is in contrast to the friendliness with other people, where we are supposed to be reserved and prudent. Lost in selfishness we cease to reflect upon ourselves. What has been compassion or affection degrades itself and becomes sexual desire and pleasure. Then there arises a dirty bog. People not only allow each other to be lukewarm, but they also start to be drawn into the depth in one. We can understand this easily when we take up one example, the quarrel between a man and his wife. The quarrel is done not only irresponsibly, but its sensual, peripheral pleasure leads man into the bottom of this earth. How could we seek freedom of the transcendental world in this situation? This is in the opposite direction. That's why he states that dirt comes out of it.

    In this stanza we have to see clearly how Buddha saw such things as a family and a family life. These are the very things to be thrown away. For example, there is no room for our discussion concerning how to educate our children at home. We see here how scholars of education are snobbish. My teacher Rev. Akegarasu never allowed a book on education to enter into his collection of books. I think it is because he saw more snobbishness in education than in any other field of study. If I am to point at the typical example of "the quiet person" in our country, I think of such people as Prince Shotoku and Shinran Shonin are those. However, we must not overlook the fact that there was, in their respective lay life, as incomparably sharp separation from family life. If people, standing on their snobbish self-centered viewpoint, indulge in wishful thinking and interpret the life of Prince Shotoku and Shinran Shonin as the life amenable to their worldly mentality, it is a laughable thing. It is easy to see in Dogan, the separation from the worldly world. (Dogan was a famous Zen Master in the 12th cent. who lived in a monastery in China and was never married, never had a family, and who lived far away from the world). However, much more sharpness is required to see into that of Prince Shotoku and Shinran Shonin (both of who had a family). The very fact that this stanza consisting of two lines is being put at the beginning of the sutra of the quiet person makes us straighten ourselves in front of the Buddha-Dharma, in front of the Buddha. If I did not say this is a fatal blow on one's crown of the head, how could I think of any other expression? Here is Buddha-Dharma, no, here is religion. This is also the case with Jesus Christ. He meant this when he said that he had come to this world, not to bring peace but to throw swords.

Stanza 2

*The person who cuts off and throws away what has already come into being and who does not create the cause to bring something into being again. The person who does not rely upon what is now coming into existence and who takes away the cause of it. This kind of person is called "the quiet person" who goes his independent way and this kind of great person lives his own life peacefully.

"Coming into being", which is said here, means "coming into being subjectively." If we understand this objectively and logically, this does not mean anything. "Cutting off and throwing away" means "watching". It rather means gazing at or watching intently, the fact of it. It is a clear awareness and introspection. Here we can look through and understand fully from what kind of cause things have occurred. For example, we see love and lust coming out of ignorance and darkness. If we can clearly recognize that love and lust have originated from such ignorance, then, in this awareness, we can transcend the darkness. "Not creating the cause" means this awareness.

What is expressed is "coming into existence" means a state of mind that we are going to feel desire now. "Not relying upon it" means not being indulgent and whimsical. In other words, it means that we watch intently the desires and reflect on it. And we see where this desire originates. We see how this desire is being quenched. For example, we see it coming from our self-conceitedness, arrogance, the over-estimation of ourselves, selfishness, and over-indulgence and from self-satisfaction. We see it coming out of the fact that we are not watching the world, the essence of things, carefully. In other words, we know that it comes out of our ignorance about ourselves and the world. If one has come to this awareness one experiences a 180 turn around and feels that one has to recognize truth and starts to seek truth. "Taking away the cause of it" means something as follows: Knowing that one does not know anything about anything; that one is drifting here and there and is led astray by illusions. One, urged by one's inner voice, starts to investigate the essential truth. Here, one can take away the cause of desire.

"Going on his independent way" means "going on his way of introspection." Having nothing to do with others (applies to "society" in general), not negotiating with them and completely ignoring others and of the worldly world, he just watches his individual being intently. For example, it is something like the thoroughly clear understanding of oneself that one is the only bad person in the whole world (applies to himself and also as a universal confession). If one has come to this awareness that all people exist absolutely, one by one, then this kind of awareness is real independence. An independent person never cares about other people. He does not interfere with other people's lives and tamper with it. The quietness of this person lies in the fact that he leaves other people to their absolute freedom. The person who is alone and is watching himself intently, does not make clamor. It is because he has no more contact and relationships with other people and there is no more possibility for him to quarrel with them. For example, the 10th article of the 17 articles (of Prince Shotuku) teaches us that even though people may get angry with you, you should reflect on yourself and be afraid of your faults. When a person listens to these words he is quiet as ever in front of the anger of other people.

Buddha says "this kind of person is a <u>great</u> person". It is because this person is not invaded by others. Peaceful life means the life of Daturaku (Emancipation or Drop out). The bottom of his self falls off and the world can be seen as it is by the quiet person. He rather sees there, boundless light and boundless life of eternal life and the only thing he can do is admire it. That is why he is peaceful. There is only the life of actional intuition and the life of Heijo-tei for him who has no more self. This life we say "peaceful". As mentioned above, the way which leads to this peace lies always in introspection. It is the realm of introspection that one does not create the cause to bring something into being and that one gets rid of it. The secret of the quietness in the independent and awakened person is being exposed here.

Stanza 3

*The person who thinks carefully by what things is being composed and who destroys the cause from which all things originate. And, the person who does not give freedom to desires, who takes away the cause of them.
*This kind of person as the "quiet person" sees the end where our life expires, stays far away from illusion and delusion and he is never in opposition with things and goes on his own way.

To think carefully means to think subjectively. It is the position that one is always aware that this world is the world for one. It is the position that one is required to think carefully about; by what part of one's personality this world is being temporarily formed. It is the position or attitude that one contemplates on how one should deal with and contact various things such as accidents and matters occurring in the world. The position of the one, as it were, is to find the cause of an entangled matter in one's attitude concerning the matter. Matters do not get so complicated if one's attitude toward them is proper. For example, why does something like the Second World War happen? It happens as a consequence of relative and antagonistic positions and attitudes and as the consequence of the revengeful "an eye for an eye, tooth for tooth" relationship. It is an attachment to <u>our side</u> (a product of self-love). It is our greed and our self interest and selfish desires. It is our egoism. It gives rise to various complicated matters. Linzai (Lin-chi) aptly said Hei-jo-bu-ji, that is, there is no complication in our flat, ordinary life. The first line of this stanza describes the "bu-ji, that is, "no complication".
Where there is open-heartedness which enables one to live life without attachment, without stagnation and in harmony with the perpetual changing of things, there is no disturbance. There arise no serious matters. When one is cheerful and flexible enough to accept all mutation and changes, oriented by the truth of continuous change, is instantly

"bu-Ji", without complication. When one is living in accordance with actional intuition all the time and is not wasting one's time in leisurely thinking; in short, when one is in "Hei-jo-tei", (flat ordinary state), one does not have any disturbance. It is the birth in wisdom that one destroys the ignorance about the truth about continues change, from which all things originate.

It is said here that such a man of wisdom "sees this end where our life expires". He probes to the bottom of life and realizes that man's life is not so serious a matter. He comes to the realization that man cannot possibly do any great thing about good and evil no matter how desperately he may try. What can a man do? All things done by human beings are nothing but trifles. The only great thing in this world is the working of Eternal life itself. This Shinran Shonin called "the Greatest Work...."

"To stay away from illusion" means that one is away from the illusive, self-conceited attachment to the Self-Power that one could do something great. …. "To never be set up in opposition with things".... "To go on his way" means that one functions in the way of Eternal life uniquely as an individual thing. …. The quietness of this wise man comes from the incessant creative life where he is never opposed to others but is always at one with all things in the world. His quietness lies in his following his own creative way and in his not being hampered by others. To go on one's way in this way means that one becomes the expression of Life and lives its life; the life filled with Truth is made possible here. Here our good-for-nothing, trivial self is being watched through and through. Without this introspection it would be impossible for one to go on one's own way.

Stanza 4

*The person who knows very well to what people are attaching to and who is not allured by one of these attachments .
*This person who has clearly gotten rid of his greedy mind.
*This kind of person as "the quiet person" is not disturbed by anything no matter what may happen for he has already gone to the other shore.

What does a man attach to? He attaches to those things which make him forget his miserable reality. For example, he attaches to those things which are ready to flatter him and are capable of appeasing his desire for money and fame. He sticks to those things which satisfy his self-conceit and pride and which lead him to ecstasy. In short, he attaches to self-satisfaction. On the other hand, he tries to evade things which could expose his miserable reality as it is. He hates things which lead to his self-negation and loves those things which are connected to his self-affirmation. In other words, he attaches to self-love. In this way we find attachment to one's self; persistent adherence to one's self is at the root of all human attachments.... People are usually induced deeper and deeper; endlessly into what satisfies their self-love. They finally lose self-control and sink deep into a bog where they completely lose their own self. The quiet person is the one who knows the misery of this. Therefore he is a person who has clearly gotten rid of his greedy mind. The quiet person is the one who is serious enough to see his reality and is not disturbed by it. He is the one who does not indulge in himself and does not spoil himself. He never falters in-between his two selves. He can calmly watch his own nature and he is a steady, well-settled person. This is the quiet person.

The reason why he is not disturbed by anything is thorough-going as said here in this stanza. It is because he has already gone to the other shore. No matter what kind of affair may arise in this world, the person who is good-for-nothing in this world has nothing to do with it. Nothing whatever can become the cause of his disturbance or excitement. What a terrible thing is being said here! This kind of person is "the quiet person". If I put it conversely, it means that the person who has already gone to the other shore cannot be disturbed at all by any kind of happening in this world. People are still cute while they are disturbed and excited by things and fellow creatures in this world. Buddha was the very person who was not disturbed and excited by any happening in this world. When Prince Shototu was informed of the assassination of the Emperor Suzaku, he is said to have said that it was all the inevitable retribution of karma. There was no surprise in him at this point. There was only the recognition of reality.

Stanza 5

*The person who has overcome everything is the person who has known everything and has understood the final cause of all things very well. The person, who has thrown away everything and has put an end to his lust and has become emancipated, is not polluted by anything.

*This kind of person is also called "the quiet person" by the wise.

Overcoming everything means that one sees all things as they are and one does not leave this attitude of seeing at all and one cannot be disturbed by what he sees, as everything which is happening one after another is being seen. How is it being seen? Everything is being seen as a matter inside the world of self-awareness. In the last analysis, everything affecting us from the outside has cause in us; in this way, everything as our matter is within us. If one supposes that things independently exist to the outside of oneself, we will inevitably be disturbed by them. One will stand in opposition to others. However, when everything is seen as a matter within oneself, it is embraced and absorbed completely into one's being. In this way it can be transcended. Overcoming everything means self-awareness and self-awareness has the capacity to transcend the duality ….. (Between external and internal).

Here I want to take up the example which shows the "overcoming everything". (This is the quotation from Prince Shyoku's 17 articles Constitution.) "Therefore when other people get angry with you, you should reflect on yourself and be concerned about your own faults." "Even if you alone have attained truth, you should act just as ordinary people act." These are the examples. These examples teach us to overcome ourselves…… "Knowing everything" means that one always recognizes that this world is the world as one. As is one's subjective world that is the world of one's self-awareness. One also recognizes the truth of self-awareness working as continuous change at the basis of this world. All things are reflecting on what we are now. In proportion as our ignorance increases this world becomes darker. The more wisdom we have, the brighter becomes this world. "Knowing everything means intuitive awareness of this world as the space less and timeless world. Once we have known this world as the world of Eternal Life, we can say for the first time we know everything.

"Understanding the final cause of all things very well" means that one copes with all matters with one's "actional intuition". (He uses the term: "actional intuition" quite often to indicate one's immediate response to a given situation that is derived intuitively by seeing directly into things, not by round-about thinking attached to a static understanding.)

Facing various problems of life, coming and going continuously in front of our eyes, one sees them by acting and one acts by seeing them. This kind of life applies to "Understanding the final cause of all things very well." This is O-mu-sho-ju-ni-sho-go-shin. (As we don't have any place to live in, we live in our mind.) One can understand things very well if one does not have any fixed concept and when one is in the state of suchness, where one is acting freely being at one with all things; we call this very state "understanding the final cause of all things very well." This "understanding" does not mean to have logical or objective knowledge about things.

"Not being polluted" means that one is not opposed to things. One puts everything in one's heart. In the great world of Oneness where one is many and many is one, everything is with its individual life and at the same time all people including you and me are being creative elements for the creative world. In this phrase of "not being polluted ", emancipated and free life where there is no opposition is being described.

"Throwing away everything" means not to be dependent upon this world, including what is called "our self". Not becoming our self made to exist by our environment, but becoming the world itself, becoming Eternal Life, we live and act, which is being expressed in "throwing away everything". Everything exists in "Nothingness". This is what is really expressed in "throwing away everything".

"Putting an end to one's lust" means that one does not live in one's small limited love; one lives in the great compassion of Tathagata which loves all senescent beings. It also means that one becomes at one with the untiring creativity of the Eternal Life. This is where we can find freedom and quiet emancipation. We call this the state of "Oneness".

++

R. Adams

The objectivity seen in the external world now becomes subjectively seen within ourselves. As this is the case, there is no dualistic external or internal as the two are inseparable. Therefore we should not get caught by external things aside from our subjective being. At the same time we should also clarify what is going on within us. This leads to clarification as to the cause of whom and what is happening in the world; as the world and people are either fighting or loving each other. We have to carefully examine what is involved as to the causes and reasons. And the causes and reasons follow self-love; as the roots of the problems going on in the world are so often attributable to this fact. Insofar as ourselves is concerned, the roots of one's evil begins with the ego, fortified by self-love or the static shell-of-self. We have to break out of this shell, so hardened and fixed within our notions of self. Seeing into this is our real difficulty, struggle, and even impossibility – the only real impossibility that we ultimately have to face with our total effort.

The solution is to throw away our limited and relative thinking that we depend on and that prevent us in discovering the causes which contribute to our difficulty. These go against and prevent continuous change which is functioning within life itself, and also against the organic life moving within us. Being in accord with our organic being, however, we are well-settled, happy, peaceful, and emancipated. We are emancipated from our own "stuck-in-the-mud" mind, as everything takes place in our own mind.

Herein we live in a state of nothingness, as everything comes down to emptiness. No study is needed here. No education is needed, either. Here is where I am free. Free to do as I wish, free to do and go about my own way in spacious freedom. And all the difficulties and struggles are part of this spacious freedom, as they are all part of the reality of life that we live in. This is the reality of the world itself. Then these are the creative paths we can take as an attitude that is needed for dwelling in the transcendental Buddha-Consciousness and awareness. This awareness is at the heart of Eternal Life. Nothingness is the soul of the tathagata of Eternal Life.

Such a shout comes from here. Such brightness comes from here, as an expression my total freedom. I meet with the sun, I am the sun, I meet with all things in life itself; I am life itself, taken as it comes. In the universe of One, I experience the One Soul of the universe.

"Spacious Freedom" . R. A.

One of Reverend Akegarasu's favorite prints was that of a man lassoing Mt. Fuji and trying to pull it down. With his eyes bulging and his whole body twisted and bent over in the effort, he is trying to do the impossible in overcoming this huge mountain. With such single-minded effort is there any Vow that can't be accomplished? So too, is our life. All those I respect the most had their own mountain to contend with. The impossible task before them, they accomplished their deepest aspiration to which they could say – so brightly as fulfilling: "I made it!" Spacious freedom is given to those who earn it. And in this spacious freedom there is a quiet joy of bringing down one's own mountain.   (R. A.)

Addenda *Refresh*

Do I have any virtues; can I have any virtues? Searching my mind I see that I have none. This question came upon me while attending a memorial service this evening for a temple member who had just passed away wherein the word, virtue, was mentioned. Later I realized that the only virtues I can have is that which was given to me by the teacher. In thinking about what this virtue is, it is that of a fully realized human being. Here the essence of this human being is that of bowing. It is not the typical mundane form of bowing that of the generic type; or even in gratitude of showing one's appreciation which is one of the aspects, but that of an uncontrollable kind that suddenly gushes out in tears. Here, even the words themselves do not appear nor are they uttered, yet with these tears come one's deepest feeling of bowing that we as humans can have that transforms ice into water. Then the phrase, "thus comes" that is attached to the word, tathagatha, gushes out from the depths of our being as the most essential and organic change going on in our mind that produce such tears. The nembutsu (Namu Amida Butsu) is the most organically spiritual essence of our being linked to the power beyond self (other power). Again, the tathagatha must be created within our being and consciousness, otherwise it exists only as an abstraction just as are so many other words we use in our Buddhist vocabulary. While good as instructional tools, yet until these words are fully chewed and digested, so to speak, and assimilated within our lives, they can exist as two-dimensional abstractions with no real life to them. Here the nembutsu can very well fit into this pattern. So too, the figure of Amida Buddha, which the word nembutsu is taken from can be treated this way as well, and so you get into a dichotomy between the words and even the misunderstanding of the actual meaning that the words imply. In this process the meaning of Amida Buddha gets lost and forgotten, and we just resort to what it is the others are doing – the whole process becomes mechanical! This is most unfortunate, as we then fail to be students and seekers into the very nature of our life itself. The very nature of our life is to be a spiritual human being which gives us the feeling of life itself as we live it. Thus we must *become* the nembutsu. In the same sense as Dharmakara came to in the Larger Sutra, so too, we must seek into what it was that caused him to become the bowing Amida Buddha. Otherwise we will be chanting the nembutsu just paying our respects reverentially as a ritual. Thus the nembutsu can become so formalized that it can lose its original meaning. Whereas bowing without being able to help it out of an inner necessity is listening to the "thus comes" emanating from our spiritual essence. Actual spiritual life cannot be fixed by ritual, any more than we as humans can be ritualized. We can still practice it as a ritual, but we should at least know that it is only a ritual, not the real thing. Indeed, this can be another one of our delusions thinking that we, by performing such practices, can be made virtuous.

The nembutsu is solemn. In solemn reverence my whole body and mind bends downward focusing on an individual I deeply respect. In expressing this essence, without any intention, my mind is clarified, emptied – to receive the only virtue that can be given to me by a power I have no control over, nor can claim as my own – nor described, nor set down in so many words – but which exists only through experiencing it. Or, I can say that this is the main thing that my teacher gave me, as I observed and listened to this man of nembutsu. Here too, I experienced it as I joined with him in oneness through many of his speeches and lectures. I felt it. Quietly I think it's no wonder this nembutsu comes now, almost to tears. "How difficult it is to be human." This was his nembutsu, both for his teacher, and all of life. This kind of reverence is not so cheap nor can it be put in a small box of what we might call standardized religion, with no real life to it.

In attending a memorial service for one of the temple members this evening I felt a solemnity along with the rest of the attendees who were already seated. At the end of the service, friends, and parishioners were offering incense along with the nembutsu (bowing) in front of the incense burner situated in front of the Hondo (Alter). Right after giving incense I turned and met the deceased person's wife who was seated in a wheel chair. As soon after I had seen her face I burst into tears uncontrollably. "I'm so glad to see you. So glad to see you" I kept repeating, all the while bursting into tears. Tears and snots were running down my nose to such an extent that I had to run to the bathroom. Fred's wife always smiled whenever I met her. He was always so serious, but she always wore a smile. (Once I even told her that her bright smiling face reminded me of Amida Buddha!). This had been an emotionless memorial service, and now I feel that I broke up this rather static atmosphere with such a shout or loud burst of emotion that must have shocked and moved the audience that reverberated throughout the ten quarters! But it was all uncontrollable.

A little later I met with one of the ministers of the temple and she remarked that the two of us, Fred and myself, didn't always get along and that there was some disagreement between us regarding the Dharma, which was true. But here I am, having such tears with the wife of the departed that brought me to a nembutsu that took over my whole being, and that cleared away all such difficulties.

Death brings us to a point of solemnity like no other that we can experience. In the matter of death we come down to the reality that teaches us the truth about our lives in no other way as well. We can choose life or we can choose death or either can come about naturally. This then is the final truth in our lives, so everyone must face it. Death is indeed the final transformation, which in Buddhism is called: "parinirvana", which is a Pali term for complete combustion. But then, death has another meaning to our lives here on earth – that unless I die I cannot be reborn. This death is what Rev. Haya Akegarasu referred to as: "Total cremation of self is my only enlightenment." What was left from the flames of self-cremation was the cool flame of his naked being. No need here to go into the circumstances that led up to his enlightenment except to say he experienced, in a spiritual sense, complete combustion; not only of the relative self but the total self, leaving Self alone as most noble. This shining Self is now the Ordinary person in the world helping all the lonely ones. As such he enters his land as a lion and with a roar that can be heard throughout the ten quarters, as he roams about freely!

So what was coming out of this rather lukewarm religious setting empty of real emotion was the shout of a nembutsu which came out of my organic being that so awakened the audience of attendees that I could feel a kind of shock, being suddenly overwhelmed with emotion. Was it because I had been working on my papers that over a period of time built up to a point where in the nembutsu of tears gushed out uncontrollably given the proper circumstances? This birth comes with this nembutsu – this shout provided the emphasis for an audience that was so far unmoved. I could sense that. This is a Buddhist memorial service, what does Buddhism have to say about life and death? Yes, it is somber and respectful, all funerals are. But beyond that what is it that is missing? This is what I observed and how I responded. It was deeply or subconsciously done, with no pre-conceived idea. So the man has gone to the other shore of the Pure Land, experiencing pari-nirvana, or complete combustion, and now we are dealing with the living who are there for his memorial.

His granddaughter speaks in the eulogy about what she has to say about her grandfather that enlightens us about the way he lived and his reasons for coming into Buddhism, for in that he was raised in an Orthodox Jewish family. He was put in an orphanage after his mother passed away. He turned to education and taught in two high schools here in Chicago. He became increasingly a seeker of truth after traveling extensively and reading extensively and became attracted to Japanese culture and then religion, even growing a Japanese garden. He came to the temple to study religion and exchange views about the Dharma, even starting a study class of his own. Eventually towards the end of his life he made a Ti Sarana and was given a Buddhist name. He got very involved with temple activities becoming the secretary of religious activities, and etc. So all in all he was taking what he considered to be the necessary steps towards eventual enlightenment. But his age took over and he became debilitated to such an extent that he lost his hearing and his sight. He quietly passed away on December of this year. Listening to this eulogy I feel that his granddaughter really captured his heart, something that was not very evident to many of his students. But his wife did, and through her I responded as I did when I met with her seated in the wheel chair having her own difficulties. The difficulties of our life are indeed to seek the truth. And through these difficulties comes the nembutsu experiencing Buddha's compassion.

At this time the nembutsu is like the tathagatha that blows away the dust that has settled on our judgments, opinions, and views, regarding how we feel about the other person. Then one realizes that the tathagatha is itself the nembutsu and the nembutsu is the tathagatha. In other words, the nembutsu is the expression of the tathagatha (continuous change) in which one's thoughts held onto previously have been negated and I am once again able to see things afresh. From this fresh sight I now appreciate Fred and see him as a human being struggling with the truth, especially given his background. He once said that he came to Buddhism for spiritual reasons. I think that he questioned the religious traditions that he grew up with and turned to Buddhism for answers, and in doing so he became a student of a tradition that was distinctly different. This is not easy for one invariably retains or clings to the tradition of his or her ethnicity; which by the way includes one's family, if not a dramatic change in one's spirituality.

Buddhism begins with impermanence. It does not begin with the belief in a Supreme Being because it is seen as a fixed entity outside of one's self where exists a dichotomized relationship, wherein the object of one's belief exists on the basis of an absolute in terms of permanence; i.e., as a God, or "Atman". This is the very thing that Shakyamuni the Buddha broke free of after much difficulty of struggle and self-introspection. Thus in Buddhism a 180 degree change in our understanding is necessary in order to fully understand that the absolute is indeed impermanence which not only allows us to see the world along with our self as subject to continuous change; but allows us to flow with it as one whole moving experience, being at one with the totality of life itself. Thus our true spirituality moves immediately from a fixed set of beliefs and religious practices based upon them as well as superstitious and sentimental practices dispelled, along with the ego-shell of the mind that created them. Thus the enlightened one who is awakened to the spiritual essence of one's life no longer needs nor clings to the conceptualized form of a God.

The "gushing out" is an expression of the infinite life and compassion within us. This is a crucial point. For the infinite is not "out there" in some other-worldly place, but is within our very own being. In other words, we ourselves have the capability of self-realization in throwing off the yokes of our bondage. This is the stage of our understanding called the "gateless gate", the final stage of our spiritual development, having gone through the religious stages preceding it. This is where we are religious persons following religious precepts attempting to be good persons and religious persons. Here we are still trying to maintain our control. But in terms of "gushing out" we go beyond this control and become alive in an area wherein there is no control – thus comes life itself. This is the transformation. So from here there is no gate since we are already in it – the spacious freedom where I am allowed to do as I wish, or where the will of the spirit takes me.

So the nembutsu, seen from this vantage point is the human expression of the infinite within our self. This is an amazing feature which is so far away from all orthodox religious practices. How welcome is this teaching when we really realize it, this essence of Pure Land Buddhism that brings us to Amida Buddha and the nembutsu.

How joyous it is when I think of it. To live in darkness and coldness, stupidity and delusion, and to see the light; the light that gives us this life that comes up as the shout of one's total being, as within the feeling expressed through the nembutsu.

Dear Rev. Marvin Harada,   Oct. 19, 2015

We are all members of the sangha who listen and learn from the teachings of Shakyamuni. These teachings include all those of our teachers who carry on the long tradition of opening our lives to the way he laid down for us to walk. All of our teachers including its founder, Shakyamuni, the one who created the sangha, was also a member, giving us the true teachings of the Buddha-Dharma that enable us to find our way. To enlighten us as to the true nature of self, that opens our eyes to see ourselves as we truly are in the world as it truly is. What a fundamental and universal truth it is. Hearing the truth, the world of the Buddha opens....

The eternal incomplete is the complete, as is the movement of going forward; seeking and finding my way into the creation of life itself, by turning a negative into a positive. This is the transforming essence of our life as within the creation of life.

Thank you so much for your letter and book by your teacher, Gyoko Hagar, as I have been in the process of going through it. Buddhism and its teachings is the process of deepening into the very core of our being whereas we can come up with our very own shout of total freedom and independence. I encourage your efforts, for how wondrous are these Buddha-lands we have to discover for ourselves.

In 2001, soon after he passed away, I decided to write a book that was dedicated in his memory. I went straight forward with a project that I knew the teacher, Reverend Gyoko Saito, would have wanted, as he wrote for others as well as for himself. To do so I had to live the life of the teacher. To merely write a book about him would not qualify as an authentic realization of his life's work. Therefore, I could not just copy his articles, but get a feeling for his life in terms of self-reflection into my own life as being at one. Being at one with the teacher is most important. This has been going on since 1963 when I first met him.

To that end I am finishing the book that I long ago started. In one way it's been a long struggle; sometimes seeming to be impossible, for I had such limited tools, such as language skills, as well as an in extensive knowledge of Buddhism itself. But as I went forward listening, learning, and hearing the teachings, I gained knowledge in so many ways that somehow came to me and inspired me to go forward no matter what. The result is a book of 260 pages in which I've done my best to capture the essence of the teacher's life and my life up to this point as well.

In your lecture here at the Buddhist temple in Chicago on the 24th of August and Reverend Akegarasu's memorial service the following Sunday, I got the impression that you expressed yourself as your own art. Reverend Akegarasu always enjoyed listening to his friends who expressed their life through their own art.

But besides this you gave us some of your translations of Akegarasu's lectures. In this case it was his commentary on the Larger Sutra which consisted of some 26 pages. We are presently using it as teaching for our sutra discussion class. I find it to be extremely useful insofar as giving me a broader and deeper understanding into the life of this sutra. His storehouse of the Dharma allows us to enter and gather whatever needed to enlighten our understanding. And it has done so expeditiously. Thank you for giving us these pages.

In another one of his articles he expresses the fact that each of us has within us a noble being. In other words, all of us, whether Buddhist or non-Buddhist alike can touch upon the deepest part of our life – referred to as the core or "roots" as it were, and come up with this most vibrant life expression as our own art.

But to find out our most noble self we first have to discard that smallish self, buried as it is in false beliefs that are evidenced by our artificial coverings, decorations, and delusions. And then the fear of death, all of which sends us into darkness and foreboding. Amidst this fear the light of Amida Buddha comes through!

Think of others who we owe our life to – so we are not alone, our very existence was given to us. And the very power of life that enabled us to do so many things was not of our power alone, but of a power of life beyond our limited self – so just entrust yourself to this incomprehensible power and you shall be free. Namu Amida Butsu is how I recognize myself as to the servant unto the master; the master being as life itself. The flame within is this noble being, its spirit shining in all directions, encompassing the Sun itself, as it embraces all sentient beings unconditionally.

In Care, Roger

"Lilly Pond" R. Adams

Dear Friend,   Nov. 26, 2015

    This morning I felt a little somber. This matches the overcast and rainy weather we're having, plus the fact that I'll not be able to meet with the family for Thanksgiving this year due to the fact that three of its members are sick, others are out of town, and with the roads all torn up and so on, and so my cousin cancelled it.
    Added to that, after listening to the way in which worldly affairs have taken a disturbing turn after the Paris terrorist attacks and, in this country as in California, amount to a gloomy picture of what is going on in the world today. A crisis of events has reached a flash point of proportions that is nearly out of control. This is the set-up of the secular world and its contentious and never ending conflicts.
    But out of this sense of darkness come the thought of my friends. Since I had some of my articles on the kitchen table in front of me, and in glancing over them I decided that it would be a good time (having this open space) to send a few to you. As I re-read them over I suddenly awoke to a living Dharma – and I became joyous!
    Then I thought: Why must we hold back? Why can't we just shout our life as being naked? So out of this sense of positive thinking is what encourages me to go forward and drop all the separation that pulls me and so many others apart.
    With that I'm delighted. The mind that is naked is the mind that is empty. All things come – they just come. And in this "just come" the great movement of life flows and gushes like a river that cuts through and jumps over rocks, or hitting them straight on, or going around them, transcending the blockages; with the power of pushing me into the unknowable creation of life itself as in the will of the spirit.

"Yellowstone"   R. A.

    The beginner's mind is the mind that is open to receive everything, and is like that of a child's mind. I throw everything else aside and just cherish and welcome all those I meet. This is the welcoming Buddha-Dharma I want to practice. As I do that then my life is fulfilled. Then this is the real reason for the book. Exposing the life of the teacher and my life as well, and to share it with all others is my real wish and deepest aspiration.

                                       Gassho, Roger

FAREWELL MESSAGE   Gyoko Saito 1981

Time really flies like an arrow. It's like only yesterday that I came to Chicago, but actually it was 25 years and 6 months ago. On the morning of May 10, 1956, I arrived in downtown Chicago by Santa Fe train after a long trip of two nights and three days.

Half my life is in Chicago. Therefore it is impossible for me to say farewell. But the time has come. I have to say farewell and thank you to all of you readers of this bulletin, because this is my final chance to write and express my feeling.

My first impression of Chicago was the one I had when I arrived in the railway station. It was unusually windy and clouded over. Paper and trash were blowing through the air. It's as if a very stormy life was about to appear. The uncertainty for my new life in Chicago, plus this threatening weather, really gave me a powerful impression at first glance.

And in fact, as soon as I jumped into Mr. Eizo Nishi's car, a terrible rainstorm broke out, pouring buckets of water on our heads. There was fierce lightening, and the sound of thunderbolts was huge. I had never experienced anything like it in Japan. When I think back, after 25 years in Chicago, it was a signal for me, who was then only 29 years old and never experienced real life, to let me know what real life was all about.

In fact, it was really true. The first Sunday in Chicago was Mother's Day Sunday, and I was asked to give a talk to the Issei gathering (first generation Japanese immigrants). The contents of my talk were the struggle of Kierkegaard's Highest Wish and Abyss and the Goethe and Nishida's philosophies and so on. Naturally the Issei people, who had experienced real life thoroughly and tasted its bitterness and difficulties, did not understand what I was talking about. Their response was: we don't understand you. The more I became honest with myself in talking to the Isseis, the more honest and extreme their response got. One brave Issei said, "Please talk to us in naniwa-bushi style!" – the melodramatic story-telling style developed during the Tokugawa. I was shocked. "Honestly," I thought to myself, "I'm going to quit!"

But then when I thought back I realized that behind the Issei's faces there were the faces of my parents. "If I cannot convince the Issei people by my talks, which means my talks couldn't be understood by my parents either." So, realizing that, for the first time I started to learn the True Teaching. In that sense, after I lost my Teacher, the Issei people in Chicago became the real Teacher for me.

Of course I did not understand English at all. Living in Chicago without

English, it was if I had suddenly become deaf and mute. It was a new experience. From the top of the sophistication of 29 years of life, suddenly you live the life of illiteracy and muteness and dumbness. It was a shock.

I was supposed to go to school to learn English, but the learning process ended in a very short time, because the Temple had just purchased its present building and was starting to move from the South Side to the North Side. I remember that for nearly half a year I slept in the basement where the judo shower room now is. Later on I moved to what is now the kitchen.

More important, the building had been a warehouse of Goldblatts', for over ten years without heat, so all the walls needed plastering. But at the time the temple couldn't afford to pay for it, so it was decided to get volunteer help from temple members. There were good plasterers, like Mr. Kanemoto and Mr. Tachi Goya, but they had their own apartments and were mostly busy, so it ended up with Mr. Shitsuke Maeda assisted by Saito. I started out as an apprentice, just mixing the plaster for him, but he encouraged me and then promoted me to be a plasterer. Even today, if anyone asks me to do plastering I am quite confident I could do a good job.

But meantime I lost most precious, important time that I was supposed to spend studying English. Circumstances did not allow me to. Then the only way I could learn English was through tutoring. Out of my desperate wish, I grabbed hold of Lee Burgess, a young artist who had come to make signs for the 1957 Festival. Through practically nothing but body language, sign language, I started to learn from him.

During the day time I was too busy, so late at night was the only time for him to teach me English. I remember, once he came to the temple in the morning. "What happened?" I asked him. "I got fired." I honestly looked around and asked him, "Where is the fire?" but somehow he got the message across that he no longer had a job. Because of staying up till one, or even three, with me every night, he couldn't wake up early enough to get to work on time. (He did get another job…and another…)

Lee also taught me how to drive. He had a junky car. I had practiced only once, when Reverend Kubose let me drive around the block and I stepped on the gas instead of the brake and drove into a concrete wall. He got a bump on the head, so he quit teaching me.

Lee took me to the Wilson and Lake Shore Drive intersection and told me, "I don't care about my junky car, but please take care of your life and mine – and let's go!" And for the first time I drove on a highway. When we reached downtown safely, he said, "I'll take the El back to the Temple and wait for you there." Boy, I never begged so hard in my life as that time! Finally he agreed to ride back with me, and we reached the Temple at last. As soon as I sat down on a chair, I had a terrible bloody nose, out of the high tension.

These incidents are just symbolic of the inner stormy life in Chicago for 25 years. But during that period I did change two Caucasian men's perfect Standard English - Lee Burgess and Roger Adams. Then I had less difficulty communicating with people in English!

But still the essential struggle was to really seek the Teaching that can be relevant to the life of the Issei people. Twenty-nine years of my life was nothing but going to school to learn that I have to wash away all the book knowledge and sophistication and be a naked human being first. Taste the struggle in real life.

Even though I regularly held discussion classes in English for 25 years, I never asked the Issei people to join with me in a study class. I just waited and waited for over 20 years. And finally, a couple of years ago, Issei people asked me to hold a study class. Then for the first time I felt my mission was accomplished.

There are so many things I can say about the contents of my stormy life in Chicago that it is endless.

One thing that I can say is that Chicago is my life, most precious life. Though close to 26 years of my life, I don't how many people I bumped into and made an inevitable in-en. Not just with one generation, but in many cases, I have been privileged to get to know three generations of temple members and friends, and share life together with all these people. They are the contents of my life. I owe my whole life to them, therefore I cannot just say, "Grateful, thankful." It is my life.

Chicago will never become just a memory, even when I move to Los Angeles. As I grow, as I deepen my understanding of life, people in Chicago, past and present, will grow together with me. In that sense, though I'm moving to Los Angeles physically and saying farewell to you all, your being in the inner part of my life will be together with me as long as I live.

With the greatest gratitude and thankfulness, temporarily I will end my writing.

(Last article in B.T.C. Bulletin, 1981)

Sunday afternoon break-time at Maida Center retreat. Berkeley, Ca. 8/1/2000

Photos of Maida Center retreat showing some of the attendees surrounding Reverend Saito, 8/1/2000, his last retreat.

WATER THAT FLOWS INTO THE SEA

    The ice that melts and becomes the water that flows into the sea
becomes indistinguishable from the flavor of the sea.
The more ice the more water, the more water, the deeper the ocean.
                                                    – Shinran Shonin

How beautiful are these phrases by Shinran expressing the ice of the mind and how the nembutsu of tears melt this ice, becoming the water as indistinguishable from the flavor of the sea – the deeper the nembutsu, the deeper the ocean.   May Blossom Time – 2015   R. A.

                          *   *   *

When I looked at the moon I saw beauty. A full moon with a halo....
That's purity. Suddenly the way opened, and I smiled.

Here there is nothing to study. No struggle to endure. All the study, words, and struggles add to the depth like fertilizer for the shout of fresh life. The moon reflected the light that was within myself, yet was covered up by things that blocked or dimmed its brightness, like the ugly stuff that is carried around like useless baggage that needs to be disposed of. How miraculous is this transformation, this emptiness, as is the very flow of life.

The flash of truth is that of *shinjin*. Fully alive, my mind dwells only on the Dharma of truth; that is, the mind that is emptied of self is cleared of discrimination, fixed beliefs, and false understandings, all based on the delusions of self. Cleared of these, I can enjoy the spacious freedom as is the Great Spirit of the unknowable life. I feel from its depth – as deep as this open space is tonight – a gratitude for the completion of a project that I started long ago. Not just for a book, but for the aspiration itself.

                                                        R. Adams 11/7/2015

www.ingramcontent.com/pod-product-compliance
Lightning Source LLC
Chambersburg PA
CBHW080052190426
43201CB00035B/2185